XML and Java™

DEVELOPING WEB APPLICATIONS

Hiroshi Maruyama
Kent Tamura
Naohiko Uramoto

Addison-Wesley

An imprint of Addison Wesley Longman, Inc.

Reading, Massachusetts • Harlow, England • Menlo Park, California
Berkeley, California • Don Mills, Ontario • Sydney
Bonn • Amsterdam • Tokyo • Mexico City

The publisher offers discounts on this book when ordered in quantity for special sales. For more information, please contact:

Corporate Government & Special Sales
Addison Wesley Longman, Inc.
One Jacob Way
Reading, Massachusetts 01867

Library of Congress Cataloging in Publication Data
Maruyama, Hiroshi, 1958–
    XML and Java : developing Web applications / Hiroshi Maruyama, Kent Tamura, and Naohiko Uramoto.
      p.   cm.
    ISBN 0-201-48543-5. — ISBN 0-201-61611-4 (CD-ROM)
    1. XML (Document markup language) 2. Java (Computer program language) 3. Web sites—Design. I. Tamura, Kent, 1965– .
II. Uramoto, Naohiko, 1972– . III. Title.
    QA76.76.H94M28   1999
    005.7'2—dc21   99-18618
                                                                             CIP

Acquisitions Editor: Mary O'Brien
Production Coordinator: Jacquelyn Young
Compositor: Stratford Publishing Services
Cover Designer: Simone Payment

ISBN 0-201-48543-5
Text printed on recycled and acid-free paper.
1 2 3 4 5 6 7 8 9 10 - MA - 0302010099

First Printing, May 1999

Contents

Acknowledgments

This book would not have been possible without the generous help of many people. In particular, we would like to express our thanks to the following people.

- Bob Schloss, David Epstein, and many other researchers in IBM's Research Division for their valuable discussions and encouragement.

- Mike Pogue and his team at Java Technology Centre, Cupertino, California, for greatly improving the quality of our *XML for Java* parser and providing product-level support, as well as their intensive and ongoing discussion regarding the use of JavaBeans.

- Michael Pauser and Dan Chang for providing us with the source code of SQLX and the related material that we used in Chapter 6.

- Tom Rowe, Jim Amsden, and others in the WebSphere team in Raleigh, North Carolina, for their comments on the earlier manuscripts and their strong encouragement.

- Kazuyo Yagishita for her "Travel Planning Application" demo, which was presented at the IBM Fair '98, and which was the original form of the sample shown in Chapter 8.

- Kazuo Iwano, our Lab Director, and our colleagues at IBM Tokyo Research Laboratory, who provided us with their warm support.

- The comments and suggestions of the six technical reviewers, which were extremely valuable for improving the quality and accuracy of this book.

- The copyeditor, Laura Michaels, for her tremendous effort correcting the grammar and style of our English.

- And the people at Addison Wesley Longman: Mary O'Brien, Elizabeth Spainhour, and Jacquelyn Young.

Finally, we thank our families, Minako and Mari Uramoto; Naoko, Ryuichi, and Yuka Maruyama, and Kazufumi and Kimie Tamura.

CHAPTER 1

Overview of Web Applications, XML, and Java

1.1 Introduction

In this book, we discuss how two new technologies, *XML* and *Java*, will change applications on the World Wide Web (Web) and how they will enable the development of new types of applications. **XML**, for Extensible Markup Language, is a new specification that enables Web page designers to create their own, customized tags to provide functionality that is not available using the current markup language used for many Web applications, the HyperText Markup Language (HTML). **Java** is a high-level, general-purpose programming language, developed by Sun Microsystems, that has several features that make it well suited for use in Web applications.

In this book, we "marry" the two technologies, giving you the basic notions and programming techniques that will enable you to design and implement applications for the Web using the two. The book is not intended to be either a primer or a reference on XML or Java. There are plenty of books available, with more coming out all of the time, for those who need a quick or more thorough understanding of either technology.[1] We assume that you have at

---

[1] We recommend that you have on hand reference books for both XML and Java. We usually use the following when writing our programs:
- W3C XML 1.0 Recommendation, `http://www.w3.org.TR/REC-xml`. We refer to the Recommendation often in this book.

least a basic understanding of both and some experience writing simple Java programs. Your having written one or more Web applications or possessing a background in designing and building business applications also would be helpful in understanding the material we present here. This book is intended for anyone desiring to maximize the effect and usefulness of their applications on the Web, including managers charged with exploiting Web technology in current and future enterprise endeavors, people responsible for developing the strategic use of B2B communications, and software vendors who provide products to users of the Web.

One of the wonderful things about the Web is that many useful resources can be downloaded at no charge, for example tools, language processors, and sample programs, as well as the latest information about technologies, old and new, including XML and Java. Two Web sites that you must know about are the following:

- `http://www.w3.org/`. This is the official site of the **World Wide Web Consortium** (W3C), the international consortium of companies involved in developing open standards so that the Web will evolve in a single direction rather than being split among competing factions. XML is a project of the W3C, so all of the official documents on XML should be available from this site.

- `http://java.sun.com/`. This is the home of Java. The latest information about Java is available here, including the latest Java Development Kit (JDK), which can be downloaded from the site.

The world of the Internet and the Web changes rapidly, so there are many things that we could not include in this book, often because they were not available at the time of this writing. It is your responsibility to check whether the information in this book is current and compliant with the latest standards. For your reference, Appendix C contains other useful links, as well as books.

We use a number of sample programs in this book in order to strengthen our discussion. These programs, as well as all of their source code, is included on

---

- The Java Series of books by Addison-Wesley, and in particular its *The Java Class Libraries, Second Edition, Volumes 1 and 2*, by Patrick Chan and Rosanna Lee (ISBN 0-201-31002-3 and 0-201-31003-1, respectively). Also see *The Java Class Libraries, Second Edition, Volume 1: 1.2 Supplement*, by Patrick Chan, Rosanna Lee, and Doug Kramer, available in Spring 1999 (**ISBN** 0-201-48552-4).

the CD-ROM that accompanies this book. We encourage you to run them and to understand how they work. Each was designed and coded by one or more of us (the authors) and tested using JDK version 1.1.7B running on Windows NT 4.0 with Service Pack 3. Of course, they should run as well on any other platform, provided it has a Java Virtual Machine (JVM).

The CD-ROM also contains IBM's **XML for Java** version 1.1.9. This is a Java implementation of an **XML processor**, a software module used to read XML documents and provide application programs with access to their content and structure. XML for Java was originally written by one of the authors (Kent Tamura) at the IBM Research, Tokyo Research Laboratory, and has an excellent reputation for its robustness and its compliance with the W3C XML standards.

1.1.1 Organization of This Book

This book is organized as follows. Part 1, consisting of Chapter 1 through Chapter 4, introduces XML and Java and reviews basic programming techniques of both.

Chapter 1, Overview of Web Applications, XML, and Java. The rest of this chapter explains the Web application and introduces XML and Java.

Chapter 2, Parsing XML Documents. This chapter discusses the XML processor and shows its most basic functionality, *parsing*, which analyzes XML documents and makes them available to application programs as structured data. It also introduces the **Document Object Model** (DOM), the standard API for dealing with an object tree, as well as two event-driven APIs.

Chapter 3, Constructing and Generating XML Documents. Once all of the logical application processes are finished, the results need to be returned to the client. Or, during the processing, an application might need to make a request to another Web application. This chapter discusses how to generate XML documents from the internal structure and to assure that the generated XML document is valid.

Chapter 4, Manipulating DOM Structures. This chapter explains how to manipulate DOM structures, the standard internal data structure for XML documents. As an example, we develop an XML-to-XML mapping tool.

Part 2 consists of Chapter 5 through Chapter 8 and is organized around the three major application areas of XML: document management and metacontent, databases, and messaging. At the same time, we also introduce the key

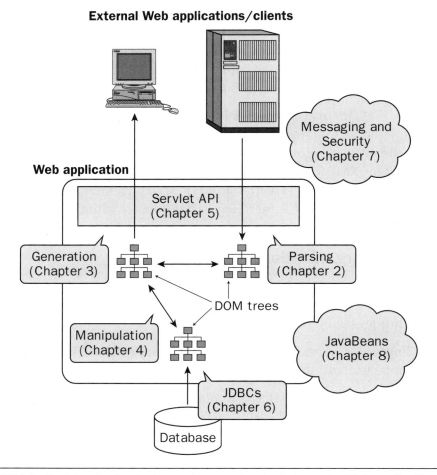

FIGURE 1.1 Enabling technologies and processing techniques for Web applications

enabling technologies for developing Web applications in each chapter: servlets, Java Database Connectivity (JDBC), security, and JavaBeans. Figure 1.1 illustrates how these key enabling technologies as well as the basic processing techniques covered in Part 1 fit in a typical XML-based Web application.

Chapter 5, Managing Documents and Working with Metacontent. This chapter covers managing XML documents within a Web application, as well as how XML can aid in searching *metacontent*. It introduces the *servlet*, the server-side Java framework for Web applications that enables Web applications to interact with external clients and other Web applications.

Chapter 6, Interfacing Databases and XML. Many Web applications are connected to *backend database systems*. This chapter describes the use of XML in conjunction with relational databases.

Chapter 7, Exchanging Messages Securely on Internet. This chapter explores the use of XML as a standard format for automating B2B *message exchange*. Messages must be meaningful to the recipient but also unreadable by anyone else. So this chapter also covers the major concern in messaging: *security*.

Chapter 8, Developing Applications Using JavaBeans. This chapter discusses the use of *software components,* a new approach to rapid application development. The cost of Web application development can be significantly reduced if common components such as parsers and generators can be made easily reusable. This chapter focuses on Java's software component package, *JavaBeans,* which is expected to boost the software productivity for both the client and server sides, in XML-enabled applications.

We also provide some useful information in the appendixes.

Appendix A, About the CD-ROM. The contents of the CD-ROM that accompanies this book and instructions on how to use it are described here.

Appendix B, Using Other XML Processors. Several noncommercial XML processor implementations are available in addition to XML for Java. This appendix covers how the sample programs on the CD-ROM can be combined with these other XML processors.

Appendix C, Useful Links and Books. This is a useful, although not complete, compilation of links on the Internet and suggested books that relate to XML and Java.

Appendix D, XML for Java API Reference.

Appendix E, XML-Related Standardization Activities. A number of standards are being defined on top of XML. This appendix covers the important ones.

Appendix F, DOMHash Definition. DOMHash, described in Chapter 7, is our proposal for defining a digest (hash) value for XML documents. This appendix is the complete definition of this proposal.

Next, we briefly discuss Web applications—what they are and some of their advantages.

1.2 What Is a Web Application

A **Web application** is any application or system of applications that uses the **hypertext transport protocol**, or HTTP, as its primary transport protocol. HTTP is the underlying protocol used by the Web, so this definition encompasses the applications used on the Web.

The Web was originally designed as a means to deliver static pages to users on the Internet. When a **Web browser** sends an HTTP request to a **Web server**, the Web server fetches the requested file from its file system and returns it through the HTTP connection to the browser. This process is depicted in Figure 1.2.

However, what the Web server returns does not necessarily need to be a static page (file) stored on the server. It could instead be the *output of a program*. This is typically made possible by the use of the **Common Gateway Interface**, or CGI. CGI is a specification for transferring information between a Web server and a **CGI program**, that is a program that can accept parameters from an HTTP request and return data as if it were a stored page. Although simple and somewhat crude, CGI is one of the most common ways for Web servers to create pages dynamically on demand.

An example usage of CGI is the retrieval of a stock quote from a real-time stock quote service. In this case, when the Web server receives a request for a quote, it

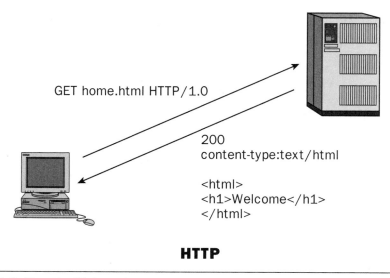

GET home.html HTTP/1.0

200
content-type:text/html

```
<html>
<h1>Welcome</h1>
</html>
```

HTTP

FIGURE 1.2 How the Web works

invokes an external database retrieval program to fetch the quote and then returns the quote as a dynamically-generated Web page to the browser. In other words, the Web server together with the database retrieval program acts as an application program that responds to HTTP requests. Thus, it is a Web application.

1.2.1 The Three-Tier Model

Web applications today are usually built by following the **three-tier model**. The three-tier model came about because of the perceived need to separate *business logic* from the GUI and the backend database. According to the model, three separate and well-defined processes, or modules, run on different platforms:

1. The *graphical user interface* (GUI), that is, the browser, which runs on the user's machine

2. The *application program* or *programs* that run on the Web server and that actually process the data (the business logic level)

3. A *database management system* that stores the data that tier 2 requires (the backend)

It was the explosive expansion of the use of Web browsers coupled with the use of CGI that made three-tier applications possible as well as practical. The model has several advantages over the more traditional single-tier or two-tier models, particularly for Web applications, including these:

- Web browsers are ubiquitous, so applications can be accessed from any platform.

- Applications can share the same look and feel.

- Its modularity makes it easier to modify or replace one tier without affecting the other tiers.

Although this three-tier configuration is the most popular way to build a new application today, XML opens up new possibilities regarding the creation of new application systems by combining two or more Web applications.

1.2.2 Example of Using XML: Web Applications That Call Web Applications

An essential aspect of the three-tier model is tier 1, the use of a browser as the universal interface between user and middle tier (application). However, a request to a Web application need not originate from a human user. It also can originate from another program using the same model and the same protocol, HTTP, used by human users. This could be considered a *Web application model*, in which Web applications connect to other Web applications. In this section, we explain how this works and give an example to illustrate the concept. We also show how XML can be used to go beyond the functionality of HTML.

Our example is an application, called PowerWarning, that accesses a Web site and uses the information obtained from the site to produce a prescribed result. More specifically, using PowerWarning we access a weather information site on the Web to obtain the current temperature for a particular location. Based on the temperature and if certain conditions have been met, the application sends a notice to clients of the service alerting them of the condition. For example, suppose one of our clients is a shopping mall in White Plains, New York. The application is to monitor the temperature in White Plains and issue a power

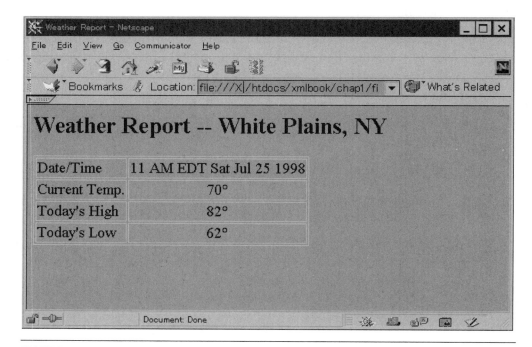

FIGURE 1.3 Sample page from the weather information Web site

overload warning if the temperature is above 100 degrees for more than three consecutive hours. We know that the weather information is available from the Web at `http://www.xweather.com/White_Plains_NY_US.html`. Figure 1.3 shows a sample HTML page returned from the site. Its source is given next.

```
[1]  <html>
[2]  <head>
[3]  <title>Weather Report</title>
[4]  </head>
[5]  <body>
[6]  <h2>Weather Report -- White Plains, NY</h2>
[7]  <table border=1>
[8]      <tr><td>Date/Time</td><td align=center>11 AM EDT Sat Jul 25
         1998</td></tr>
[9]      <tr><td>Current Temp.</td><td align=center>70&#176;</td></tr>
[10]     <tr><td>Today's High</td><td align=center>82&#176;</td></tr>
[11]     <tr><td>Today's Low</td><td align=center>62&#176;</td></tr>
[12] </table>
[13] </body>
[14] </html>
```

We need our application to

1. obtain this page every hour,

2. extract the pertinent temperature information from it, and

3. test whether the temperature has exceeded 100 degrees for more than three continuous hours.

To have PowerWarning extract the pertinent temperature information from the Web page, we could have it follow any of several strategies.

Strategy 1:   *For the current temperature of White Plains, go to line 9, column 46 of the page and continue until reaching the next ampersand.*
            However, any experienced programmer can point out problems with this rather quick and dirty strategy. For example, making a slight change in the page such as inserting a blank line above or removing whitespaces to the left of the designated start location will prevent the PowerWarning application from functioning properly (it won't be able to find the temperature), even though the page will still display fine to users, as shown in Figure 1.3.

Strategy 2:   *For the current temperature of White Plains, go to the first* `<table>` *tag, then go to the second* `<tr>` *tag within the table, and then go to the second* `<td>` *tag within the row.*

This much better strategy will withstand small changes that do not alter the appearance of the page. However, what will happen if the Web page designer decides to add a "cool" masthead to the page by using a `<table>` tag to put many small GIF images together, as is done in many fancy Web pages? In this case, going to the first `<table>` tag will not return the temperature for White Plains, as the masthead would be in the first table and the temperature would be in the second table on the page.

The problem so far is that HTML was originally designed to represent a *presentation structure* of a document, which would have such structural parts as a header, a title, paragraphs, headings, and so on, so its tags were designed for this purpose. However, HMTL does not include tags to represent *logical data*, such as the current temperature. To extract data from an HTML page, we need to embed the data in a document-oriented tag.

The problem of how to treat data in an HTML page is further complicated by many of the current Web pages not complying well with the HTML specification. HTML is so simple and easy to understand and use that people who often do not have a good grounding in the HTML specification are developing Web pages. These casual Web page "designers" tend to be satisfied with their pages if the pages simply display properly on their own browsers. Ensuring the pages conform to the HTML standard is not done. As a result, browsers tend to be quite tolerant of errors in the HTML syntax so as to allow such pages to display without a lot of problems. But this in turn just encourages less sensitivity to proper HTML syntax. Because of this, it is not always easy to parse an HTML page, particularly in order to extract data.

1.2.3 Enter XML

XML solves the problem of how to extract data such as the weather information. With XML, we can define a structure that directly represents data, in this case the temperature of a specified location. For example, the weather information site could return, instead of an HTML page, the following XML document.

```
<?xml version="1.0"?>
<!DOCTYPE WeatherReport SYSTEM
"http://www.xweather.com/WeatherReport.dtd">
<WeatherReport>
    <City>White Plains</City>
    <State>NY</State>
    <Date>Sat Jul 25 1998</Date>
    <Time>11 AM EDT</Time>
    <CurrTemp unit="Farenheit">70</CurrTemp>
    <High unit="Farenheit">82</High>
    <Low unit="Farenheit">62</Low>
</WeatherReport>
```

This XML document is a *logical representation* of the weather data; that is, this representation is independent of the page's presentation structure and thus of how it will display on a screen. In our example, we define the XML tag <CurrTemp> to represent the current temperature data. We then devise a third strategy for extracting the current temperature of White Plains.

Strategy 3:   *For the current temperature of White Plains, N.Y., go to the* <CurrTemp> *tag.*

Of course, for this strategy to work this tag needs to be used in the weather information site application so that our application will be able to find it. Thus obtaining the agreement of the site to use the tag is necessary before we can put our strategy into place. If the site administrator at the weather reporting site agrees to use this tag in the site's application, the tag would be defined in the application's grammar called a **Document Type Definition** (DTD). This DTD would be published and thereby be made available to anyone wanting to use the site in a manner similar to our PowerWarning application. In a sense, the published DTD acts as the specification of the weather information site's Web application at http://www.xweather.com/.

> **NOTE:** The fact that an XML page is a logical representation of data makes serving different types of clients easier. This is shown in Figure 1.4. The logical representation is converted into an appropriate representation depending on the type of the client. For example, for application programs, including PowerWarning, the data format might be the XML representation itself and so no conversion is needed. For personal computer (PC) users, however, the preferred representation might be HTML. And if the client is a cellular phone or a personal digital assistant (PDA), the contents might need to be converted into a very compact representation such as Wireless Markup Language (WML). In Chapter 4, we describe one technique to do such conversions called the *LMX processor.*

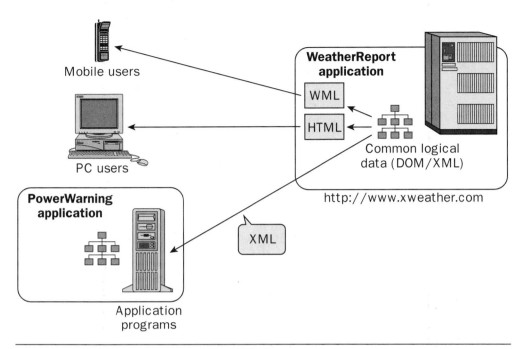

FIGURE 1.4 Serving different types of clients using XML's logical representation

Now our PowerWarning application has a more direct way to extract data, and one that will not be affected by changes in the Web page's appearance.

This example demonstrates but one of many things that we can achieve by using XML. Suppose our PowerWarning application works well as described previously and is popular with our client, the shopping mall. So we decide to provide this service to other clients through our own Web site, located at www.powerwarning.com. Subscribers to our service would connect to our site and set their own parameters, such as

- the city to be monitored,

- the condition that would prompt the issuance of a warning, such as temperature and duration, and

- the method of notification, for example, by pager or electronic mail (e-mail).

PowerWarning would then periodically poll the weather information sites of specified cities and issue warnings to subscribers when preset conditions were met.

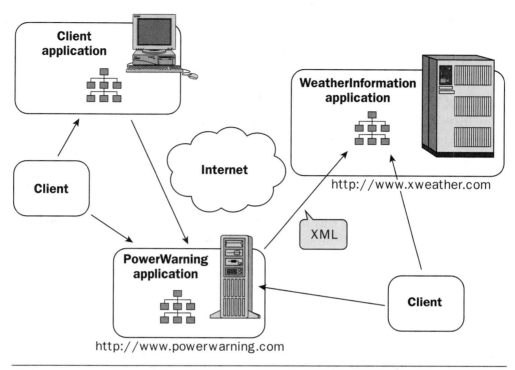

FIGURE 1.5 Web application model: connecting a web of Web applications

As you can see, the Web application model surpasses the three-tier model. While the three-tier model connects users with backend systems, the Web application model, a "web of Web applications," connects Web applications with other Web applications. This is shown in Figure 1.5. And the choice for such communication? XML.

1.3 Some XML Basics

XML will be one of the key technologies of future Web applications. In this section, we give an overview of XML and its possible application areas.

1.3.1 Development of XML

XML and HTML both derive from the *Standard Generalized Markup Language,* or SGML (ISO8879), which was defined in 1986 as an international standard for document markup. The first HTML specification was published by the W3C in 1992 as a markup language specific to Web pages. Most existing browsers support HMTL version 3.2. and the latest ones support version 4.0, which was issued in April 1998.

Discussion on XML started in 1997, and the first version, 1.0 Recommendation, was issued by the W3C in February 1998. In this book, we base our discussion of XML on this 1.0 Recommendation. You are encouraged to check the latest publications at the W3C Web site, `http://www.w3.org/`. Also, we list in Appendix E several important ones to keep your eyes on.

First, HTML

With free Web browsers such as IE and Navigator being deployed universally, HTML has become one of the primary means to mark up documents delivered via the Web. Its advantages include the following:

• It has a simple syntax with a fixed tag set.

• It makes it easy to create multimedia documents by incorporating images and audio.

• It enables many other documents to be linked together.

HTML has been enhanced many times in its history. However, one of its most significant disadvantages remains, and that is its fixed set of tags. The only way to add functionality to HTML (via new tags) is to take a proposal detailing the desired functionality to the W3C and put it on the discussion table. The discussion process can be lengthy, however, and not all proposed tags are general enough to be included in the HTML specification.

This problem of limited flexibility can be solved with XML.

Enter XML

XML is an *extensible* markup language. With XML, you can define your own set of tags by means of a DTD. As an example of how this can be useful, consider that while HTML is powerful enough for formatting Web pages, it might not be best for marking up large documents that are to be printed on paper. For example, HTML does not support automatic numbering of chapters and sections, or allow you control over page breaks, or format mathematics with ease (as those of you familiar with Don Knuth's TeX formatting system for mathematics can attest). XML offers the opportunity to create richer documents than HTML can produce by introducing appropriate tags. Because of this flexibility, XML is considered to be the next generation markup language for general documents.

It is even possible to convert an existing HTML document into a well-formed XML document. HTML-compatible browsers ignore non-HTML tags, thus they can display XML documents that contain some HTML tags. Both Lotus and Microsoft are planning to use an XML document with mixed HTML and non-HTML tags as the native document format for their word processors.

Not many Web pages are authored in XML, yet. However, many emerging document markup proposals are based on XML. In addition, XML can be used for such fields as metacontent, databases, and messaging as well. We discuss each of these new areas in later chapters in the book.

> **NOTE:** Many Web-related standards are defined by the W3C. Unlike ANSI and ISO, it is not an official standards body. For this reason, it issues its decisions as recommendations, not as international standards. However, in practice, its recommendations have the same authoritative standing as international standards issued by other standard bodies such as ANSI and ISO.
>
> The W3C publishes several levels of documents.
>
> - **Note**. A Note is a proposal by one organization or a group of organizations and is the most informal level of document. If a Note is determined to merit formal discussion, with the purpose of arriving at a decision whether to go forward with it, it is sent to a Working Group for that formal discussion.
> - **Working Draft**. A Working Draft is the result of the efforts of a Working Group. Working Drafts are published and made public in order to encourage feedback from interested parties.
> - **Proposed Recommendation**. If the Working Group arrives at a favorable consensus, it issues a Proposed Recommendation. It is submitted to the W3C member organizations for a vote. If approved, it then becomes a Recommendation.
> - **Recommendation**. A Recommendation is a standard in the usual sense.
>
> Each formal W3C publication has a unique document name, whether a Note, Working Draft, Proposed Recommendation, or Recommendation.

1.3.2 Validity and Well-Formedness of XML Documents

As this book is not intended to be an introduction to or reference manual of XML, we do not discuss the details of the XML specification. However, we do want to explain one important concept: the difference between *validity* and *well-formedness.*

Recall that in XML, you can define your own tag set using a DTD. Following is an example of a DTD.

```
<!ELEMENT WeatherReport (City, State, Date, Time, CurrTemp, High,
Low)>
<!ELEMENT City (#PCDATA)>
<!ELEMENT State (#PCDATA)>
<!ELEMENT Date (#PCDATA)>
<!ELEMENT Time (#PCDATA)>
<!ELEMENT CurrTemp (#PCDATA)>
<!ELEMENT High (#PCDATA)>
<!ELEMENT Low (#PCDATA)>
<!ATTLIST CurrTemp Unit (Farenheit|Celsius) #REQUIRED>
<!ATTLIST High Unit (Farenheit|Celsius) #REQUIRED>
<!ATTLIST Low Unit (Farenheit|Celsius) #REQUIRED>
```

NOTE: SGML traditionally has a syntax for its DTD that is separate from the SGML syntax. XML inherited this tradition: Its DTD syntax differs from the XML syntax. However, using the same XML syntax for both documents and DTDs could be beneficial. This is because then the same mechanism in the XML processor could be used to analyze both the DTD and the XML document. This is a hotly debated issue by the XML community. Proponents argue that the current DTD syntax is ugly and not easily extended and that if the expressive power of DTD's is to be enriched, the syntax must be changed. However, opponents say that there are many existing DTDs, so the current syntax should be retained.

Another hot topic is how to deal with complex data types. The XML 1.0 Recommendation includes no way to specify the data type of a particular element or attribute. For example, the contents of the `CurrTemp` element can be any string, according to the current XML DTD. This means that `<CurrTemp>97</CurrTemp>` and `<CurrTemp>Hello World</CurrTemp>` will be considered equally valid by the XML processor, even though obviously Hello World is not what is wanted. If we could specify the data type, we could ensure that the correct data is extracted by specifying that the contents of this element should be a number and if it is not, then the validity check will fail.

Given these issues and the benefits they promise, we will not be surprised if in the near future an alternative way of writing DTDs becomes popular.

Validity

Validity means that the XML document meets the validity constraints (VCs) specified in the XML 1.0 Recommendation. For a document to be checked for validity, it must include the `<!DOCTYPE>` declaration at the beginning of the XML document, which specifies the DTD according to which the document will be validated; for example,

```
<!DOCTYPE WeatherReport SYSTEM
"http://www.xweather.com.WeatherReport.dtd>"
```

where the URL is the location of the DTD. If the `<!DOCTYPE>` declaration is not included, the XML processor will not perform validity checking. In this case, it will perform only a check for *well-formedness*, which is discussed in the next subsection.

The XML processor reads the document's DTD and checks its validity based on the VCs. VCs focus on the *logical structure of elements.* That is, VCs require that all tags are defined in the DTD, that all elements appearing within an element follow the content model defined in the DTD, that all attributes are declared in the DTD, and so on.

Usually an application needs to know all tags that appear in the document in order to process them correctly. Given an element with an unknown tag name, the application will have no clue what to do with it, even though that name might be meaningful to humans. For example, the tag `<Invoice>` might be understandable to English-speaking people but it is as meaningless as the Japanese `<seikyuusho>` to an application that does not know the semantics of the tag. Therefore, when you want to process XML documents, you will usually be interested in documents that are valid against the DTD you are working with.

However, XML is designed so that an XML document can be parsed without an explicit DTD's being defined, provided it contains no **external entities**, that is, entities defined in a DTD. (External entities may be used only in an XML document that has a `<!DOCTYPE>` declaration.) This is one of XML's big differences from SGML. In SGML, all documents must have a DTD. In the case of HTML, the DTD is known and fixed, so there is no need to include a DTD at all.

Well-Formedness

Well-formedness means that the XML document meets the set of well-formedness constraints (WFCs) defined in the 1.0 Recommendation. Whereas validity mainly deals with the logical structure of elements, well-formedness focuses on the *physical structure,* such as tag matching. For example, in XML every start tag, such as `<TR>`, must have a corresponding end tag, such as `</TR>`. Otherwise, a tag must be an **empty tag**, a tag that has an explicit slash at the end of it, as in `<City/>`. This contrasts with SGML and HTML, both of which can be parsed without having explicit end tags as long as there is no parsing ambiguity.

Other constraints that determine well-formedness include these:

- Attribute names must be unique within an element.

- Attribute values must not contain the character "<".

XML documents that are not well-formed should be rejected by the XML processor.

Note that *a valid document is always well-formed but a well-formed document is not necessarily valid.* For example, a well-formed document may contain unknown tags. Would it ever make sense to allow such a thing? The answer is yes, because not all tags need necessarily be understood by any one application. For example, you might want to allow some text with HTML markups in a certain field, such as a comment. Even though the content cannot be understood by the application that receives the document, it can be submitted to an external browser upon request to display the HTML tagged comment on the screen. Another good example of not requiring validity is rendering. In this case, even if a browser encounters an unknown tag, usually it can be simply skipped without resulting in a disaster.

1.4 Application Areas of XML

XML is so powerful and so flexible that many groups of people are considering using it for different purposes, not just marking up documents. In this section, we briefly discuss these areas by grouping them into three "camps" that are specifically important for Web applications. In Chapters 5 through 7, we go into more detail on each.

- Use XML to describe *metacontent* regarding documents or on-line resources.

- Use XML to publish and exchange *database* contents.

- Use XML as a *messaging format* for communication between application programs.

1.4.1 Metacontent

In 1997, XML was thought of mainly as the language for **metacontent**. Metacontent is information about a document's contents, such as its title, author, file size, creation date, revision history, keywords, and so on. Metacontent can be used, for example, for searching, information filtering, and document management.

As an example of the usefulness of explicit metacontent, suppose you want to search documents that were written by U.S. President Bill Clinton. If you use the current Web search engines and input "Bill Clinton" as the search keyword, you likely will get thousands of hits. Most of these hits will be just *noises,* mentions of Bill Clinton in the bodies of documents, not all of which were written by him. Your search would be much more productive if you could express the search query as "find documents whose Author element contains the words 'Bill Clinton'."

Unfortunately, no such element, or tag, is defined in HTML. Further, it is unlikely that the HTML specification will be extended in the near future to include one. This is because of several reasons.

1. In the past, the HTML specification was too rapidly extended. This was because of the "browser war" that occurred between Netscape and Microsoft in the mid-1990s. At that time, these companies sought to add more and more functions to their browsers by defining their own proprietary HTML tags, without having the tags standardized by the W3C. This led to incompatible browsers, which in turn diminished the value of the Web-based three-tier model for Web applications. Since then, both companies generally try to get their new extensions standardized with the W3C before incorporating them into their browsers. But since the release of HTML 4.0 in April, 1998, the W3C seems to be more cautious in further extending HTML.

2. Extending HTML does not solve all of the problems with metacontent in that other resources, such as image files, audio and video files, and other content types, might require metacontent extensions as well.

3. The third reason concerns performance. HTML has the TITLE and META tags that can accommodate some metacontent. But these tags, when used, are *inside* an HTML document, so search engines cannot refer to the information without downloading the entire HTML file. It is not efficient to download, for example, a 100-Kb HTML file just to check if the TITLE tag contains a certain character string, particularly when there are hundreds of such files available from a Web site. If the metacontent of all the documents available on a site were put in a single file, the search performance would be greatly improved.

For these reasons, a metacontent description that is *external* to the file has received a lot of attention. XML is considered to be the best vehicle for defining a metacontent syntax because of its extensibility, flexibility, and readability. RDF, CDF, and OSD mentioned in Appendix E are examples of such metacontent formats defined in XML. Chapter 5 is devoted to the use of XML for metacontent.

1.4.2 Databases

Many three-tier applications extract data from backend database systems. Usually, the results are transformed via the `<table>` tag of HTML and displayed on the screen. If data is delivered as an XML document that preserves the original information, such as column names and data types, it can be used by the client for other purposes than just displaying on the screen. For example, it might be possible to load the data into a spreadsheet and do some computation such as calculating sums and averages. Chapter 6 gives examples of how XML can be used to interface with databases.

1.4.3 Messaging

The hottest application area of XML is **messaging**. Messaging is the exchange of messages between organizations or between application systems within an organization.

Messaging among companies has traditionally been done by **Electronic Data Interchange** (EDI), which has been widely used in industries such as finance and manufacturing since the 1970s. In the United States, ANSI defined the X12 standards, a set of EDI messaging standards for various industries. In Europe, the standard for EDI is EDIFACT.

In its long history, EDI has greatly contributed to automating B2B transactions. However, even though virtually every corporation is now connected to a single network and can send messages to anybody else, not all of them are using EDI. Instead, they use traditional means such as fax and telephone, for example to send and receive orders and invoices. In particular, many small companies cannot participate in the EDI world because of the high cost of building and operating an EDI system. For example, many EDI systems require a value-added network (VAN), not the ubiquitous Internet. While there are many good reasons why a VAN is more desirable than the Internet, such as increased security, reliability, and availability, a VAN also is more expensive than the Internet (which is required for Web access and e-mail anyway). Also, an EDI system is not like an off-the-shelf software that you can install on your PC and be ready to do business right away. Rather, a skilled vendor is needed to build an EDI system.

It is natural that a small company that already has an Internet connection would want to do B2B messaging with their partners using inexpensive, off-the-shelf software. Even for a large company that already has an EDI system, B2B on the Internet can be a good opportunity to invite new small partners to join and connect to its own infrastructure. Thus B2B messaging on the Internet, sometimes termed *Internet EDI,* is getting attention nowadays.

There have been two major technical problems with B2B messaging on the Internet. One is insufficient security. The Internet is a public network, and until recently there has been no protection against attacks such as eavesdropping and forgery. If messages are stolen or modified during transmission, B2B messaging will be almost useless. Fortunately, the recent advancement of public key-based cryptography has remedied most of the security problems in communication. Using modern cryptographic protocols such as SSL, which we discuss in Chapter 7, and secure mail formats such as S/MIME, the Internet has become as secure as any other network, including VANs and intranets.

The other technical problem is agreeing on a standard message format to use. Here, XML can play a role. Among the skills needed to build an EDI system is a good understanding of the X12 or EDIFACT message format. We do not know the exact number of people who are knowledgeable of these formats, but we are sure that it is at least an order of magnitude smaller than the population that knows HTML. Since XML and HTML are closely related, it should be easy for people who are familiar with the basic HTML syntax to understand the gist of XML. A DTD together with a few message examples should give a fairly good understanding of the message format, enough to start building a prototype implementation. Thus, with XML, the threshold for participating in a message-exchanging community can be quite low.

1.5 Why Use XML in Web Applications

We have shown that several areas are being considered for applying the XML technology for different goals. However, XML is not the only or most efficient way to achieve these goals. For example, to express numerical data why not use a binary format instead of a long character string such as a pair of tags like `<CurrTemp></CurrTemp>`. Or, instead of using HTTP with XML to transmit data over the Internet using a standard data format, why not use IIOP or a Remote Procedure Call (RPC)? These latter, sophisticated, communication methods are much more efficient in terms of both communication bandwidth and computation power.

So what are the benefits of using XML in the application areas discussed in the previous section? There are at least three:

- Simplicity

- Richness of the data structure

- Excellent handling of international characters

1.5.1 Simplicity

The first and the largest benefit of XML is its simplicity, particularly compared to binary formats. Suppose you define a message in a binary format, such as "the value of parameter X is represented as a 4-byte integer in the network byte order, beginning at the twelfth octet from the top of the message." To understand this binary message, you would have to look at its hexadecimal dump and understand the message content bit-by-bit, a tedious and time-consuming task. Although new tools can be created to display and edit binary messages such as this, this is an additional task to undertake.

By contrast, XML is a character-based format and therefore human-readable. Further, XML messages can easily be read, created, and modified by using standard and common tools such as text editors or UNIX's string search tool, grep. This all makes understanding and analyzing XML messages much easier than their binary counterparts.

In XML, tags can be named with understandable strings. Suppose that you have developed a decent Web application that you want to promote. As a Web application, it receives an HTTP request and returns an XML document as a response (rather than relying on more efficient methods such as IIOP). You provide your data in XML, so you also publish a DTD that describes its syntax. Assume that a potential partner would like to do business with you. By accessing your Web site, it learns that you provide an XML-based Web application for automatic B2B messaging. By studying your DTD, it finds that it includes tags in plain English, such as `<Time>` and `<Date>`. Taking advantage of XML's simplicity, the company's engineers can develop glue code that connects its own business application to your Web application just by using off-the-shelf XML and Web application tools.

Another example of XML's simplicity is its ability to represent tree-structured data. But why would you want to use XML to represent tree-structured data instead of the widely used Abstract Syntax Notation 1 (ASN.1)? ASN.1 is a binary protocol representation scheme for tree-structured data. One of its popular uses is for the *X.509 digital certificate.* (We discuss the X.509 digital certificate, authentication, and other security issues in Chapter 7.)

ASN.1 is carefully designed so that it minimizes the size of data. A very efficient protocol engine can be realized by combining an ANS.1 message with a good ASN.1 parser implementation. In short, ASN.1 is optimized for efficiency. However, because of this it has complicated bit arrangements that make understanding it hard. You can use automatic protocol generation tools to save some of the effort involved here, but good tools cost thousands of dollars.

By contrast, XML has similar ability to represent tree-structured data, but it is much simpler and is easier to understand and to work with.

One thing stands out from the history of the Internet: "Simplicity wins, efficiency loses."[1] In the Internet world, the rule of the game is called *openness,* that is, accessibility and availability to the public. Even if you have an unparalleled technology, it will not win in the market without receiving wide support from the majority of the affected population. A technology that is relatively less efficient but open and easy to understand compared with its competitors will have a better chance to win in the Internet world.

1.5.2 Richness of Data Structure

Although simple, XML is powerful enough to express complex data structures. Different applications require different structures for representing data. Currently, an XML document has essentially a rooted tree structure. However, other possible data structure might be better suited for a particular type of data, for example tables and graphs. A table is the logical data structure of relational databases. A graph can represent shared elements and cycled paths. More complex structures, however, require more computation.

---

[1]From a talk given by Adam Bosworth of Microsoft in May 1998 at IBM's Almaden Research Center in California.

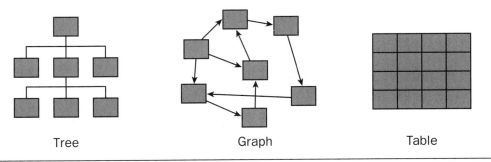

Tree   Graph   Table

FIGURE 1.6 Data structures: Tree, graph, and table

For many applications, a tree structure is general and powerful enough to express fairly complex data. It is a sensible balance between expressive power and simplicity. In addition, there are ways to represent graphs and tables in a tree, although doing this might be rather inefficient. Thus XML has sufficient power to express complex data structures to satisfy the need of most applications.

1.5.3 International Character Handling

One substantial benefit of using XML that should not be underestimated is its capability to handle international character sets. Even if you are designing a very simple message format, this point alone is reason enough to adopt XML.

Today, business is often international in scope. This is especially true regarding Web applications because the Internet easily leaps national borders. It is only natural that business transactions will contain, for example, street names in Chinese or person names in Arabic. The XML 1.0 Recommendation is defined based on the ISO-10646 (Unicode) character set, so virtually all the characters that are used today all over the world are legal characters. We discuss character sets and encoding more in Chapter 2.

> **NOTE:** Do not confuse character sets with character encodings. A **character set** defines a set of characters regardless how they are represented in a binary computer. A **character encoding** specifies a mapping between a character set and particular binary representation of the characters. Therefore one character set may have many different encodings.

1.6 Java's Role in Web Applications

In the previous section, we described the basics of XML and discussed its use in Web applications. In this section, we touch on the other important technology that is the topic of this book—Java.

Many of you might think of Java as a programming language used to make your Web pages "cool" by adding animation and other dynamic features. However, we believe that Java is essential for developing Web applications. We tell you why in this section.

Java is a general-purpose, object-oriented programming language developed by James Gosling and others at Sun Microsystems. Java was originally intended as a programming language for embedded systems such as those in TV set-top boxes and cellular phones. However, soon after announced by Sun in May 1995, Netscape Communications adopted it as the programming language for extending its browser's functions. Thereafter, it rapidly gained popularity as Web page designers discovered they could use it to add to their pages dynamic features such as animation and simple interactions with the user.

A popular mechanism for doing this is the **Java applet**, a small Java program that can be downloaded from a Web server and run on a user's computer by

> **NOTE:** Executing a downloaded program is not always safe. To counter this, all Java-enabled browsers have default security checks that make all Java applets downloaded from the Web "safe," called the **sandbox** model. The sandbox is a Java security mechanism in which the downloaded applet runs and is thereby prevented from performing sensitive operations, such as accessing local files and the network. Thus applets in the sandbox have limited functionality. The latest versions of browser allow the user to give applets that are *trusted* the permission to do more things. An applet is considered trusted if it has been *digitally signed* to prove that it was created by a trusted software publisher and that it has not been tampered with. Users can enable digitally signed applets to do more operations than applets in the sandbox typically would be allowed to do, such as writing files in specific directories. In this way, Java applets can be used for more-productive purposes than just providing animation. A good example of this is e-Suite by Lotus Development Corporation. Functionally, e-Suite is a full office suite product—it contains spreadsheet, word processing, presentation graphics, and so on, functionalities. These are actually implemented as a set of signed applets, and thus no installation process is required.

using a Java-compatible browser, such as Netscape Navigator and IE. However, it does take some time to download the applet. Because of this, other (faster) ways to add dynamic features to Web pages, such as animated GIF, JavaScript, VBScript, and DHTML (Dynamic HTML), are becoming more popular among Web page designers. Thus the client-side application of Java has diminished as Java is no longer necessarily the choice for adding Web page animation. By contrast, however, the use of Java on the server side is growing. We discuss this more shortly, but first we consider the advantages of Java as a general-purpose programming language.

1.6.1 Advantages of Java as a Programming Language

Java has a number of advantages as a general purpose programming language for server-side applications:

- Platform independence

- High productivity

- Built-in Internet support

- Good support for international characters

Platform Independence

The most widely known characteristic of Java is its independence from platforms such as CPU architectures and operating systems. Java programs are compiled into *bytecodes,* which in turn are interpreted by the interpreter built in a JVM. This means that compiled bytecode (in a sense, binary executable code) can run on any platform that has a JVM. Sun Microsystems' catch phrase "Write once, run anywhere"™ attracted many software vendors who had been struggling to port a single software to many different platforms.

Of course, there is no such thing as free lunch. Since Java bytecodes are interpreted, the runtime execution speed is in general slower than that of C or C++, sometimes by an order of magnitude. However, this difference has been dramatically reduced by the introduction of just-in-time (JIT) compilers that translate bytecode into machine native code at runtime.

Although platform-independence alone is a good enough reason to select Java as a programming language, it has other important advantages over C and C++ that we discuss next.

Safety

Java programs are much safer compared to C and C++; that is, they are less likely to have fatal errors. Java has no pointers. Also, array indexes are always checked at runtime so that they do not exceed the array boundaries. Further, memory management is the responsibility of the JVM, so there should be no problem with memory leaks, which are one of the hardest bugs to identify. This means that the majority of the fatal bugs that are common in C and C++ programs would never occur in Java programs. So your Java programs should contain fewer bugs and therefore be safer than C and C++ programs developed with the same amount of effort.

High Productivity

Java programming is generally more productive than C and C++ programming. It was designed by incorporating the latest object-oriented software engineering results, from the ground up. Java standard libraries also make a heavy use of *design patterns*, which make them extremely flexible. Other language features that contribute to higher productivity include

- clear separation between the interface and the implementation,

- absence of easy-to-mistake constructs such as multiple inheritance and operator overloading, and

- language-level support for threads and monitors (data object for synchronization).

Built-in Internet Support

Java's network library package (`java.net`) contains a wealth of Internet connectivity routines. In particular, the classes `URL` and `URLConnection` handle the details of the HTTP protocol and make connecting to a Web server very easy.

Support for International Characters

As in XML, Java uses Unicode as the character set. From JDK 1.1 on, the JVM is equipped with conversion tables that contain major character encodings. In addition, based on the current locale setting, the Java library automatically chooses appropriate representations of date, currency, and character encodings.

By contrast, the standard C or C++ library does not support Unicode; it is only for ASCII. Although there are vendor-specific libraries available that deal specifically with Unicode, a C or C++ programmer still needs to be always aware of what is being used.

1.6.2 Servlets

Another essential feature that makes Java a perfect language for writing Web applications is the *servlet.*

Most early Web applications were written in scripting language, such as Perl, and were invoked by the simple but crude CGI mechanism. CGI is a great idea that enables dynamic content generation, but it has several limitations— notably the overhead of processing one request is sometimes prohibitively high. This is because each time a CGI program is executed, a new process is started. As one way to address these problems, Web server providers such as Netscape Communications provide APIs as *user exits* (aka *entry points*) that can be directly called from the Web server. In Netscape servers, these APIs are called *NSAPI.* The server is configured so that when a certain URL is accessed, a speci-fied dynamic link library (DLL) is loaded to the process space of the server and the DLL is called through the standard C calling sequence as if it is a part of the server code. Since the application program (DLL) runs in the same process space as the server, there is no process-switching overhead and thus it is very efficient. This method has a large drawback, however. Consider that if a CGI program crashes, the termination of the process has no immediate conse-quences either on any other processes running on the server or on the server itself. By contrast, if an application is running in the server's process space, memory or pointer bugs could crash the server, as well as have serious conse-quences for other applications (DLLs) running in the same process space.

A Java alternative to this method is the **servlet**. A servlet is a mechanism to invoke a Java program. It is the server-side Java framework for Web applica-tions that enables Web applications to interact with external clients and other Web applications. Here is how it works. When a URL is requested, the associ-ated Java class (servlet) is executed. The servlet runs in a JVM that resides in the same process space as the server, so no process-switch overhead is incurred. Further, because Java has no pointers and no out-of-bound array access, buggy servlets never crash the server or other applications running in the same JVM. Thus the servlet is an ideal mechanism for Web applications due to its effi-ciency and safety.

In addition to these essential advantages, Sun Microsystems has provided servlet libraries that help ease Web application development. These libraries allow for extracting HTTP header values, parsing X.509 certificates used in secure sockets layer connections (we discuss this in Chapter 7), and processing server-side includes. We cover servlets in Chapter 5.

1.6.3 Java Database Connectivity

It has been said that the total on-line data stored in various kinds of computers today is on the order of peta bytes (10^{15} bytes). A large part of this data is stored in relational database systems (RDBMSs), which allow the flexible and efficient retrieval and updating of data while preserving the integrity and consistency of the data. Java also provides Web applications a means to access databases, the Java API called **Java Database Connectivity** (JDBC). With it, you can write a single database application that can be run on different platforms and interact with different databases.

Since the onset of the Web, a lot of documents have been added to the mass of on-line data, in the form of HTML. HTML documents are served from ordinary file systems, so no special management systems are necessary for storing, editing, and retrieving them. However, file systems provide only minimum management capabilities, such as access control and mutual exclusion, so HTML documents must be rather static. This means that they are not suitable for information that dynamically changes (such as stock quotes). Still, HTML documents contribute a very small fraction of the total on-line data compared to the data in database systems.

The three-tier model allows the data in database systems to be served through the ubiquitous HTTP/HTML infrastructure. Many vendors provide products for accessing database systems from the Web. Some are positioned as *Web publishers* of a database system, while others are *connectors,* a part of a Web application server that enables application programs to access backend database systems. In either case, data from RDBMSs is converted to an HTML expression (normally using the `<table>` tag) and embedded in an HTML document.

A typical example of such a system can be found at the official 1998 Winter Olympic Games Web site. The results of the games were collected by the computers at the game sites and fed to a centralized database system. The data was made immediately available to the public through the Web. In this system, HTML pages were dynamically generated by accessing the game result databases. RDBMSs and their connectors to HTTP/HTML used in this application contributed to realizing the robust, efficient, and reliable working system, as well as reducing the cost of application development.

Publishing database contents as HTML pages makes them available to a large number of Internet users. By converting database contents into XML, they can reach a more important audience: application programs. In fact, some vendors think XML is best utilized as a data interchange format between databases.

JDBC, defined by Sun Microsystems, has the advantage of enabling Java programs to execute Standard Query Language (SQL) statements and thereby to interact with SQL-compliant databases, which are most databases. This, coupled with Java's ability to run on most platforms, enables a single Java database application to run on different platforms and interact with different DBMSs. Thus Web applications that need to access databases should do so through JDBC. We discuss JDBC in Chapter 5.

1.6.4 JavaBeans

Another advantage of using Java is **JavaBeans**, the software component model for Java. JavaBeans allows the rapid development of an application by putting together existing software components by using a visual builder. It is anticipated that many JavaBeans such as database access beans, transactional beans, and even possibly XML beans that are readily assembled with a standard Java-Bean builder will be provided by many independent vendors. In Chapter 8, we develop a Web application using JavaBeans.

1.7 Summary

In this chapter, we first showed the goals and the structure of this book. We then discussed

1. what a Web application is and how Web applications can be used in B2B scenarios,

2. the basics of XML and its application areas, and

3. the merits of using Java in Web applications.

The following chapters will take you through Web application programming using XML and Java.

Parsing XML Documents

2.1 Introduction

In this chapter, we discuss the parsing of XML documents using an XML processor. **Parsing** is the process of reading a document and dissecting it into its elements that can then be analyzed. In XML, parsing is done by an *XML processor,* the most fundamental building block of a Web application. In particular, we show you how to set up your programming environment in XML for Java. Next, we discuss how to read, parse, and print a simple XML document. We finish by explaining how to do basic programming using three common APIs: DOM, SAX, and ElementHandler.

2.2 XML Processors

As explained in Chapter 1, an **XML processor** is a software module that is used to read XML documents and provide application programs with access to their content and structure. Several XML processors written in Java are available. Recall from Chapter 1 that some are **validating** processors, while others are **nonvalidating**. When reading an XML document, a validating processor checks the validity constraints and the well-formedness constraints defined in the XML 1.0 Recommendation, issued in February 1998, and reports any violations. A nonvalidating processor checks only the well-formedness constraints.

In this book, we use XML for Java, a validating XML processor, one of the most robust and faithful implementations of XML processor. The complete current release of XML for Java is included on the accompanying CD-ROM and conforms to the 1.0 Recommendation. Or you can download it from IBM's Web site at `http://www.alphaworks.ibm.com/formula/xml/`. XML for Java comes with a free commercial license, meaning you may freely distribute it within your own products. Just be sure to read the licensing information in `license.html`, located on the CD-ROM. However, the behavior of any conforming XML processor is highly predictable, so using another conforming XML processor should not be difficult, if you so choose. Appendix B compares some of the major XML processors.

2.3 Introduction to XML for Java

The validating processor XML for Java is a Java class library and therefore requires basic Java programming skills to use. To begin using it, you need to set up your programming environment as follows:

1. Install the JDK (Java Development Kit).

2. Install XML for Java.

3. Update the CLASSPATH environment variable.

XML for Java is written in Java 1.1, so you first need to have the JDK version 1.1.7B or later version installed on your system. We developed our sample programs in JDK 1.1.7B. If needed, you can download the latest release from Sun Microsystems' Web site, `http://java.sun.com/`. At the time of this writing, JDK 1.2 has just been released. XML for Java has been tested against this version, so you should be able to use it as well. In the samples in the book, we assume you have installed JDK in `c:\jdk1.1.7B`.

The second step in setting up your programming environment is to install XML for Java (if not already done). In developing our sample programs, we used XML for Java version 1.1.9. The CD-ROM that accompanies this book contains version 1.1.9. To install XML for Java:

1. Create a directory for XML for Java on your system, and call it `xml4j`.

2. On the CD-ROM, move to the directory containing XML for Java and locate the zipped file containing the program, `xml4j_1_1_9.zip`.

3. Unzip `xml4j_1_1_9.zip`. Note, the zip tool you use needs to support long filenames.

In the samples in the book, we assume you have installed XML for Java in
`c:\xml4j`.

Note that because XML for Java is written in Java, it theoretically can run in any
operating system platform on any hardware that supports Java 1.1. However,
different platforms might differ, for example in how to set environment variables. We use Windows (NT and 95/98) in our command line input/output
examples in this book. If your platform is other than these, you should replace
the command prompts and certain shell commands with those appropriate for
your platform.

The third step in setting up your programming environment is to set the environment variable CLASSPATH to tell the Java interpreter where to find the Java
class libraries. To execute the samples in this book, you must have in your
CLASSPATH the jar file `xml4j\xml4j_1_1_9.jar`. You might also want to
include the current directory (.) in your CLASSPATH. You can set both of these
in Windows 95/98 by using the following command:

```
c:\xml4j>set CLASSPATH=.;c:\xml4j\xml4j_1_1_9.jar;c:\xml4j\
xml4jSamples_1_1_9.jar
```

In NT, you set it the same as for the above.

You also might want to add this command line to your profile to avoid having
to type it every time you bring up a new command prompt. In Windows 95/98,
you would add it to the `autoexec.bat` file. In NT, you would add it by right-
clicking My Computer and then left-clicking System Property/Environment tab
and adding the new variable CLASSPATH in the Environment dialog.

To see if the installation was successful, move to the installation directory
(`c:\xml4j`) and enter the following command:

```
c:\xml4j>java samples.XJParse.XJParse -format data/personnel.xml
```

This should open a formatted output of a sample XML file named
`personnel.xml`. If it does not, double-check your installation, especially the
CLASSPATH environment variable.

An alternative way to tell the Java interpreter where to find the Java classes that
doesn't involve setting CLASSPATH is to enter the following command:

```
c:\xml4j>java -classpath
.;c:\xml4j\xml4j_1_1_9.jar;c:\xml4j\xml4jSamples_1_1_9.jar
samples.XJParse.XJParse -format data/personnel.xml
```

Now you are ready to try the sample programs on the CD-ROM. Go to the `samples\chap2` directory, which contains all of the samples in this chapter. Note, in our samples we use "R" for the CD-ROM drive; you should substitute the correct letter for your own CD-ROM drive. Enter the following command to launch the program `SimpleParse` to read the document `department.xml`:

```
R:\samples\chap2>java SimpleParse department.xml
```

You will see nothing. However, this is expected because this sample program produces no output.

All of the sample programs in the book are included on the CD-ROM. Take a few moments to explore the CD-ROM before moving on to the next section.

2.4 Reading an XML Document

In this section, we show you how to read a simple XML document, called `department.xml`, using XML for Java. This document represents a set of employee records in a department and is shown next.

```
<?xml version="1.0"?>
<!DOCTYPE department SYSTEM "department.dtd">
<department>
    <employee id="J.D">
        <name>John Doe</name>
        <email>John.Doe@foo.ibm.com</email>
    </employee>

    <employee id="B.S">
        <name>Bob Smith</name>
        <email>Bob.Smith@foo.com</email>
    </employee>

    <employee id="A.M">
        <name>Alice Miller</name>
        <url href="http://www.trl.jp.ibm.com/~amiller/"/>
    </employee>
</department>
```

The DTD of this document is given in a separate file, `department.dtd`, shown next. The meanings of the tags should be self-explanatory.

```
<!ELEMENT department (employee)*>
<!ELEMENT employee (name, (email | url))>
```

```
<!ATTLIST employee id CDATA #REQUIRED>
<!ELEMENT name (#PCDATA)>
<!ELEMENT email (#PCDATA)>
<!ELEMENT url EMPTY>
<!ATTLIST url href CDATA #REQUIRED>
```

Next, we read `department.xml` using XML for Java. We run the sample program, `SimpleParse`, located in `samples\chap2` on the CD-ROM, using the following command:

```
R:\samples\chap2>java SimpleParse department.xml
```

This program, as in the previous section, produces no output. However, we know that XML for Java did its job, for `SimpleParse`

- opened the document `department.xml`,

- found that `department.dtd` is the document's DTD,

- read that DTD and analyzed `department.xml` according to the syntax defined in the DTD, and

- created a corresponding data structure in memory, a structure that can later be referred to or manipulated by application programs such as a Java object.

The fact that you see no output means that there were no violations of well-formedness or validity constraints.

Listing 2.1 gives the source code of `SimpleParse`. Although a very short program, it shows the basics of how you can use XML for Java.

Listing 2.1 `SimpleParse.java`: Reads and parses an XML document

```
[1] import org.w3c.dom.Document;
[2] import com.ibm.xml.parser.Parser;
    import java.io.FileInputStream;

    public class SimpleParse {
        public static void main(String[] argv) {
            if (argv.length != 1) {
                System.err.println("Require a filename.");
                System.exit(1);
            }
            try {

[13]            FileInputStream is = new FileInputStream(argv[0]);
                                    // Opens the specified file.
```

```
                                    // Starts to parse.
[15]          Parser parser = new Parser(argv[0]);
                                    // @XML4J
[16]          Document doc = parser.readStream(is);
[17]                            // Error?
[18]          if (parser.getNumberOfErrors() > 0) {
[19]              System.exit(1);     // If the document has error,
[20]                                  // the program terminates.
[21]          }
[22]                                  // Codes for process will be here.
[23]      } catch (Exception e) {
[24]          e.printStackTrace();
[25]      }
      }
    }
```

> **NOTE:** In the sample programs in this book, we generally avoid using XML for Java-specific features. When we do use such features in Part 1, we mark the affected lines with the comment @XML4J.

To work with this program, we need to import two classes from two packages:

- In line [1], the class Document, from `org.w3c.dom`, which is an interface that represents the whole XML document

- In line [2], the class `Parser`, from the package `com.ibm.xml.parser`, which contains the main routines for XML for Java and is used to parse an XML document

Note, later we will need to import other classes in the `com.ibm.xml.parser` package, so we could tell the compiler to import all of the classes in the package, as follows:

```
import com.ibm.xml.parser.*;
```

In this book, however, we chose to explicitly list all of the classes used in each example so that you can know what classes are actually used.

The most important part of this program is the following three lines:

```
[13] FileInputStream is = new FileInputStream(argv[0]);
```

Creates an input stream for reading a file.

```
[15] Parser parser = new Parser (argv[0]);
```

Creates an instance of a `Parser` object.

```
[16] Document doc = parser.readStream(is);
```

Passes the stream to the parser.

In this code fragment, `argv[0]` refers to the first command line argument, which is the name of the file to be opened. `Parser` requires the filename as its argument when it is created because it uses the filename in error messages, if any. If parsing succeeds without errors, an instance of the class `Document`, which as mentioned earlier represents the entire document structure, is created. It is assigned to the variable `doc`. You can access the root element of the structure using `doc` and can visit and edit its child elements. (However, the program simply ends without doing anything.)

For the sake of completeness, this program also contains a test for the command line arguments (line [7]–[9]), a test for the number of errors during parsing (line [19]–[21]), and an exception handling (line [23]–[25]).

You might think that this program has no practical value because it does not produce any output. However, it is very useful as a syntax checker. It can tell you whether the input XML document is well formed and valid. To show you how this works, we give an invalid document, `department2.xml`, to `SimpleParse`.

```
<?xml version="1.0"?>
<!DOCTYPE department SYSTEM "department.dtd">
<department>
  <employee id="J.D">
    <name>John Doe</name>
  </employee>

  <employee id="B.S">
    <name>Bob Smith</name>
    <email>Bob.Smith@foo.com</email>
  </employee>

  <employee id="A.M">
    <name>Alice Miller</name>
    <url href="http://www.trl.jp.ibm.com/~amiller/"/>
  </employee>
</department>
```

Note that the first employee (John Doe) does not have an `email` or `url` tag. This violates the DTD, which requires that an `employee` tag must have both a `name` tag and either an `email` or a `url` tag. Thus `department2.xml` is not a valid document and `SimpleParse` generates the following error message when reading it.

```
R:\samples\chap>java SimpleParse department2.xml
department2.xml: 6, 13: Content mismatch in '<employee>'. Content
model is "(name, (email|url))'.
```

This message tells you that the content of the `employee` element is invalid according to the content model defined in the DTD. In this case, the `getNumberOfErrors()` method returns a value greater than zero, and the program terminates with return value 1.

> **NOTE:** Actual error messages may differ depending on your locale setting. Java 1.1 can switch resources, such as messages, based on the current locale setting. XML for Java uses this capability to switch error messages. Currently English and Japanese error messages are distributed in the package. If you are running XML for Java in a Japanese environment, the previous message will be shown in Japanese.

We have shown a simple program that reads an XML document using XML for Java. Although simple, it serves as a basis for more complex programs and can be used as an XML syntax checker. In the next section, we show how to generate an XML document from the internal structure.

2.5 Working with Character Encoding in XML Documents

Every conforming XML processor must support at least two Unicode encodings: UTF-8 and UTF-16. UTF-8 and UTF-16 are variable-length encodings of the Unicode character set.

UTF-8 subsumes ASCII; that is, every ASCII character (0x00–0x7F) has the same encoding in UTF-8. Non-ASCII characters have longer encodings; for example, most Chinese characters are represented in 3 bytes in UTF-8. UTF-16 uses 2 bytes for representing even U.S. English characters.

Some XML processors, including XML for Java, support conversion to and from other locale-specific encodings used in different parts of the world. For example, XML for Java supports more than 30 encodings, including European, Japanese, Chinese, and Korean.

The XML 1.0 Recommendation allows you to specify the character encoding of an XML document by declaring it in the first line of the document, for example,

```
<?xml version="1.0" encoding="UTF-16"?>
```

How can an XML processor recognize that this document is encoded in UTF-16 before reading this line? Isn't this a chicken-and-the-egg problem? The answer is that an XML usually starts with `<?xml`. Thus the processor can read the first 4 bytes of the file and determine the basic scheme of encoding (ASCII-compatible encoding basis such as UTF-8, 16-bit basis such as UTF-16, and so on). Only a limited set of characters are allowed in the first line, so it is sufficient to parse the line. After parsing the `encoding` attribute, the processor resets its encoding rule to the specified one. If the processor cannot determine the basic encoding scheme after looking at the first four octets, it assumes that the encoding is UTF-8. Therefore, a document with an encoding other than UTF-8 must start with `<?xml`.

2.6 Printing an XML Document from a Parsed Structure

Our second sample program, `SimpleParseAndPrint`, shown in Listing 2.2, is a minimum modification to `SimpleParse` that prints an XML document to standard output after reading and parsing it. It differs from `SimpleParse` in the addition of the following lines.

```
[1] import com.ibm.xml.parser.TXDocument;
[2] import java.io.PrintWriter;
    ...
   [27] ((TXDocument)doc).print (new PrintWriter (System.out));
```

Listing 2.2 `SimpleParseAndPrint.java`: Reproduces an XML document from a parsed structure

```
[1] import com.ibm.xml.parser.Parser;
[2] import com.ibm.xml.parser.TXDocument;
    import java.io.FileInputStream;
    import java.io.PrintWriter;
    import org.w3c.dom.Document;

    public class SimpleParseAndPrint {
    public static void main(String[] argv) {
        if (argv.length != 1) {
            System.err.println("Require a filename.");
            System.exit(1);
        }
        try {
            FileInputStream is = new FileInputStream(argv[0]);
                                                    // Opens the
                                                    // specified file.
                                                    // Starts to parse.
            Parser parser = new Parser(argv[0]);    // @XML4J
            Document doc = parser.readStream(is);   // @XML4J
            if (parser.getNumberOfErrors() > 0) {   // Error? @XML4J
                System.exit(1);                     // If the document
                                                    // has error,
                                                    // the program
                                                    // terminates.
            }
            // Prints to the standard output in XML format.
   [27] ((TXDocument)doc).print(new PrintWriter(System.out));
                    // @XML4J
            // Codes for process will be here.
        } catch (Exception e) {
            e.printStackTrace();
        }
    }
}
```

Recall that the variable `doc` holds the instance of the class `Document` that represents an entire internal structure of an XML document. `Document` is an interface, so the variable `doc` actually holds an instance of `Document`'s implementation class, `TXDocument`, which is provided by XML for Java. `TXDocument` has a `print()` method that takes a `java.io.Writer` as its argument and generates an XML document from the internal structure. In this example, the output goes to the standard output (System.out), with the character encoding determined by the current locale. Note that TXDocument and print() are implementation-specific, so you need to use something else if you are using a different XML processor.

> **NOTE:** As is always true for good (long-lived) software, XML for Java contains names inherited from its early development days. TX originally referred to Tokyo Research Laboratory's XML processor (IBM has seven research laboratories worldwide, of which Tokyo is one). So it likely will not really mean anything to you. It was intentionally left as a prefix in later releases of XML for Java. This is because without some uncommon prefixes the class names such as Element and Text would be too general so that application programmers might be forced, at times, to specify the full class name, as in com.ibm.xml.parser.Text, if it is confusing with other classes. We wanted to have something uncommon as our prefix. TX is as meaningless as any other random prefix, so why not TX?

Following is the output of the program.

```
R:\samples\chap2>java SimpleParseAndPrint department.xml
<?xml version="1.0"?>
<!DOCTYPE department SYSTEM "department.dtd">
<department>
  <employee id="J.D">
    <name>John Doe</name>
    <email>John.Doe@foo.ibm.com</email>
  </employee>

  <employee id="B.S">
    <name>Bob Smith</name>
    <email>Bob.Smith@foo.com</email>
  </employee>

  <employee id="A.M">
    <name>Alice Miller</name>
    <url href="http://www.trl.jp.ibm.com/~amiller/"/>
  </employee>
</department>
```

Note that the input file department .xml is exactly reproduced in the output. XML for Java is designed to preserve the appearance of the input as much as possible, including whitespaces and line breaks. More on the handling of whitespace is in Chapter 3.

2.7 Programming Interfaces for Document Structure

In the previous two sections, we showed how to read and print an XML document. Next, we explain how to process an XML document by accessing internal structure, as well as how to do additional useful tasks.

To process an XML document by accessing internal structure, we need to use APIs (application program interfaces). The XML 1.0 Recommendation defines the precise behavior of an XML processor when reading and printing a file, but it says nothing about which API to use. In this section, we discuss two widely used APIs used in XML processors:

- **Document Object Model (DOM)** (Level 1), a tree structure-based API issued as a W3C Recommendation in October 1998.

- **Simple API for XML (SAX)**, an event-driven API developed by David Megginson and a number of people on the xml-dev mailing list on the Web. Although not sanctioned by any standards body, SAX is supported by most of the available XML processors because of its simplicity.

We also discuss *ElementHandler,* an event-driven proprietary API provided by XML for Java. Following is a brief comparison of the three APIs. We cover each in more depth in the next three subsections.

In DOM, an XML document is represented as a tree whose nodes are elements, text, and so on. An XML processor generates the tree and hands it to an application program; see Figure 2.1. DOM provides a set of APIs to access and manipulate these nodes in the DOM tree. A DOM-based XML processor creates the entire structure of an XML document in memory, so it is suitable for applications that operate on the document as a whole. In particular, the use of DOM is best suited for the following situations:

- When structurally modifying an XML document, for example, sorting elements in a particular order or moving some elements from one place in the tree to another

- When sharing the document in memory with other applications

An XML processor with SAX does not create a data structure. Instead, it scans an input XML document and generates events, such as the start of an element, the end of an element, and so on (see Figure 2.1). The application program

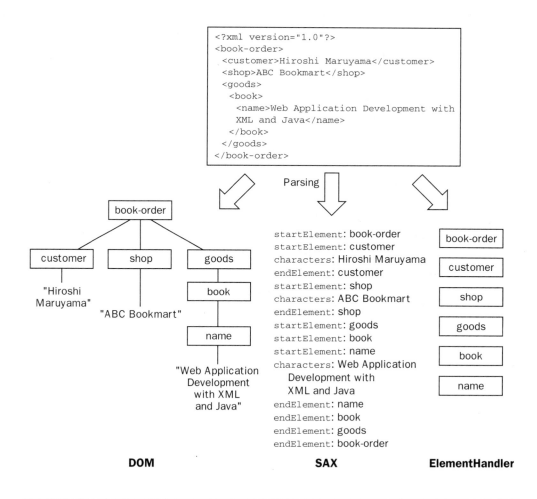

FIGURE 2.1 Comparison of DOM, SAX APIs, and ElementHandler

intercepts these events and does whatever is appropriate for the task at hand, such as getting element names or attribute values. SAX is more efficient than DOM because it does not create an explicit data structure. Therefore it is good for the following occasions:

1. When dealing with a large document that does not fit in memory

2. When doing tasks on elements that are irrelevant to the surrounding document structure, counting the total number of elements in a document, or extracting the contents of a specific element

ElementHandler is event-driven like SAX but creates a DOM tree. It provides a callback function when the parser encounters elements that are specified by the programmer. It is suitable for an event-driven task when the application program also needs to manipulate the internal structure of an element.

In the following subsections, we take the simple task of extracting information from an XML document that has a set of attribute and value pairs and explain how these three API can be used for this task.

2.7.1 Document Object Model

This section introduces the object structure defined by the *Document Object Model* (DOM). The term *document object model* has been used to refer to a model that defines the structure of an HTML document, thereby allowing scripting languages such as JavaScript to access the elements of the structure. You might have experience writing JavaScript programs that manipulate the value of an input field within a Form element. For example, `document.forms(1).username.value` refers to the value of the input field with the name "username" in the first `Form` element in an HTML document. This expression is used to access the HTML DOM or IE and Navigator. However, some expressions cannot be interpreted because the current HTML object models are browser-dependent. Thus you generally should prepare different pages suited for each type of browser that might be displaying your scripts.

The W3C set up a working group, the DOM Working Group, whose goals include defining a common, interoperable document object model for HTML, as well as one for XML. The HTML and XML object models have much in common. The Working Group has recently published a W3C Recommendation, the *Document Object Model (DOM) Level 1 Specification*, which consists of two parts:

• Chapter 1: Document Object Model (Core) Level 1

• Chapter 2: Document Object Model (HTML) Level 1

We use only Chapter 1 in this book, since the object model for XML is defined there. Also, in this book, we use DOM to mean the object model for the core (Chapter 1 of the DOM Specification).

DOM defines a set of Java interfaces to create, access, and manipulate internal structures of XML documents. XML is a language for describing tree-structured data. In XML, an element is represented by a start tag and a matching end tag (or an empty-element tag). An element may contain one or more other elements between its start and end tags. Thus an entire document is rendered as a nested tree. For example, our previous department example `department.xml` can be depicted as shown in Figure 2.2.

Each pair of start and end tags corresponds to an *Element* node, represented by the boxes in the figure, such as `document` and `employee`. Each chunk of text surrounded by two tags corresponds to a *Text* node, represented by the strings in the figure. These nodes are defined as *objects* in DOM. Primarily, DOM defines a platform- and language-neutral interface for application programs in terms of a standard set of objects. To help interoperability, it defines APIs, called *language bindings*, for Java, ECMAScript, and the Object Management Group interface definition language (OMG IDL). The current DOM specification, Level 1, is expected to evolve via the incorporation of additional features.

From an object-oriented programming viewpoint, the DOM API is a set of interfaces that should be implemented by a particular DOM implementation. XML for Java is one example of such a DOM implementation. Table 2.1 shows the interfaces defined in DOM (Core) Level 1.

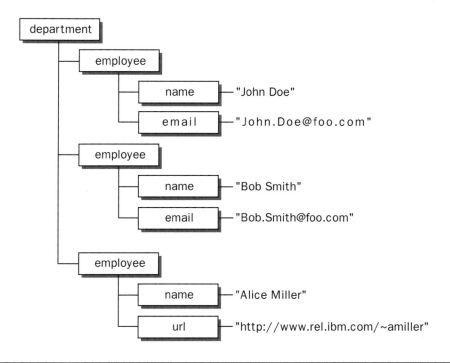

FIGURE 2.2 Structure of an XML document in DOM (`department.xml`)

TABLE 2.1 Core Class Interfaces of DOM Level 1 (based on REC-DOM-19981001)

CLASS INTERFACE NAME	DESCRIPTION	IMPLEMENTATION CLASSES IN XML FOR JAVA
Node	The primary data type representing a single node in the document tree	Child or Parent
Document	The entire XML document	TXDocument
Element	An element and any contained nodes	TXElement
Attr	An attribute in an Element object	TXAttribute
ProcessingInstruction	A processing instruction	TXPI
CDATASection	A CDATASection	TXCDATASection
Document Fragment	A lightweight document object used to represent multiple subtrees or partial documents	TXDocumentFragment
Entity	An entity, parsed or unparsed, in a DocumentType object	EntityDecl.EntityImpl
EntityReference	An entity reference, as it appears in the document tree	GeneralReference
Document Type	A DTD, which contains a list of entities	DTD
Notation	A notation declared in the DTD (a notation declares, by name, the format of an unparsed entity)	TXNotation.NotationImpl
CharacterData	A parent interface of Text and others, which require operations such as insert a string and delete a string	TXCharacterData
Comment	A comment	TXComment
Text	Text	TXText
DOMException	An exception thrown when no further processing is possible; normal errors are reported by return values. Note that this is an abstract class.	TXDOMException
DOMImplementation	A placeholder of methods that are not dependent on specific DOM implementations	NA
NodeList	An ordered collection of nodes; items in the NodeList are accessible via an integral index, starting from 0	NA
NamedNodeMap	A collection of nodes that can be accessed by name	NA

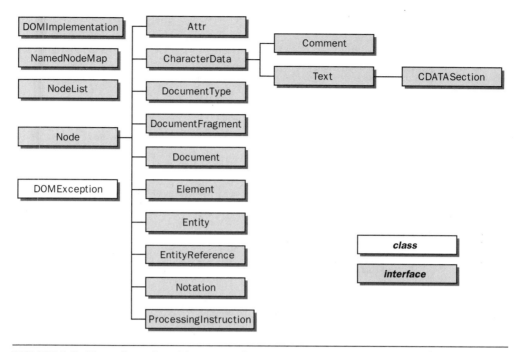

FIGURE 2.3 Class/interface hierarchy of DOM (Core) Level 1 specification (W3C Recommendation)

Figure 2.3 shows the class hierarchy of the DOM (Core) Level 1 interfaces. Note that Node is the primary data structure that constructs a tree structure. DOM tree constituents such as Element, Text, and Attr are all defined as interfaces derived from Node.

Working with DOM

Next, we look at DOM in action. The process consists of two phases: parsing an XML document and accessing the DOM tree. A common action for XML documents is to extract text from elements. Using the sample program MakeEltTblDOM.java, we extract key-value pairs from the XML document keyval.xml, which is shown next.

```
<?xml version="1.0"?>
<keyval>
  <key>URL</key>
  <value>http://www.ibm.com/xml</value>
  <key>Owner</key>
  <value>IBM</value>
</keyval>
```

The complete listing of the program is shown in Listing 2.3.

Listing 2.3 `MakeEltTblDOM.java`: Extracts key-value pairs and stores them in a hash table (DOM-based implementation)

```java
import com.ibm.xml.parser.Parser;
import java.io.FileInputStream;
import java.io.InputStream;
import java.util.Hashtable;
import org.w3c.dom.CDATASection;
import org.w3c.dom.Document;
import org.w3c.dom.Element;
import org.w3c.dom.EntityReference;
import org.w3c.dom.Node;
import org.w3c.dom.Text;

public class MakeEltTblDOM {

    static public void main(String[] argv) {
        if (argv.length != 1) {
            System.err.println("Missing filename.");
            System.exit(1);
        }
        try {
            InputStream is = new FileInputStream(argv[0]);
                                                        // Opens the
                                                        // specified file.
                                                        // Starts
                                                        // parsing.
            Parser parser = new Parser(argv[0]);        // @XML4J
            Document doc = parser.readStream(is);       // @XML4J

            if (parser.getNumberOfErrors() > 0) {       // Checks if
                                                        // there are
                                                        // errors.
                                                        // @XML4J
                System.exit(1);
            }
            // The document is well-formed.

            // Creates a hashtable for string key-value pairs.
            Hashtable hash = new Hashtable();

            String key = null, value = null;
```

```
            // Traverses all of the children of the root element.
[36]        for (Node kvchild = doc.getDocumentElement().
            getFirstChild();

[38]            kvchild != null;
[39]            kvchild = kvchild.getNextSibling()) {

                if (kvchild instanceof Element) {   // When child is
                                                    // an element

                    if (kvchild.getNodeName().equals("key")) { // If
                        tag name is "key," store its content in vkey.

                        key = makeChildrenText(kvchild);

                    } else if (kvchild.getNodeName().
                    equals("value")) {

                        // If tag name is "value", extracts the text
                        // content from the child.
                        value = makeChildrenText(kvchild);
                        // Checks if key is specified and
                        // stores the key-value pair in the
                        // hashtable.
                        if (key != null) {
                            hash.put(key, value);
                            key = null;
                        }
                    }
                }
            }
            // Displays the hashtable.
            System.out.println(hash);

        } catch (Exception e) {
            e.printStackTrace();
        }
    }

[68]    private static String makeChildrenText (Node node){
        // Creates a StringBuffer to store the result.
        // StringBuffer is more efficient than String.
        StringBuffer buffer = new StringBuffer();
        return makeChildrenText1 (node, buffer);
    }
```

```
        private static String makeChildrenText1 (Node node, StringBuffer
        buffer){

            // Visits all of the child nodes.
[78]        for (Node ch = node.getFirstChild();
                ch != null;
                ch = ch.getNextSibling()) {
                // Recursively calls, if the child may have children.
[82]            if (ch instanceof Element || ch instanceof
                  EntityReference) {
                    buffer.append(makeChildrenText(ch));
                // If the child is text, appends it to the result buffer.
                } else if (ch instanceof Text) {
                    buffer.append(ch.getNodeValue());
                }
            }

            return buffer.toString();
        }
    }
```

Suppose we want to get the strings "URL" and "http://www.ibm.com/xml."
First, we find the specified element, such as key or value, in a DOM tree
obtained by parsing and then we extract the text from it. The program reads an
XML document from the file and creates a DOM tree in the variable doc. Next,
it scans all of the child elements of the root element to locate key elements
and value elements.

```
        // Traverses all of the children of the root element.
[36]    for (Node kvchild = doc.getDocumentElement().getFirstChild();
[38]          kvchild != null;
[39]          kvchild = kvchild.getNextSibling()) {
        ...
        }
```

The getDocumentElement() method (line [36]) returns the root element of
the document. The getFirstChild() method returns the first child element of
an element. Together, these extract the first child element of the root element
and assign it to kvchild, a variable of type Node. For each iteration, the next
element is retrieved by the getNextSibling() method (line [39]). With DOM,
this is a standard way to iterate on the child nodes of a given node. The interface Node has other methods to access various other information of the node.
Chapter 4 covers DOM programming in more detail.

The private method `makeChildrenText()` (line [68]) (which simply calls `makeChildrenText1()`) extracts all of the text in the descendant nodes and returns the concatenation of it. It is necessary because `key` elements and/or `value` elements may have subelements recursively. You can see how the program recursively descends into subtrees. The point here is the test on whether an element may have child nodes (either it is an `Element` or an `EntityReference`) at the line [82]. If it is, then the process goes recursively into the child nodes.

```
        . . .
        // Visits all of the child nodes.
[78]    for (Node ch = node.getFirstChild();
            ch != null;
            ch = ch.getNextSibling()) {
            // Recursively calls, if the child may have children.
[82]        if (ch instanceof Element || ch instanceof EntityReference) {
                buffer.append(makeChildrenText(ch));
            // If the child is a text, append it to the result buffer
            } else if (ch instanceof Text) {
                buffer.append(ch.getNodeValue());
            }
        }
```

> **NOTE:** XML for Java provides a number of useful methods for the class `TXElement`. One is `getText()`, whose functionality is the same as `makeChildrenText()`'s. You can replace the line
>
> `value = makeChildrenText(kvchild);`
>
> with
>
> `value = ((TXElement)kvchild).getText()`
>
> and remove the definition of method `makeChildrenText()`. The method `getText()` is used in Section 2.7.2.

The output of this program is the following.

```
R:\samples\chap2>java MakeEltTblDOM keyval.xml
{URL=http://www.ibm.com/xml, Owner=IBM}
```

In this subsection, we introduced DOM, the object model for XML documents, and showed a simple program that uses the DOM API. DOM is one of the most fundamental APIs for dealing with XML documents by computer programs.

Chapter 3 and later make heavy use of DOM. Chapter 4 has more on programming techniques using DOM. In addition, we provide the complete Java binding of DOM in Appendix D. In the next subsection, we cover the other fundamental API, SAX.

2.7.2 Event-Driven APIs

In Section 2.7.1, we surveyed the method of using the DOM API to access the structure of an XML document. An alternative to DOM to access the document structure is to use an event-driven API. An application that wants information about document structure, such as the element type name of each element, attribute names appearing in an element, and attribute values of each attribute, can register **handlers**, a type of callback function, to the XML processor. The processor notifies the handlers of events such as the start of a new tag and the existence of data characters. Unlike when using the DOM API, which is recursive, the entire process is *one-pass,* that is, any application-specific operations are performed during parsing.

In this subsection and the next, we describe two different event-driven APIs. One is the *Simple API for XML* (SAX), which is supported by most XML processors, and the other is *ElementHandler,* which is specific to XML for Java. We first show how SAX can be used for the simple rewriting of XML documents.

Simple API for XML

SAX is designed as a lightweight API that does not involve the generation of internal structures. Applications must register event handlers to a parser object that implements the `org.sax.Parser` interface. SAX has three handler interfaces: `DocumentHandler`, `DTDHandler`, and `ErrorHandler`. (It also provides the default implementation class `HandlerBase` for the default behavior of all of these interfaces.)

`DocumentHandler` is the most important and most often used interface because it is called whenever an element is found. You would typically use `DocumentHandler` as follows. (This is also illustrated in Listing 2.4.)

First, you import the `Parser` interface:

```
import org.xml.sax.Parser;
```

Next, you create an instance of a SAX driver:

```
Class c = Class.forName ("com.ibm.xml.parser.SAXDriver");
```

`"com.ibm.xml.parser.SAXDriver"` is a SAX driver provided by XML for Java. Using this driver, you create a `parser` object:

```
Parser parser = (Parser)c.new Instance();
```

This is a standard technique in Java to dynamically specify a class to be instantiated at runtime. Note that `Parser` is an interface defined in the SAX package.

Next, you register an instance of class `MyHandler` as a DocumentHandler:

```
parser.setDocumentHandler(new MyHandler());
```

`MyHandler` can be programmed by implementing the `DocumentHandler` interface or by subclassing the adapter class, `HandlerBase`. You can define only the methods you need.

Table 2.2 shows the methods defined in the `DocumentHandler` interface.

TABLE 2.2 `DocumentHandler` Methods

METHOD	DESCRIPTION
`startDocument ()`	Receives notification of the beginning of the document.
`endDocument ()`	Receives notification of the end of the document.
`startElement (String name, AttributeList atts)`	Receives notification of the beginning of an element.
`endElement (String name)`	Receives notification of the end of an element.
`characters (char ch [], int start, int length)`	Receives notification of character data.
`ignorableWhitespace (char ch [], int start, int length)`	Receives notification of ignorable whitespace in element content.
`processingInstruction (String target, String data)`	Receives notification of a processing instruction.
`setDocumentLocator (Locator locator)`	Receives an object for locating the origin of SAX document events. The `Locator` object gives information on the location of the event, such as line number and column position.

Sax defines several event types and associated methods. It can be helpful to understand how these methods are called during the parsing process, so our first SAX sample program, `NotifyStr.java` reports all of the SAX events to the standard output. Listing 2.4 shows the complete listing.

Listing 2.4 `NotifyStr.java`: Traces the methods of `DocumentHandler`

```java
import org.xml.sax.AttributeList;
import org.xml.sax.HandlerBase;
import org.xml.sax.Parser;
import org.xml.sax.Locator;
import org.xml.sax.SAXException;

public class NotifyStr extends HandlerBase {
    static public void main(String[] argv) {
        try {

            Class c = Class.forName(argv[0]);        // Gets a class
                                                     // object for SAX
                                                     // Driver.
            Parser parser = (Parser)c.newInstance(); // Creates an
                                                     // instance of
                                                     // the class.
            NotifyStr notifyStr = new NotifyStr();   // Creates a
                                                     // document
                                                     // handler,
            parser.setDocumentHandler(notifyStr);    // and registers
                                                     // it.
            parser.parse(argv[1]);

        } catch (Exception e) {
            e.printStackTrace();
        }
    }

    public NotifyStr() {
    }

    public void startDocument() throws SAXException {
        System.out.println("startDocument is called:");
    }

    public void endDocument() throws SAXException {
        System.out.println("endDocument is called:");
    }
```

```
    public void startElement(String name, AttributeList amap) throws
    SAXException {
        System.out.println("startElement is called: element name="
          + name);
        for (int i = 0; i < amap.getLength(); i++) {
            String attname = amap.getName(i);
            String type = amap.getType(i);
            String value = amap.getValue(i);
            System.out.println("  attribute name="+attname+"
              type="+type+" value="+value);
        }
    }

    public void endElement(String name) throws SAXException {
        System.out.println("endElement is called: " + name);
    }

    public void characters(char[] ch, int start, int length) throws
    SAXException {
        System.out.println("characters is called: " + new String(ch,
    start, length));
    }
}
```

This program takes a SAX driver class as the first command line argument and the filename of an XML document as the second argument. To run the program using XML for Java as the SAX driver, you have to supply `"com.ibm.xml.parser.SAXDriver"` as the first argument. Following is the output of `NotifyStr.java`.

```
R:\samples\chap2>java NotifyStr com.ibm.xml.parser.SAXDriver
department.xml
startDocument is called:
startElement is called: element name=department
startElement is called: element name=employee
    attribute name=id type=CDATA value=J.D
startElement is called: element name=name
characters is called: John Doe
endElement is called: name
startElement is called: element name=email
characters is called: John.Doe@foo.ibm.com
endElement is called: email
endElement is called: employee
startElement is called: element name=employee
    attribute name=id type=CDATA value=B.S
```

```
startElement is called: element name=name
characters is called: Bob Smith
endElement is called: name
startElement is called: element name=email
characters is called: Bob.Smith@foo.com
endElement is called: email
endElement is called: employee
startElement is called: element name=employee
    attribute name=id type=CDATA value=A.M
startElement is called: element name=name
characters is called: Alice Miller
endElement is called: name
startElement is called: element name=email
characters is called: Alice.Miller@jp.ibm.com
endElement is called: email
endElement is called: employee
endElement is called: department
endDocument is called:
```

With this output, you should be able to understand when these methods in the listing are called. For example, when the parser recognizes a start tag, the method `startElement` is called and the name of the element is printed.

To highlight the differences in programming with DOM, we show in Listing 2.5 the SAX version of the program for extracting key-value pairs given in Listing 2.3.

Listing 2.5 `MakeEltTblSAX.java`: Extracts key-value pairs and stores them in a hash table (SAX-based implementation).

```java
import java.io.File;
import java.io.FileInputStream;
import java.io.InputStream;
import java.net.URL;
import java.util.Hashtable;
import org.xml.sax.AttributeList;
import org.xml.sax.HandlerBase;
import org.xml.sax.Parser;
import org.xml.sax.SAXException;

public class MakeEltTblSAX extends HandlerBase {
    static public void main(String[] argv) {
        if (argv.length != 2) {
            System.err.println("Usage: java MakeEltTblSAX
            <SAX-class-name> <xml-filename>");
```

```
            System.err.println("When you use IBM's XML for Java,
               com.ibm.xml.parser.SAXDriver is for SAX-class-name");
            System.exit(1);
         }
         try {
            Class c = Class.forName(argv[0]);          // Gets a class
                                                        // object for SAX
                                                        // Driver.
            Parser parser = (Parser)c.newInstance(); // Creates an
                                                        // instance of
                                                        // the class.
            MakeEltTblSAX makehash = new MakeEltTblSAX();
                                                        // Create a
                                                        // document
                                                        // handler,
            parser.setDocumentHandler(makehash);        // and registers
                                                        // it.


            parser.parse(argv[1]);

            System.out.println(makehash.m_hash);
         } catch (Exception e) {
            e.printStackTrace();
         }
      }

      Hashtable m_hash;
      public MakeEltTblSAX() {
         m_hash = new Hashtable();
         m_state = STATE_OTHER;
         m_textbuf = new StringBuffer();
      }

      int m_state;
      static final int STATE_KEY = 0, STATE_VALUE = 1, STATE_OTHER = 2;
      StringBuffer m_textbuf;
      String m_key;

[55]  public void startElement(String name, AttributeList amap) throws
      SAXException {
         if (name.equals("key")) {
            m_state = STATE_KEY;                        // Stores the status.
            m_textbuf.setLength(0);
         } else if (name.equals("value")) {
```

```
                    m_state = STATE_VALUE;              // Stores the status.
                    m_textbuf.setLength(0);
                }
            }

[66]    public void endElement(String name) throws SAXException {
            if (name.equals("key")) {
                m_key = m_textbuf.toString();
                this.m_state = STATE_OTHER;
            } else if (name.equals("value")) {
                m_hash.put(m_key, m_textbuf.toString());
                this.m_state = STATE_OTHER;
            }
        }

[76]    public void characters(char[] ch, int start, int length) throws
        SAXException {
            if (m_state == STATE_KEY || m_state == STATE_VALUE) {
                m_textbuf.append(ch, start, length);
            }
        }

        public void endDocument() throws SAXException {
            m_textbuf = null;
            m_key = null;
        }
    }
```

This program produces exactly the same result as in Listing 2.3, as follows:

```
R:\samples\chap2>java MakeEltTblSAX com.ibm.xml.parser.SAXDriver
keyval.xml
{URL=http://www.ibm.com/xml, Owner=IBM}
```

Note that in this sample program, the SAX driver's name is specified in the command line. Also, there is no XML processor-dependent code in this program. MakeEltTblSAX.java should run with any SAX-compatible XML processor, with proper SAX driver class.

As this example shows, for any element in the tree three methods are called, in this order (arguments are omitted):

- startElement()

- characters() (possibly multiple times)

- endElement

However, as these are called independently of each other, the application program is responsible for keeping track of with which element an event is associated. In `MakeEltTblSAX.java`, the variable `m_state` holds the state of the process if the current tag is `key` or `value`. It is set in the `startElement()` method, as shown next.

```
[55] public void startElement(String name, AttributeList amap) throws
     SAXException {
         if (name.equals("key")) {
             m_state = STATE_KEY;
             m_textbuf.setLength(0);
         } else if (name.equals("value")) {
             m_state = STATE_VALUE;
             m_textbuf.setLength(0);
         }
     }
```

The variable `m_state` is reset in the `endElement()` method.

When text is found (that is, the `characters()` method is called), the program checks whether it appears in a context of either `key` or `value`, and if so, concatenates the string to the buffer.

```
[76] public void characters(char[] ch, int start, int length) throws
     SAXException {
         if (STATE_KEY == m_state || STATE_VALUE == m_state) {
             m_textbuf.append(ch, start, length);
         }
     }
```

When `endElement()` is called, the assembled text strings are stored in the hashtable.

```
[66] public void endElement(String name) throws SAXException {
         if (name.equals("key")) {
             m_key = m_textbuf.toString();
             this.m_state = STATE_OTHER;
         } else if (name.equals("value")) {
             m_hash.put(m_key, m_textbuf.toString());
             this.m_state = STATE_OTHER;
         }
     }
```

ElementHandler

IBM's XML for Java allows you to register an element handler to a particular element name before starting to read an XML document. An element handler is called whenever the parser encounters the specified element. In this subsection, show how an element handler can change the structure of an input document using the ElementHandler API.

As with SAX, an application using ElementHandler can receive events about elements. The two differ in that ElementHandler creates a DOM tree, while SAX does not. On the other hand, an element handler can be attached to elements only—you cannot catch events of other types.

ElementHandler is particularly useful when you need to modify some element while preserving the overall structure. We use `SimpleFilter.java`, shown in Listing 2.6, to illustrate the use of ElementHandler for this purpose.

Listing 2.6 `SimpleFilter.java`: Modifies the structure of an XML document

```
      import org.w3c.dom.Document;
      import com.ibm.xml.parser.Parser;
      import com.ibm.xml.parser.TXDocument;
      import com.ibm.xml.parser.TXElement;
 [5]  import com.ibm.xml.parser.ElementHandler;
      import java.io.FileInputStream;
      import java.io.PrintWriter;

      // Note: This class is XML4J specific.

      public class SimpleFilter implements ElementHandler {

[13]  public TXElement handleElement(TXElement el) { // ElementHandler.
                                                    // @XML4J
          String addr = el.getText();
          TXElement e = new TXElement("url");
          e.setAttribute("href", "mailto:"+addr);
          return e;
      }

      public static void main(String[] argv) {
          if (argv.length != 1) {
              System.err.println("Missing filename.");
              System.exit(1);
          }
```

```
            try {
                FileInputStream is = new FileInputStream(argv[0]);
                Parser parser = new Parser(argv[0]);    // @XML4J

[30]        parser.addElementHandler(new SimpleFilter(), "email");
                                                    // Registers
                                                    // ElementHandler.

            Document doc = parser.readStream(is);    // Starts parsing
                                                    // @XML4J

            // Error?
            if (parser.getNumberOfErrors() > 0) {    // @XML4J
                System.exit(1);    // If the document has error,
                                    // the program terminates.
            }

            // Generates a modified XML document.
            ((TXDocument)doc).printWithFormat(new PrintWriter
            (System.out));                          // @XML4J

        } catch (Exception e) {
            e.printStackTrace();
        }
    }
}
```

This program converts the email tags into the url tags. For example,

```
<email>John.Doe@foo.com</email>
```

is converted to

```
<url href="mailto:John.Doe@foo.com"/>.
```

An element handler is a class that implements the com.ibm.xml.parser. ElementHandler interface. So, first you need to import that interface into your program, using the following line:

```
[5] import com.ibm.xml.parser.ElementHandler;
```

Since ElementHandler is an interface, you must define a class that implements it. ElementHandler has only one method, handleElement(), to be implemented by its implementation class.

> **NOTE:** If you are familiar with C or C++ and not very familiar with Java 1.1's event model, you can consider an element handler as a sort of a callback function. These are, of course, separate concepts, but at least you can get a glimpse of the idea.

The class `SimpleFilter` implements an element handler. In the method `main()`, we create a new instance of this element handler and register it as the handler of the element `email` in the following line:

```
[30] parser.addElementHandler(new SimpleFilter(), "email");
```

During the parsing, when an `email` element is created after recognizing an end tag (`</email>`), the `handleElement()` method of the element handler is called. Here is the implementation of this method.

```
[13]   public TXElement handleElement(TXElement el) { // ElementHandler
           String addr = el.getText();
           TXElement e = new TXElement("url");
           e.setAttribute("href", "mailto:"+addr);
           return e;
       }
```

The newly generated `email` element is passed through the argument `el`. The program obtains the text string in this element (such as `"John.Doe@foo.com"`) by calling `getText()` (this is functionally equivalent to the `makeChildrenText()` method in Section 2.7.1) and setting it to the variable `addr`. Then, another element named `url` is created and the address is set to its `href` attribute. Finally, this new `url` element is returned as the return value of this method, replacing the original `email` element in the resulting DOM tree. In this way, `<email>John.Doe@foo.com</email>` is replaced by `<url href="mailto:John.Doe@foo.com"/>`.

Following is the result of executing the program.

```
R:\samples\chap2>java SimpleFilter department.xml
<?xml version="1.0"?>
<!DOCTYPE department SYSTEM "department.dtd" >
<department>
    <employee id="J.D">
        <name>John Doe</name>
[7]        <url href="mailto:John.Doe@foo.ibm.com"/>
    </employee>
    <employee id="B.S">
```

```
                  <name>Bob Smith</name>
[11]              <url href="mailto:Bob.Smith@foo.com"/>
              </employee>
              <employee id="A.M">
                  <name>Alice Miller</name>
[15]              <url href="http://www.trl.jp.ibm.com/~amiller/"/>
              </employee>
          </department>
```

As you see, the `email` tags of John Doe, Bob Smith, and Alice Miller have been replaced by the `url` tags (lines [7], [11], and [15]).

> **NOTE:** In XML for Java, validity constraints are checked after ElementHandler is called. In other words, the constraints are applied to the modified structure. Therefore the `url` element must be declared in the DTD.

You can attach as many element handlers as you like to any element names. By default, the `handleElement()` method is called after the parser sees the end tag of an element. For example, if you have an element handler attached to `employee`, it is called when the parser sees an `</employee>` tag.

```
<department>
    <employee id="J.D">
        <name>John Doe</name>
        <email>John.Doe@foo.com</email>
        <title>Manager<title/>
    </employee>
<department>
```

For this input, all of the complete element structures for `name`, `email`, and `title` are available to the element handler of `employee`. On the other hand, the element for `department` is not yet complete, so it is not available to you. Exceptions to this are the attributes of the parent tag—XML for Java provides methods for accessing them. For the details, refer to Appendix D for the interface specifications.

Java 1.1 introduced a powerful concept called *inner class* into Java language syntax whereby you can embed a class definition within an expression as an anonymous class. Inner classes are particularly useful for element handlers because you do not need to give a separate name for each element handler. In the previous example, we defined `SimpleFilter` as an implementation of

ElementHandler and registered it as an element handler of `email`, as shown next.

```
parser.addElementHandler(new SimpleFilter(), "email");
```

With an inner class, we can embed a class definition in place of new `addElementerHandler()` as follows.

```
parser.addElementHandler(new ElementHandler() {
    public TXElement handleElement(TXElement el) {
        String addr = el.getText();
        TXElement e = new TXElement("url");
        e.setAttribute("href", "mailto:"+addr);
        return e;
    }
    , "email");
}
```

The entire rewritten program is shown in Listing 2.7.

Listing 2.7 `SimpleFilter2`: Modifies the structure of an XML document (inner class-based version)

```
import org.w3c.dom.Document;
import com.ibm.xml.parser.Parser;
import com.ibm.xml.parser.TXDocument;
import com.ibm.xml.parser.TXElement;
import com.ibm.xml.parser.ElementHandler;
import java.io.FileInputStream;
import java.io.PrintWriter;

// Note: This class is XML4J specific.

public class SimpleFilter2 {

    public static void main(String[] argv) {
        if (argv.length != 1) {
            System.err.println("Missing filename.");
            System.exit(1);
        }
        try {
            FileInputStream is = new FileInputStream(argv[0]);
            Parser parser = new Parser(argv[0]);                // @XML4J

            parser.addElementHandler(new ElementHandler() {  // @XML4J
                public TXElement handleElement(TXElement el) {
                    String addr = el.getText();
```

```
                        TXElement e = new TXElement("url");
                        e.setAttribute("href", "mailto:"+addr);
                        return e;
                    }}
                    , "email");

            Document doc = parser.readStream(is);    // Starts parsing.
            // Error?
            if (parser.getNumberOfErrors() > 0) {    // @XML4J

                System.exit(1);                      // If the document
                                                     // has error,
                                                     // the program
                                                     // terminates.
            }

            // Generates the modified XML document
            ((TXDocument)doc).printWithFormat(new PrintWriter(System
                out));

        } catch (Exception e) {
            e.printStackTrace();
        }
    }
}
```

Using element handlers, you can write simple filter programs, such as to search particular tags and to substitute and insert elements.

The next example, in Listing 2.8, is functionally equivalent to MakeEltTblDOM.java (Listing 2.3) from Section 2.7.1. Comparing these two programs, you will see the difference between the two approaches. In MakeEltTblDOM.java, a specific element is searched after creating a whole DOM tree. In MakeEltTblEltHandler.java, element handlers are called in the course of parsing.

Listing 2.8 MakeEltTblEltHandler.java: Extracts key-value pairs and stores them in a hashtable (ElementHandler-based implementation)

```
import java.io.FileInputStream;
import java.io.InputStream;
import java.util.Hashtable;
import com.ibm.xml.parser.ElementHandler;
import com.ibm.xml.parser.Parser;
import com.ibm.xml.parser.TXElement;
```

```
// Note: This class is XML4J specific.

public class MakeEltTblEltHandler implements ElementHandler {

    Hashtable hash = new Hashtable();
    String key = null;

    public TXElement handleElement(TXElement el) { // ElementHandler.
                                                    // @XML4J

        String name = el.getNodeName();    // Gets an element name.
                                            // If the name is "key",
                                            // stores the content.
        if (name.equals("key")) {
            this.key = el.getText();
        } else if (name.equals("value") && this.key != null) {
    // If the element name is "value" and, the variable key is
    // not null, stored key and value to the hashtable.
            this.hash.put(this.key, el.getText());
            this.key = null;
        }
        return el;
    }

    static public void main(String[] argv) {
        if (argv.length != 1) {
            System.err.println("Missing filename.");
            System.exit(1);
        }
        try {

            InputStream is = new FileInputStream(argv[0]); // Opens the
                                                            // specified
                                                            // file.

            Parser parser = new Parser(argv[0]);     // @XML4J

            MakeEltTblEltHandler handler = new MakeEltTblEltHandler();
            parser.addElementHandler(handler, "key");    // Registers
                                                          // ElementHand-
                                                          // ler. @XML4J
            parser.addElementHandler(handler, "value"); // @XML4J

            parser.readStream(is);                       // Starts parsing.
                                                          // @XML4J.
```

```
                        // Error?
                        if (parser.getNumberOfErrors() > 0) {    // @XML4J
                            System.exit(1);
                        }

                        System.out.println(handler.hash);        // Prints the
                                                                 // hashtable.

                    } catch (Exception e) {
                        e.printStackTrace();
                    }
                }
            }
```

Running this program produces exactly the same result as MakeEltTblDOM.java.

```
R:\samples\chap2>java MakeEltTblEltHandler keyval.xml
{URL=http://www.ibm.com/xml, Owner=IBM}
```

The core of this program is the handleElement() method. This method is registered for two tag names: value and key. The tag name is obtained by calling the getNodeName() method, while the content of the tag is obtained with getText(). These methods are specific to XML for Java.

In this section, we examined the three APIs provided by XML for Java. Table 2.3 summarizes the comparison of the three approaches. You should select the one appropriate to your application.

TABLE 2.3 Comparison of DOM, SAX, and ElementHandler

	DOM	SAX	ELEMENTHANDLER
Creates a tree structure?	Yes	No	Yes
Event-driven?	No	Yes	Yes
Types of events available	N/A	Document, Element, Text, PI	Element only
Efficient for large documents?	No	Yes	Yes

2.8 Summary

In this chapter, we discussed the basics of programming using XML for Java as an XML processor. We showed how to read and generate XML documents and introduced two types of APIs: the DOM API and the event-driven APIs, SAX and ElementHandler.

With DOM, an entire DOM tree is always created before any application-specific tasks are done. By contrast, with an event-driven API you can implement a simple task easily as a one-pass process. Thus event-driven APIs can be more efficient than the DOM API. On the other hand, it is hard to randomly access different parts of a DOM tree with a one-pass process. You should consider the pros and cons of these methods and select an appropriate method.

The next chapter deals in more detail with generating XML documents.

CHAPTER 3

Constructing and Generating XML Documents

3.1 Introduction

In the examples in Chapter 2, we assumed that there was an input XML document before any process began. If you are to build an application program that takes a set of data from a backend database and generates an XML document based on that data, you might need to create a document structure from scratch. In this chapter, we present the basics of constructing an internal DOM tree. Once the structure is built, you can instruct XML for Java to generate an XML document from it.

We first discuss the generation of a DOM tree without worrying about a DTD and validity. The DOM API enables you to build a well-formed DOM tree without relying on any particular implementation of XML processor. Well-formed XML documents are very flexible and quite useful for many applications (especially for document applications).

If you use XML for messaging or exchanging structured data between application programs, validity is important. Validating XML processors check the validity on the receiving side, but generally it is more desirable to generate a valid XML document in the first place. So, we show you how to build a valid DOM tree according to a given DTD. Unfortunately, the DOM Level 1 specification has no definition for accessing DTD information. Thus, we use XML for Java's native API for parsing and examining a DTD.

Finally, we cover topics (especially, handling of whitespace) that require careful attention when generating an XML document from an internal DOM structure.

3.2 Creating an Internal Structure from Scratch

In this section, we show how to build a DOM tree without reading an external XML document. The sample program we write, `MakeDocumentWithFactory`, creates a very simple DOM tree from scratch. Recall that in the DOM tree structure, a document is represented by a `Document` object. So this is what you need first to create. Since the implementation class of `Document` in XML for Java is `TXDocument`, you must explicitly generate an object of `TXDocument` as follows.

```
import org.w3c.dom.Document;
import com.ibm.xml.parser.TXDocument;
    ...
Document doc = new TXDocument();      // @XML4J.
```

If the DOM implementation is dynamically selected at runtime, you can use Java 1.1's reflection feature to create a class object and then create an instance of it, as follows.

```
import org.w3c.dom.Document;
String documentImplClass = "com.ibm.xml.parser.TXDocument";
Document doc =
(Document)Class.forName(documentImplClass).newInstance();
```

This is a little more complicated, but it is preferable because it compiles without XML for Java and thus is more XML processor-independent.

The other DOM objects such as `Element` and `Text` also need to be created as implementation-specific objects. The `Document` interface has implementation-neutral methods for creating them. That is, `Document` is an abstract factory interface, so we use the *Abstract Factory* interface. It uses the *Factory Method* design pattern. The Abstract Factory pattern and the Factory Method pattern are well-known design patterns that, when generating a new object, make applications independent of any implementation class. A *design pattern* is a set of well-known techniques in object-oriented programming that maximize the reusability of code. Abstract Factory and Factory Method are two of these patterns. A number of these have resulted from the development of large programs. The standard Java class library uses many design patterns.[1]

For example, suppose you want to create a `person` element and set it as the root element of the document `doc`. In XML for Java, the interface `Element` is implemented by the class `TXElement`, so a naive code might look as follows.

```
Element root = new TXElement("person");      // @XML4J.
doc.appendChild(root);
```

Unfortunately, this code is dependent on the specific implementation—XML for Java. You can eliminate this kind of implementation dependency by using a factory method. Thus the previous example can be rewritten as follows.

```
Element root = doc.createElement("person");
doc.appendChild(root);
```

Now the code is solely written in the DOM API and so is more portable. Table 3.1 lists the factory methods provided by a Document object. We use these in our examples.

The `Document` object contains the information on the *prolog* part of a document, including the DTD, root node, comments, and processing instructions. The following objects can be attached as its children (remember, `Document` is also derived from `Node`):

• At most, one `DocumentType` object—this represents the DTD

• One `Element` object—this is the root element

TABLE 3.1 `Document` Object Factory Methods

```
public Element                    createElement(String tagName);
public DocumentFragment           createDocumentFragment();
public Text                       createTextNode(String data);
public Comment                    createComment(String data);
public CDATASection               createCDATASection(String data);
public ProcessingInstruction      createProcessingInstruction(String
                                  target, String data);
public Attr                       createAttribute(String name);
public EntityReference            createEntityReference(String name);
```

---

[1] We recommend *Design Patterns* written by Erich Gamma et al. (Addison-Wesley, Reading, Mass., ISBN: 0-201-63361-2) for further reading.

- Zero or more `Comment` objects

- Zero or more `ProcessingInstruction` objects

For the sample document, we have already created the root element. Next, we add a new element, `name`, as a child node of the root element (the `person` element just created).

```
Element item = doc.createElement("name");
item.appendChild(doc.createTextNode("John Doe"));
root.appendChild(item);
```

We created a `name` element to contain a text node with the content string "John Doe" and appended the element as the last child of the root element.

`Element` may take any number of the following objects as children:

- `Element`

- `Text`

- `Comment`

- `ProcessingInstruction`

By this point, we have created the DOM object tree shown in Figure 3.1. Note that you can recursively add elements to build a complex tree structure.

Finally, we generate an XML document from this DOM tree. To do this, we need to use the implementation-specific features. This is because DOM does not specify methods for generation. The following sets the version of XML.

```
((TXDocument)doc).SetVersion("1.0");
```

XML for Java does not produce an XML declaration if no version number is explicitly supplied. Currently, the only value allowed is `"1.0"`.

```
((TXDocument)doc).printWithFormat(new PrintWriter(System.out));
```

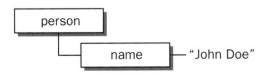

FIGURE 3.1 DOM object tree created by `MakeDocumentWithFactory`

Generates an XML document from the doc tree, with appropriate line breaks and indentation. This line is also XML for Java specific. We talk more about generating XML documents from DOM trees in Section 3.4.

The complete listing of our program, MakeDocumentWithFactory.java, is shown in Listing 3.1.

Listing 3.1 MakeDocumentWithFactory.java: Creates a document from scratch

```java
import com.ibm.xml.parser.TXDocument;
import org.w3c.dom.Document;
import org.w3c.dom.Element;
import org.w3c.dom.Text;
import org.w3c.dom.ProcessingInstruction;
import java.io.PrintWriter;

public class MakeDocumentWithFactory {
    public static void main(String[] argv) {
        try {

            // Creates a Document object.
            Document doc = (Document)Class.forName
              ("com.ibm.xml.parser.TXDocument").newInstance();

            // Makes the "person" element as the root, and adds it.
            Element root = doc.createElement("person");

            // Makes the "name" element, and adds it.
            Element item = doc.createElement("name");
            item.appendChild(doc.createTextNode("John Doe"));
            root.appendChild(item);

            // Makes the command and processing instruction.
            root.appendChild(doc.createComment
              ("Processing Instruction for application"));
            root.appendChild(doc.createProcessingInstruction("parser",
              " igonoreNextLine"));

            // Makes the "age" element, and adds it.
            item = doc.createElement("age");
            item.appendChild(doc.createTextNode("35"));
            root.appendChild(item);

            // Makes the "email" element, and adds it.
            item = doc.createElement("email");
            item.appendChild(doc.createTextNode("John.Doe@foo.com"));
```

```
            // Makes the "url" element with an attribute, and adds it.
            item = doc.createElement("url");
            item.setAttribute("href", "http://www.foo.com/~John.Doe/");
            root.appendChild(item);

            // Now the root has a name, age, email, and url.
            doc.appendChild(root);

            // Shows the XML document.
            ((TXDocument)doc).setVersion("1.0");        // @XML4J
            ((TXDocument)doc).printWithFormat(new PrintWriter(System.
              out)); // @XML4J
        } catch (Exception e) {
          e.printStackTrace();
        }
      }
   }
```

Executing this program yields the following output.

```
R:\samples\chap3>java MakeDocumentWithFactory
<?xml version="1.0"?>
<person>
    <name>John Doe</name>
    <!-Processing Instruction for application->
    <?parser igonoreNextLine?>
    <age>35</age>
    <url href="http://www.ibm.com/~John.Doe/"/>
</person>
```

You can easily modify this program, for example to connect to your database to automatically generate an employee list of your whole department in XML. Another possibility is to create a DOM tree interactively by bringing up a series of dialogs (Wizards, in Windows terminology) and ask the user to supply the data.

You might think that it could have been easier to generate an XML document directly using `System.out.println()` (or `printf()` in C or `cout` in C++, or . . .) as follows.

```
System.out.println("<?xml version=\"1.0\">");
System.out.println("<person>");
System.out.println("    <name>John Doe</name>");
...
```

In fact, most current CGI programs and servlets generate HTML pages in this way. Why do we bother creating a complex object structure rather than just using `println()`? We can give you two good reasons.

1. XML documents *must* be well-formed.

    The current browsers are amazingly forgiving about errors in HTML markup. This is partly because even though some of the tags are ignored or handled incorrectly, nothing serious happens. The information will be displayed on a screen in a reasonable way, and the human user is responsible for making sense of it. On the other hand, XML tags are supposed to be interpreted by application programs. The well-formedness of XML documents is strictly defined in the XML 1.0 Recommendation, and all conforming XML processors are required to report errors to application programs if the parsed XML document is not well-formed. There should not be errors such as missing end tags, unknown entities, or unknown characters. Creating a toy program that generates very simple XML documents might be possible with `println()`. But for complex enterprise Web applications, you should let an XML processor be responsible for generating well-formed and valid documents.

2. Creating well-formed and valid XML documents is not as easy as it might seem.

    XML is intended to be a simple, lightweight markup language. Yet, understanding every detail of the specification is not easy. For example, how can you make a difference between ignorable whitespaces and unignorable whitespaces? Or, how can you include a newline character within an attribute value? The XML 1.0 Recommendation precisely defines these details, and the XML processors in your business partner's application program will expect that your XML document complies with them. Even though you are familiar with these details, it is not productive for you to develop code that takes care of them every time you call `println()`. One of the biggest values of an XML processor is that it can handle these details for you.

XML processors are the result of intensive intellectual work. They free you from worrying about the proper nesting of tags, escaping of special characters such as the ampersand and left angle bracket, and handling of international character sets. So why not use an XML processor?

3.3 Building a Valid DOM Tree

We discussed building a DOM tree from scratch in Section 3.2. Since the document had no DTD, adding any element did not violate validity constraints.

However, in real situations in which application programs exchange data using XML, XML documents usually have a DTD so that their validity can be checked by a validating XML processor when they are received. This means that when building an internal DOM tree, you should make sure that the resulting XML document is always valid. To do this, you must be able to access the content model defined in a DTD, check the validity of the current (partially built) DOM tree, and know what element can be added at which position. XML for Java provides this functionality, called *validating generation*. In this section, we show how you can use validating generation to build a valid DOM tree, that is, a DOM tree that will generate a valid XML document. As a programming example, we develop a simple graphical user interface (GUI) tool for generating valid XML documents. Note that most of the methods described in this section are unique to XML for Java, so the sample programs in this section cannot be run with other XML processors.

3.3.1 Reading a DTD

The sample programs in Chapter 2 were intended to read an XML document. In the process of reading a document, the XML processor might or might not read a DTD as well, depending on whether a `<!DOCTYPE ... >` declaration is present. Here, we show how to read a DTD explicitly without reading an XML document.[2] The following code fragment reads a DTD from a file, `department.dtd`, using the `ReadDTDStream()` method.

```
import com.ibm.xml.parser.DTD;
...
String dtdfile = "department.dtd";
FileInputStream is = new FileInputStream(dtdfile);
Parser.parser = new Parser(dtdfile);
DTD dtd = parser.readDTDStream(is);
```

---

[2]In this section, the acronym *DTD* is used to refer to a DTD as well as to the DTD class provided by XML for Java. Do not confuse DTD with the DTD class and DTD objects; note the differences in font.

A DTD may be stored on a local hard disk, or it may be obtained from the Internet by using the JDK URL class, as follows.

```
String dtdURL = "http://www.ibm.com/department.dtd";
InputStream is = (new URL(dtdfile)).openStream();
Parser parser = new Parser(dtdfile);
DTD dtd = parser.readDTDStream(is);
```

In either case, we first create a Parser object and then call the readDTDStream method to load a DTD. The return value of this method is a DTD object.

3.3.2 Querying for Attribute Declarations

A DTD object holds information about a DTD, such as the content model of each element, attribute declarations, and entity declarations. You can query this information by using a set of methods defined in the DTD class. For example, the names of attributes defined for an element can be retrieved with the following code.

```
Enumeration en = dtd.getAttributeDeclarations("employee");
while (en.hasMoreElements()) {
    AttDef attrs = (AttDef)en.nextElement();
    String attName = attrs.getName();
    ...
}
```

Here, the method getAttributeDeclarations() takes an element name as its argument and returns an enumeration of all of the attribute definitions for the element in the form of a special class AttDef. An AttDef object represents one attribute definition, whose getName() method returns its attribute name.

3.3.3 Querying If an Element Can Be Added to a DOM Tree

Next, we show how to check if a new element can be added at a particular point of a DOM tree. We use department.dtd from Section 2.4 as our DTD. Figure 3.2 shows the process of building a valid DOM tree.

```
<!ELEMENT department (employee)*>
<!ELEMENT employee (name, (email | url))>
<!ATTLIST employee id CDATA #REQUIRED>
<!ELEMENT name (#PCDATA)>
```

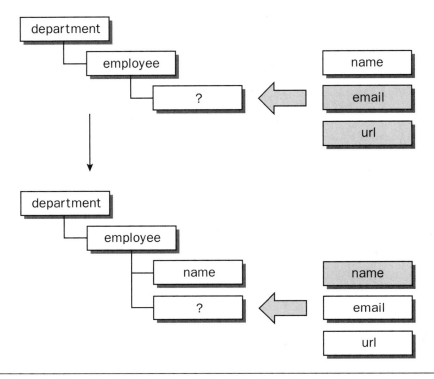

FIGURE 3.2 Building a valid DOM tree

```
<!ELEMENT email (#PCDATA)>
<!ELEMENT url EMPTY>
<!ATTLIST url href CDATA #REQUIRED>
```

We first create a `department` element as the root element and then create an `employee` as the child of `department` (assume that we have already checked the validity up to this point). What possible element can be added to `employee`? According to the DTD, only a `name` element is allowed as the first child of an `employee`, so we create a `name` element and append it to `employee`. The next possible element is either an `email` or a `url`. Thus the set of appendable elements changes dynamically during the process of building a DOM tree. And so allowing access to the DTD contents is not enough to guide the building of a valid DOM tree; both the content model and the current status of the DOM tree should be taken into account. With XML for Java, you can query what elements may be added at a particular position. We show you how next.

First, we read the DTD and create a DTD object.

```
// Reads the DTD from the file.
String dtdfile = "department.dtd";
FileInputStream is = new FileInputStream(dtdfile);
Parser parser = new Parser(dtdfile);
DTD dtd = parser.readDTDStream(is);
```

Then we create a Document object as described in Section 3.2 and add the root element (department) and its child (employee). Here, for simplicity, we assume we already know that an employee can be a child of department.

```
// Creates a Document object and root element.
Document doc = new TXDocument();
Element root = doc.createElement("department");
doc.appendChild(root);

// Appends an "employee" element. Assume it is valid as a child
// of the "department" element.
Element el = doc.createElement("employee");
root.appendChild(el);
```

Next, we extract the content type of the element employee.

```
// Gets the content type of the element.
switch (dtd.getContentType("element")) {
    case -1:
        // This element is not declared.
        break;
    case ElementDecl.EMPTY:
        // Any element is not insertable.
        break;
    case ElementDecl.ANY:
        // Any element is insertable.
        break;
    case ElementDecl.MODEL_GROUP:
    // ... continued
        break;
}
```

The possible return values of the getContentType() method have the meanings given in Table 3.2.

If the return value of getContentType() is either ElementDecl.EMPTY or ElementDecl.ANY, the process is straightforward: Either no elements are allowed or all elements are allowed. In the case of ElementDecl.MODEL_GROUP, we need to further check the appendability of an element, as follows.

TABLE 3.2 Return Values of `getContentType()`

RETURN VALUE	DESCRIPTION
`ElementDecl.EMPTY`	The element allows no child node.
`ElementDecl.ANY`	The element can have any number of child elements, in any order, as long as they are declared in the DTD.
`ElementDecl.MODEL_GROUP`	The child must follow the content model defined in the element type declaration of the element.
`-1`	The element is not defined in the DTD.

```
Hashtable tab = dtd.prepareTable("employee");
dtd.getAppendableElement(el, tab);
if (((InsertableElement)tab.get(DTD.CM_ERROR)).status) {
    // This element has an incorrect structure.
} else {
    // Continued.
}
```

First, using `prepareTable()`, we create a data structure (hashtable) that is to hold a set of `InsertableElement` objects that have element names and status (that is, whether or not this element is allowed). In this case, three `InsertableElement` objects corresponding to `name`, `email`, and `url` are created and stored in the hashtable with these names as keys. In addition, another three, special, `InsertableElement` objects are created and put into the hashtable: `DTD.CM_ERROR`, `DTD.CM_EOC`, and `DTD.CM_PCDATA`.

An `InsertableElement` object has a public member variable, `status`, that has a `boolean` value.

- If `status` of the `DTD.CM_ERROR` is `true`, then the element structure is already erroneous.

- If `status` of the `DTD.CM_EOC` is `true`, this element structure is already complete without the addition of any more child nodes.

- If `status` of the `DTD.CM_PCDATA` is `true`, then a text node can be added to this element.

Next, via a call of the `getAppendableElement()` method, insertable elements for an element as children are calculated. `getAppendableElement()` takes an element `el` and a hashtable `tab` as its arguments. If an element is appendable (it can be added as the last child) to the element `el`, `getAppendableElement()`

sets the corresponding `InsertableElement` object to `true`. Therefore, in the following code, all of the `InsertableElement` objects up to the `else` clause contain the names of the elements that can be appended to the element `el`.

```
Enumeration en = tab.elements();
while (en.hasMoreElements()) {
    InsertableElement ie = (InsertableElement)en.nextElement();
    if (!ie.name.equals(DTD.CM_ERROR) && !ie.name.equals(DTD.CM_EOC)
      && ie.status) {
    if (ie.name.equals(DTD.CM_PCDATA)) {
        // Can append the TextElement instance to el.
    } else {
        // Can append the Element instance named ie.name.
        ...
    }
    }
}
```

A More Complex Program

Next, we develop a more complex program that does validating generation. `GeneratingSample.java`, shown in Listing 3.2, is a GUI tool that allows the user to interactively build a valid XML document.

`GeneratingSample` takes a DTD file as its argument. Typing the following command causes two windows to appear on the screen, as shown in Figure 3.3:

```
R:\samples\chap3>java GeneratingSample department.dtd
```

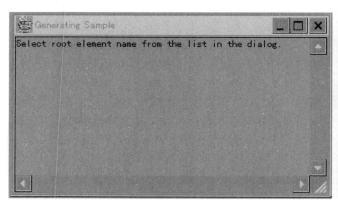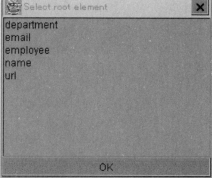

FIGURE 3.3 Sample run of validating generation

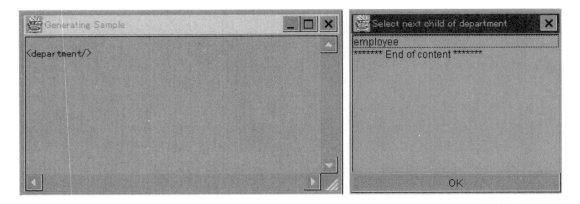

FIGURE 3.4 Sample run of validating generation after selecting `department`

Figure 3.4 shows the result of creating a root element (`department`) and selecting it as the root element.

In the left window in Figure 3.4 is a partial DOM structure consisting of an empty element named `department`. The right window shows that only the `employee` element can be appended as the first child of `department`. Selecting the `employee` element in the right window and clicking OK changes the screen to that shown in Figure 3.5.

We also can select `name`. Figure 3.6 shows the results.

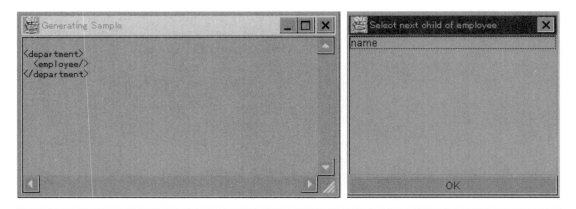

FIGURE 3.5 Sample run of validating generation after selecting `employee`

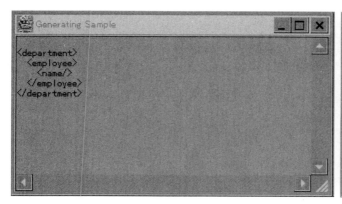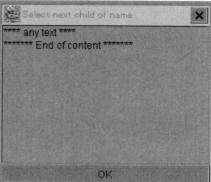

FIGURE 3.6 Sample run of validating generation after selecting `name`

In the right window are "any text" and "End of content" menus. You can select "any text" first and click OK and then select "End of content." Both "email" and "url" are then allowed as the next child to the `name` element.

The source code of `GeneratingSample` is shown in Listing 3.2. The constructor of this class contains the code just described. We do not give a detailed explanation, assuming you can understand how it works. Note, this class is XML4J specific.

Listing 3.2 `GeneratingSample.java`: A sample of validating generation

```
import com.ibm.xml.parser.DTD;
import com.ibm.xml.parser.ElementDecl;
import com.ibm.xml.parser.FormatPrintVisitor;
import com.ibm.xml.parser.InsertableElement;
import com.ibm.xml.parser.NonRecursivePreorderTreeTraversal;
import com.ibm.xml.parser.Parser;
import com.ibm.xml.parser.Stderr;
import com.ibm.xml.parser.TXElement;
import com.ibm.xml.parser.TXText;
import com.ibm.xml.parser.Visitor;
import java.awt.Button;
import java.awt.Component;
import java.awt.Dialog;
import java.awt.Dimension;
import java.awt.Frame;
import java.awt.List;
import java.awt.TextArea;
import java.awt.Toolkit;
```

```java
import java.awt.event.ActionEvent;
import java.awt.event.ActionListener;
import java.awt.event.WindowAdapter;
import java.awt.event.WindowEvent;
import java.io.StringWriter;
import java.util.Enumeration;
import java.util.Hashtable;
import java.util.Vector;

/**
    * This program depends on XML for Java entirely.
    */
public class GeneratingSample extends WindowAdapter implements
Runnable {
        static final String S_EOC = "******* End of content *******";
        static final String S_TEXT = "**** any text ****";

        public static void main(String[] argv) {
            new GeneratingSample(argv);
        }

        DTD dtd;
        Hashtable hash;
        Frame frame;
        Vector allElement;
        TextArea text;
        TXElement root;

        GeneratingSample(String[] argv) {
            try {
                String fname = null;
                for (int i = 0; i < argv.length; i ++) {
                    if (argv[i].charAt(0) != '-') {
                            fname = argv[i];      // A DTD filename.
                    } else {
                        System.err.println("Warning: Unknown option:"
                          +argv[i]);
                    }
                }
                                    // Loads DTD without a document.
            Parser pc = new Parser(fname);
            String targeturl = Stderr.file2URL(fname).toString();
            this.dtd = pc.readDTDStream(pc.getInputStream(fname, null,
              targeturl));
```

```
        if (this.dtd == null) {
            System.err.println("no DTD");
        } else {
            // Stores all declared element names in
            // allElement.
            this.allElement = new Vector();
            Enumeration en = this.dtd.getElementDeclarations();
            while (en.hasMoreElements()) {
                ElementDecl ed = (ElementDecl)en.nextElement();
                this.allElement.addElement(ed.getName());
            }

            // Makes a hashtable that has all elements and
            // InsertableElements for each element.
            this.hash = this.dtd.prepareTable((String)this.
              allElement.elementAt(0));
            en = this.allElement.elements();
            while (en.hasMoreElements()) {
                String n = (String)en.nextElement();
                this.hash.put(n, new InsertableElement(n));
            }

                            // Makes a frame.
            this.frame = new Frame("Generating Sample");
            this.frame.addWindowListener(this);
            this.frame.add(this.text = new TextArea(), "Center");
            this.frame.pack();
            centerComponentInScreen(this.frame, 384, 220);
            this.frame.show();
                            // Next, calls windowOpened().
        }
    } catch (Exception e) {
        e.printStackTrace();
    }
}

public static void centerComponent(Component com, int w, int h,
Dimension di) {
    com.setSize(w, h);
    com.setLocation((di.width-w)/2, (di.height-h)/2);
}

public static void centerComponentInScreen(Component com, int w,
int h) {
    centerComponent(com, w, h, Toolkit.getDefaultToolkit().
    getScreenSize());
```

```
    }
                                    // WindowAdapter.
    public void windowOpened(WindowEvent e) {
        new Thread(this).start();    // Next, calls run().
    }
                                    // WindowAdapter.
    public void windowClosing(WindowEvent e) {
        this.frame.dispose();
        System.exit(0);
    }

    void out() {
        try {
            StringWriter sw = new StringWriter();
            Visitor v = new FormatPrintVisitor(sw);
            new NonRecursivePreorderTreeTraversal(v).traverse(this.
               root);
            sw.close();
            this.text.setText(sw.toString());
        } catch (Exception e) {
            e.printStackTrace();
        }
    }

                            // Runnable.
    public void run() {
        this.text.setText("Select root element name from the list on
           the dialog.");
                                // Asks the user which element is the root
                                // element.
        String rootname = choice(this.frame, "Select root element",
                            sortStringVector(this.allElement));
                                // Creates the root element selected by
                                // the user.
        this.root = new TXElement(rootname);
        this.out();
        this.construct(this.root); // Constructs the valid contents of
                                    // the root element.
        System.err.println("Complete.");
    }

    /**
     * Construct valid contents of specified element.
     */
    void construct(TXElement parent) {
```

```
                                // Checks the content model: EMPTY or
                                // ANY or ...
switch (this.dtd.getContentType(parent.getNodeName())) {
    case -1:
        System.err.println("This element "+parent.
        getNodeName()+" is not declared.");
    break;
case ElementDecl.EMPTY:
    System.err.println("This element "+parent.
      getNodeName()+" is declared as EMPTY.");
    break;
case ElementDecl.ANY:
    System.err.println("This element "+parent.
      getNodeName()+" is declared as ANY.");
    break;

case ElementDecl.MODEL_GROUP:
    while (true) {
                        // Creates a list of available
                        // elements as a child of the parent.
        Vector vec = makeAvailable(this.dtd, parent,
          this.hash);
        if (vec.size() == 0) break;
        if (vec.size() == 1 && S_EOC.equals((String)vec.
          elementAt(0)))
            break;
                        // Sorts the list.
    vec = sortNames(this.dtd.makeContentElementList(parent.
      getNodeName()), vec);
                        // Asks the user which element to
                        // insert.
    String chi = choice(this.frame, "Select next child of"
      +parent.getNodeName(), vec);
                        // Appends the selected element/text.
    if (chi.equals(DTD.CM_PCDATA) || chi.equals(S_TEXT)) {
        parent.appendChild(new TXText("Some text"));
        this.out();
    } else if (chi.equals(S_EOC)) {
        break;
    } else {
        TXElement child = new TXElement(chi);
        parent.appendChild(child);
        this.out();
                        // Inserted element also must have
                        // valid contents.
```

```
                             this.construct(child);
                }
            }
            break;
        default:
            System.err.println("Internal Error.");
        }
    }

/**
    * Query available element names as children of el.
    */
static Vector makeAvailable(DTD dtd, TXElement el, Hashtable
    hash) {
    Vector v = new Vector();
    dtd.getAppendableElements(el, hash);
    if (((InsertableElement)hash.get(DTD.CM_ERROR)).status) {
        System.err.println("Element has wrong structure.");
    } else {
                            // DTD#getAppendableElements()
                            // returns a result in
                            // a hashtable consisting of
                            // InsertableElements.
                            // To return a result in Vector,
                            // checks all InsertableElements in
                            // the hashtable.
        Enumeration en = hash.elements();
        while (en.hasMoreElements()) {
            InsertableElement ie =
            (InsertableElement)en.nextElement();
            if (!ie.name.equals(DTD.CM_ERROR)
                && ie.status) {
                if (ie.name.equals(DTD.CM_EOC))
                        v.addElement(S_EOC);
                else
                        v.addElement(ie.name);
            }
        }
    }
    return v;
}

/**
    * Asks to user which String in Vector is preferred.
    */
```

```
static String choice(Frame parent, String tit, Vector v) {
        final Dialog f = new Dialog(parent, tit, true);
        final List list = new List();
        Enumeration en = v.elements();
        while (en.hasMoreElements()) {
            String el = (String)en.nextElement();
            list.add(el.equals(DTD.CM_PCDATA) ? S_TEXT : el);
        }
        Button btok = new Button("OK");
        f.add(list, "Center");
        f.add(btok, "South");
        btok.addActionListener(new ActionListener() {
            public void actionPerformed(ActionEvent e) {
                if (null != list.getSelectedItem())
                    f.setVisible(false);
                else
                    System.err.println("Select 1 item!");
            }
        });
        f.pack();
        centerComponentInScreen(f, 256, 220);
        f.show();

        String selected = list.getSelectedItem();
        f.dispose();
        System.err.println("SELECTED: "+selected);
        return selected;
}



//
// Utility methods
// Heap sort.
//
static private void fall(String[] pd, int n, int i) {
    int j = 2*i+1;
    if (j < n) {                // left exists.
        if (j+1 < n) {          // right exists too.
                                // j: bigger.
        if (0 > pd[j].compareTo(pd[j+1]))
            j = 2*i+2;
    } else {                    // only left.
    }
```

```
        if (pd[i].compareTo(pd[j]) < 0) {
                            // The child is bigger.
            String t = pd[i];
                pd[i] = pd[j];
                pd[j] = t;
                fall(pd, n, j);
            }
        }
    }
    static void heapSort(String[] pd) {
        int i;
        for (i = pd.length/2; i >= 0; i--) { // Makes the heap.
            fall(pd, pd.length, i);
        }
        for (i = pd.length-1; i > 0; i--) {
            String t = pd[0];
            pd[0] = pd[i];
            pd[i] = t;
            fall(pd, i, 0);
        }
    }

    static Vector sortStringVector(Vector v) {
        String[] as = new String[v.size()];
        v.copyInto(as);
        heapSort(as);
        v.removeAllElements();
        v.ensureCapacity(as.length);
        for (int i = 0; i < as.length; i ++)
            v.addElement(as[i]);
        return v;
    }

    static Vector sortNames(Vector base, Vector v) {
        if (null == base) {
            return sortStringVector(v);
        }
        Vector ret = new Vector();
        for (int i = 0; i < base.size(); i ++) {
            String n = (String)base.elementAt(i);
            int ind = v.indexOf(n);
            if (ind >= 0) {
                ret.addElement(n);
                v.removeElementAt(ind);
            }
```

```
        }
        for (int i = 0; i < v.size(); i ++) {
            ret.addElement(v.elementAt(i));
        }
        return ret;
    }
}
```

In this section, we showed how to ensure the validity of a DOM structure that you are building. Using these techniques, you can ensure that every XML document you create is valid. As an important consequence, a client that receives such assured-validity XML documents may skip a validation process, which is expensive in terms of program size and computation time. This could result in a significant gain if the client runs on a limited resource machine, such as Tier-0 devices (TV set-top boxes, PDAs, and cellular phones).

3.4 Generating an XML Document from a DOM Tree

In Section 2.6, we showed that by using the print() method of the class TXDocument, it is easy to generate an XML document from an internal DOM tree. Although simple generation looks simple, a few topics need serious consideration, including how to handle whitespaces and character encoding. This section deals with such topics.

According to the XML 1.0 Recommendation, a whitespace is one or more space (#x20) characters, carriage returns, line feeds, or tabs. Whitespaces are used to delimit tokens. (Note, many production rules in the Recommendation explicitly also include S, the nonterminal symbol that represents a whitespace.) In some applications, whitespaces are meaningful. However, they also are used to improve readability of XML documents. To demonstrate by how much we can improve readability by inserting appropriate whitespaces, we remove all nonessential whitespaces from our example from Chapter 2, department.xml. The result is a single, very long line shown in the following file, departmentWithNoWS.xml (because of the page width limitation, the line is wrapped but notice that there are no newline characters between them). Obviously, this is much less readable than the original file, which contains appropriate newlines and indentations.

```
<?xml version="1.0"?><!DOCTYPE department SYSTEM "department.
dtd"><department><employee id="J.D"><name>John Doe</name><email>John.
Doe@ibm.com</email></employee><employee id="B.S"><name>Bob Smith
</name><email>Bob.Smith@ibm.com</email></employee><employee id="A.M">
<name>Alice Miller</name><email>Alice.Miller@jp.ibm.com</email>
</employee></department>
```

The DOM tree for a "readable" XML document with whitespaces, however, may differ from what you might expect because XML processors preserve whitespaces in a DOM tree. Figure 3.7 shows the DOM trees for department.xml and departmentWithNoWS.xml using the visualization tool TreeView, which is included in the distribution package of XML for Java. This tool displays the DOM tree on the screen using the Swing 1.0 library.[3]

Note that in the DOM tree of department.xml, all of the whitespaces, including both newlines and space characters, are preserved. This is a required behavior of a conforming XML processor because some whitespaces are in fact meaningful in some types of applications (for example, program source code and poetry). Without knowing the semantics of the application, you do not know which whitespaces are significant and which are not.

In our department.xml example, whitespaces are not explicitly stated in the content models in the DTD. For example, the content model of the element department allows only name, email, and url as possible child elements. Will whitespaces (Text elements consisting of whitespace characters) violate the validity of the document? To allow for inserting whitespaces for readability without explicitly specifying whitespaces in the content models in a DTD, the XML 1.0 Recommendation (http://www.w3.org/TR/REC-xml) has the following rule as one of the validity constraints.

> The declaration matches children and the sequence of child elements belongs to the language generated by the regular expression in the content model, *with optional white space (characters matching the nonterminal S) between each pair of child elements* (italics ours).

Thus, although the DOM tree may have extraneous whitespaces, validation is done by ignoring those whitespaces that are not defined in the content model.

---

[3] You need to install Swing 1.0 to run TreeView with JDK 1.1. See http://java.sun.com/products/jfc for details.

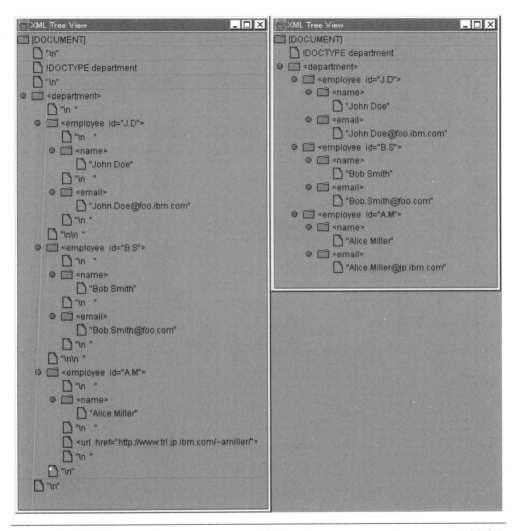

FIGURE 3.7 DOM trees of department.xml (left) and departmentWithNoWS.xml (right)

Because whitespaces are preserved, you cannot assume that the first child of
the root element department is a name element in your program. It may be
troublesome to write a code fragment that skips whitespaces here and there
in your program, especially since it is not simple to know if a particular Text
element consisting of whitespaces only is ignorable. XML for Java provides
the TXText.getIsIgnorableWhitespace() method to test if a text node is
an ignorable whitespace. Listing 3.3 (removeWSNode.java) removes all of the
ignorable whitespaces from the input.

Listing 3.3 `removeWSNode.java`: Removes ignorable whitespaces from an XML document

```java
import org.w3c.dom.Document;
import org.w3c.dom.Text;
import org.w3c.dom.Element;
import org.w3c.dom.Node;
import com.ibm.xml.parser.Parser;
import com.ibm.xml.parser.TXText;
import com.ibm.xml.parser.TXElement;
import com.ibm.xml.parser.TXDocument;
import java.io.FileInputStream;
import java.io.PrintWriter;
import java.util.Vector;
import java.util.Enumeration;

public class removeWSNode {

    public static void main(String[] argv) {
        if (argv.length != 1) {
            System.err.println("Require a filename.");
            System.exit(1);
        }
        try {
            // Opens the specified file.
            FileInputStream is = new FileInputStream(argv[0]);
            // Starts to parse.
            Parser parser = new Parser(argv[0]);
            Document doc = parser.readStream(is);
            // Error?
            if (0 < parser.getNumberOfErrors()) {
                System.exit(1);
            }
            Element root = doc.getDocumentElement();
            removeWhiteSpaceNodes(root);

            ((TXDocument)doc).print(new PrintWriter(System.out));

        } catch (Exception e) {
            e.printStackTrace();
        }
    }

    public static void removeWhiteSpaceNodes(Element parent) {
        Node nextNode = parent.getFirstChild();
```

```
          for (Node child = parent.getFirstChild();
               nextNode != null;) {
          child = nextNode;
          nextNode = child.getNextSibling();

          if (child instanceof TXText) {
              if (((TXText)child).getIsIgnorableWhitespace()) {
                  parent.removeChild(child);
              }
          } else if (child instanceof TXElement) {
              removeWhiteSpaceNodes((Element)child);
          }
        }
      }
    }
```

Note that a whitespace is ignorable only when

- it is not specified in the content model and

- it appears between two tags (or between a tag and the end of file).

Whitespaces between or adjacent to normal texts are never ignored.

There are two ways to tell XML for Java if certain whitespaces are significant:

1. Define the significant whitespaces in the content models in the DTD.

2. Use the `xml:space="preserve"` attribute in an element in which all of the whitespaces are to be preserved.

In the following XML document, all of the whitespaces within the department element are to be preserved.[4]

```
<?xml version="1.0"?>
<department xml:space="preserve">
   <employee id="J.D">
       <name>John Doe</name>
       <email>John.Doe@ibm.com</email>
   </employee>
```

---

[4]When spaces are declared nonignorable by `xml:space="preserve"`, XML for Java uses the spaces in content model matching. If the previous sample document had the document type declaration (`<!DOCTYPE department SYSTEM "department.dtd">`), the parser would output an error that the document did not match the content model.

```
<employee id="B.S">
    <name>Bob Smith</name>
    <email>Bob.Smith@ibm.com</email>
</employee>

<employee id="A.M">
    <name>Alice Miller</name>
    <url href="http://www.trl.jp.ibm.com/~amiller/"/>
</employee>
</department>
```

3.5 Summary

In this chapter, we covered how to build a DOM structure using a DOM-compliant XML processor. We also discussed the importance of ensuring that the DOM tree is valid and showed how the validating generation provided by XML for Java can be used to achieve this. Finally, we explained the treatment of whitespaces when generating an XML document from a generated DOM tree.

This chapter concludes the coverage of the basic programming skills for reading and generating XML documents using the standard APIs. In the next chapter, we discuss advanced topics of DOM tree manipulation and give a more complex example.

Manipulating DOM Structures

4.1 Introduction

We discussed parsing in Chapter 2 and document generation in Chapter 3. This covered many important aspects in processing XML documents. However, in the development of Web applications knowledge about parsing and generation is not sufficient. You also need to understand how to manipulate the internal structure. If you use SAX, you need to design the internal structure yourself. If you use DOM, you need to understand techniques for dealing with DOM trees using the DOM API.

In this chapter, we discuss basic techniques for and some considerations about manipulating DOM structures. Then we conclude Part 1 of this book by presenting a small but nontrivial application program that requires a good understanding of tree manipulation using the DOM API.

4.2 Tree Manipulation Using the DOM API

We touched briefly on traversing a DOM tree in the `MakeEltTblDOM.java` program in Chapter 2 and on generating a DOM tree from scratch in Chapter 3. This section gives you more tips on DOM programming. Because of space limitations, we cannot describe every detail of DOM. Please consult the latest DOM specification whenever you have further questions.

DOM provides a set of methods to access DOM trees. A node in a DOM tree may be one of

- `Document`,

- `ProcessingInstruction`,

- `Comment`,

- `DocumentType`,

- `Notation`,

- `Entity`,

- `Element`,

- `Text`,

- `CDATASection`, or

- `EntityReference`.

All of these interfaces are derived from the `Node` interface (see Figure 2.2 in Chapter 2). Therefore the basic structural methods such as accessing and updating parent and child nodes are defined in the `Node` interface. In this section, we show you how the methods defined in `Node` are used and some specific interfaces.

4.2.1 Accessing and Updating the Status of a Node

First covered are the four methods for obtaining and updating the status of the node itself. These have nothing to do with the structural manipulation.

- `node.getNodeType()`. Obtains the node type.

  This method returns an integer that represents the type of this node. For example, if the node is an `Element`, `Node.ELEMENT_NODE` is returned.

- `node.getNodeName()`. Obtains the name of the node.

  This method returns the name of the node. The name depends on the node type. For `Element`, it is the element name; for `Attr`, it is the attribute name; and so on. Table 4.1 summarizes the `getNodeType()` and `getNodeName()` methods.

TABLE 4.1 Summary of `getNodeType()` and `getNodeName()` Methods

DOM INTERFACE	`getNodeType()`	`getNodeName()`
Element	Node.ELEMENT_NODE	Name of element
Attr	Node.ATTRIBUTE_NODE	Name of attribute
Text	Node.TEXT_NODE	"#text"
CDATASection	Node.CDATA_SECTION_NODE	"#cdata-section"
EntityReference	Node.ENTITY_REFERENCE_NODE	Entity name
Entity	Node.ENTITY_NODE	Entity name
ProcessingInstruction	Node.PROCESSING_INSTRUCTION_NODE	PI target
Comment	Node.COMMENT_NODE	"#comment"
Document	Node.DOCUMENT_NODE	"#document"
DocumentType	Node.DOCUMENT_TYPE_NODE	Name of root element
DocumentFragment	Node.DOCUMENT_FRAGMENT_NODE	"#document-fragment"
Notation	Node.NOTATION_NODE	Notation name

- `node.getNodeValue()`. Obtains the value of the node.

  This method returns the value of the node. The value is type-dependent. If the node is an `Attr`, the value of the attribute is returned, and if it is a `Text` or a `CDATASection`, the value is the text string. The value is also defined for `Attr`, `Text`, `CDATASection`, `ProcessingInstruction`, and `Comment`. For other node types, the value is `null`.

- `node.setNodeValue(arg)`. Updates the node value.

  This method updates the value defined in `getNodeValue()`.

4.2.2 Accessing Structural Information

Since DOM is tree-structured, any structural information is given by parent-child relationships. DOM provides a set of methods to access this information:

- `node.getParentnode()`

- `node.hasChildNodes()`

- `node.getFirstChild() != null`

- `node.getLastChild() != null`

- `node.getChildNodes().getLength()>0`

- `node.getPreviousSibling()`

- `node.getNextSibling()`

For some operations, there are multiple ways to achieve the desired results.

Throughout this subsection, we use the following small XML fragment as a sample.

```
<name>
    <given>John</given>
    <family>Doe</family>
</name>
```

The `Element name` has five children:

- `Text`

- `Element given`

- `Text`

- `Element family`

- `Text`

Note that whitespaces for indentation are represented as `Text` nodes. "\n" in Figure 4.1 represents an end-of-line character. Each of `Element given` and `Element family` has one `Text` node as its child.

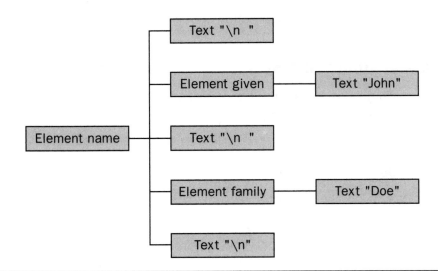

FIGURE 4.1 DOM nodes representing the sample fragment

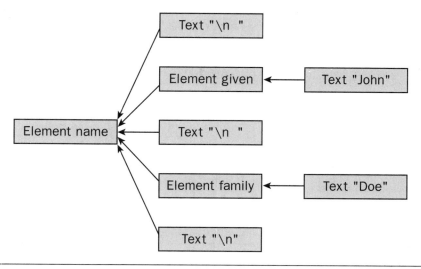

FIGURE 4.2 Using `getParentNode()`

Obtaining the Parent Node

The `node.getParentNode()` method returns the parent node of this node. If `Element name` is the root element in a document, `getParentNode()` with `name` returns the `Document node`. Figure 4.2 shows how to use this method.

Checking Whether a Node Has One or More Child Nodes

There are several methods that check whether the node has a child:

- `node.hasChildNodes()`

- `node.getFirstChild() != null`

- `node.getLastChild() != null`

- `node.getChildNodes().getLength() > 0`

Any of these works well for this purpose, but for readability we recommend the first one.

Obtaining the Next and Previous Siblings

You can use the following two methods to go back and forth among child nodes:

- `node.getPreviousSibling()`. Returns the previous sibling.

- `node.getNextSibling()`. Returns the next sibling.

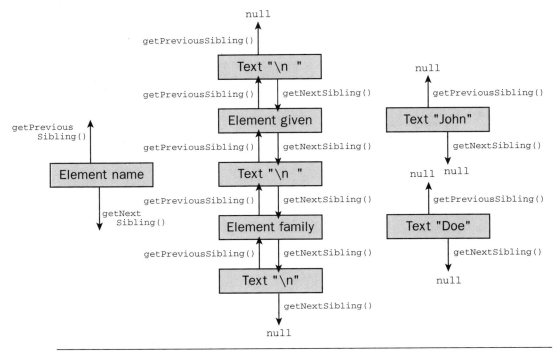

FIGURE 4.3 Using `getPreviousSibling()` and `getNextSibling()` to move among siblings

Figure 4.3 shows how to use these two methods.

Processing Children in the Order They Appear

Suppose you want to visit the five children of `Element name` in the order they appear:

1. `Text "\n  "`

2. `Element given`

3. `Text "\n  "`

4. `Element family`

5. `Text "\n  "`

To iterate on the children of a node, you have two choices:

- Use `getFirstChild()` and `getNextSibling()` —this is simple and straight-forward.

```
for (Node child = node.getFirstChild();
    child != null;
    child = child.getNextSibling()) {
    ...process child
}
```

- Create a `NodeList`, and use an index to access the children.

```
NodeList nodeList = node.getChildNodes();
for (int i = 0; i < nodeList.getLength(); i ++) {
    Node child = nodeList.item(i);
    ...process child
}
```

Figure 4.4 illustrates how this is done.

Processing Children in Reverse Order

There are two ways to process children in reverse order:

- Use `getLastChild()` and `getPreviousSibling()`.

```
for (Node child = node.getLastChild();
    child != null;
    child = child.getPreviousSibling()) {
    ...process child
}
```

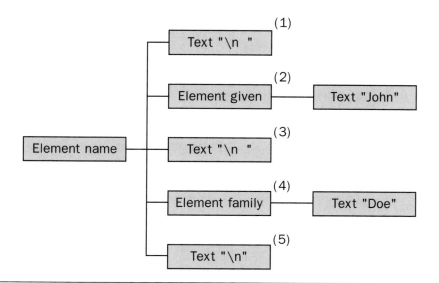

FIGURE 4.4 Two ways to process children

- Create a `NodeList` by calling `getChildNodes()`, and use `item()` to access each item in the `NodeList`.

```
NodeList nodeList = node.getChildNodes();
for (int i = nodeList.getLength() -1; i > = 0; i --) {
    Node child = nodeList.item(i);
    ...process child
}
```

Processing All Descendants (Processing Children Recursively)

You might want to visit all of the descendant nodes of a given node. Starting at `Element name` in Figure 4.5, the following code fragment visits the nodes in this order:

1. `Element name`
2. `Text "\n  "`
3. `Element given`
4. `Text "John"`
5. `Text "\n  "`
6. `Element family`

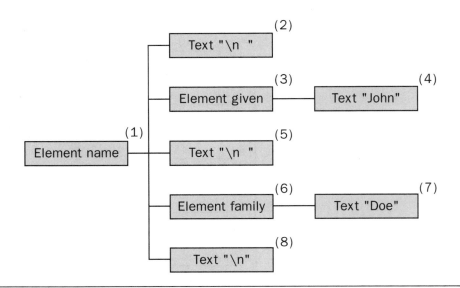

FIGURE 4.5 Processing descendants

7. Text "Doe"

8. Text "\n"

```
public void processNodeRecursively(Node node) {
    ... process node ...
    for (Node child = node.getFirstChild();
            child != null;
            child = child.getNextSibling()) {
        processNodeRecursively(child);
    }
}
```

4.2.3 A Simple Program Using the DOM API

Using the DOM API described in 4.2.2, we next write a program, PrintDOMTree.java, that displays a tree on the screen that represents a DOM tree structure. This is shown in Listing 4.1.

Listing 4.1 PrintDOMTree.java: Displays a DOM tree on the screen

```
import com.ibm.xml.parser.Parser;
import java.io.FileInputStream;
import java.io.PrintWriter;
import org.w3c.dom.Node;

public class PrintDOMTree {
    /**
     * This method is written in pure DOM.
     */
    public static void printTree(Node node, PrintWriter writer, int
      currIndent, int dx) {
        for (int i = 0; i < currIndent; i ++)
            writer.print(" ");
        switch (node.getNodeType()) {
            case Node.DOCUMENT_NODE:
            case Node.ELEMENT_NODE:
            case Node.TEXT_NODE:
            case Node.CDATA_SECTION_NODE:
                writer.println(node.getNodeName());
                break;
            case Node.PROCESSING_INSTRUCTION_NODE:
                writer.println("<?"+node.getNodeName()+"...?>");
                break;
```

```
                      case Node.COMMENT_NODE:
                          writer.println("<!-"+node.getNodeValue()+"-->");
                          break;
                      case Node.ENTITY_NODE:
                          writer.println("ENTITY "+node.getNodeName());
                          break;
                      case Node.ENTITY_REFERENCE_NODE:
                          writer.println("&"+node.getNodeName()+";");
                          break;
                      case Node.DOCUMENT_TYPE_NODE:
                          writer.println("DOCTYPE "+node.getNodeName());
                          break;
                      default:
                          writer.println("?"+node.getNodeName());
                  }

                  for (Node child = node.getFirstChild();
                          child != null;
                          child = child.getNextSibling()) {
                      printTree(child, writer, currIndent+dx, dx);
                  }
          }

          public static void main(String[] argv) {
              try {
                  Parser parser = new Parser(argv[0]); // @XML4J
                  PrintWriter pwriter = new PrintWriter(System.out);
                  printTree(parser.readStream(new FileInputStream(argv[0])),
                  // @XML4J
                          pwriter, 0, 2);
                  pwriter.flush();
              } catch (Exception e) {
                  e.printStackTrace();
              }
          }
      }
```

As input to this program, we use the following XML file, first.xml, which contains an entity reference.

```
<?xml version="1.0"?>
<!DOCTYPE root [
    <!ENTITY first "<first>Ichibanme</first>">
]>
<root>
```

```
        &first;
        <second>Nibanme</second>
    </root>
```

With `first.xml` supplied as input, the output of the `PrintDOMTree.java` program follows.

```
R:\samples\chap4> java PrintDOMTree first.xml
#document
    DOCTYPE root
        #text
        ENTITY first
            first
                #text
        #text
    #text
    root
        #text
        &first;
            first
                #text
        #text
        second
            #text
        #text
    #text
R:\samples\chap4>
```

NOTE: There are certain incompatibilities of XML for Java with the DOM Level 1 Recommendation. These result from maintaining backward compatibility of XML for Java, as well as realizing more advanced features. In the previous example, the following points violate DOM Level 1:

- A Text node appears as a child of the Document node.

- An Entity node and Text nodes appear as children of the DocumentType node.

XML for Java might be updated in the future to be more compatible with DOM.

4.2.4 Inserting, Deleting, and Replacing a Child Node

We have looked at the ways to access various parts of a DOM tree. Now we shift our attention to modifying the tree. Structural changes in a DOM tree are always done by inserting, deleting, or replacing a child node. Some types of nodes—Text, CDATASection, Comment, Notation, and ProcessingInstruc-tion—can never have a child node. Others may have constraints regarding allowed child node types, violations of which will generate a DOMException. In this section, we cover the following methods:

- node.insertBefore()
- node.appendChild()
- node.replaceChild()
- node.removechild()

Inserting a Child Node

To insert a child node, use node.insertBefore(newChild, refChild) to insert a newChild before refChild. If refChild is null, the new child is added as the last child of node. Figure 4.6 illustrates how this is done.

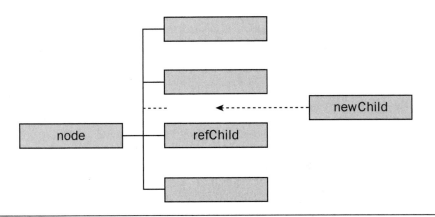

FIGURE 4.6 Using insertBefore() to insert a new child

Adding a Child Node

To add a child node, use node.appendChild(newChild) to add a newChild as the last child of node. This is equivalent to node.insertBefore(newChild, null) and is illustrated in Figure 4.7.

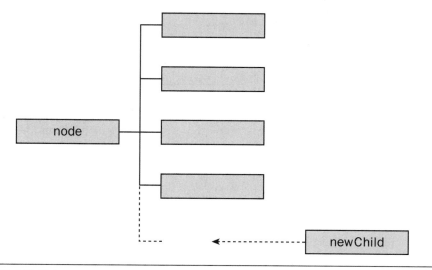

FIGURE 4.7 Using `appendChild()` to add a child

Replacing a Child Node

To replace an old child with a new child, use `node.replaceChild(newChild, oldChild)` to replace `oldChild`, which must be a child node of node, with a `newChild`. Figure 4.8 demonstrates its use.

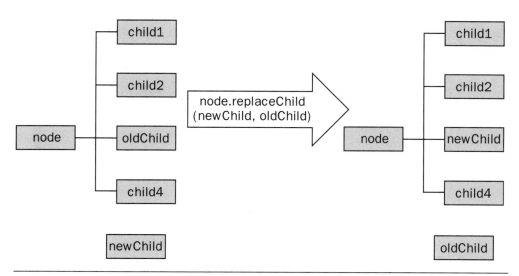

FIGURE 4.8 Using `replaceChild()` to replace a child

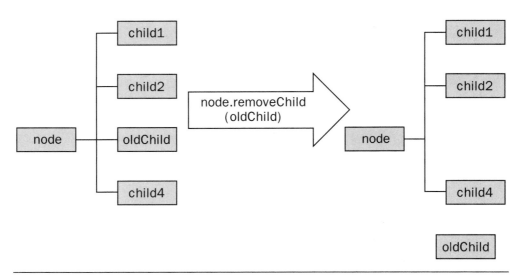

FIGURE 4.9 Using `removeChild()` to remove a child

Deleting a Child Node

To delete a child, use `node.removeChild(oldChild)` to remove `oldChild`, which must be a child node of `node`, from the children of `node`. See Figure 4.9.

By now you should be able to create and manipulate any tree consisting of `Node`s. However, to manipulate a DOM tree, you need to learn one more thing, which is discussed next.

4.2.5 DOM Tree and Attributes

An `Element` node may have attributes in addition to child nodes. Attributes are represented by the `Attr` interface, which is derived from the `Node` interface. However, you cannot obtain `Attr` objects by calling the previous methods of an `Element` node.

Following are the attribute-manipulating methods defined as part of the `Element` interface.

- `NamedNodeMap getAttributes()`

- `String getAttribute(String name)`

- `void setAttribute(String name, String value)`

- `void removeAttribute(String name)`

- `Attr getAttributeNode(String name)`

- `void setAttributeNode(Attr newAttr)`

- `void removeAttributeNode(Attr oldAttr)`

To obtain an attribute whose name is already known, use `getAttribute(String name)` and `getAttributeNode(String name)`. To obtain a list of all of the attributes, use `getAttributes()`, as follows.

```
NamedNodeMap nnm = element.getAttributes();
for (int i = 0; i < nnm.getLength(); i ++) {
    Attr attr = (Attr)nnm.getItem(i);
    ...Process attr...
}
```

Alternatively, `NamedNodeMap` has the `getNamedItem(String)` method to get an attribute by its name.

The rest of this section offers two tips and some potential pitfalls when using the DOM API.

4.2.6 How to Remove All Child Nodes

The first tip concerns how to remove all of the child nodes and make an empty node. Suppose you write the following code to remove all children of a node.

```
for (Node child = node.getFirstChild();
        child != null;
        child = child.getNextSibling()) {
    node.removeChild(child);
}
```

This looks like a straightforward implementation, but unfortunately, it does not work properly. It simply removes the first child of the node and exits the loop. Here is how it works—or more precisely, how it does not work.

1. In the initialization of the `for` loop, the first child of the node is assigned to `child` (if there are no children, this value is `null`).

2. `child != null` is `true`, so this check passes and the body of the loop is executed.

3. `removeChild(child)` is used to remove the first child from `node`. As soon as the child is removed, its internal variables are updated and `child.getParentNode()`, `child.getPreviousSibling()`, and `child.getNextSibling()` all now return `null`.

4. In the third component of `for` (that is, `child = child.getNextSibling()`), `child` is set to `null` and the loop terminates.

Even if you use `NodeList` instead of `getNextSibling()`, as shown next, it still does not work. This is because `getChildNodes()` returns not the "snapshot" of the child nodes but a "live" data structure that will be updated immediately whenever any changes are made on the node from which it was created.

```
NodeList nodeList = node.getChildNodes();
for (int i = 0; i < nodeList.getLength(); i ++) {
    node.removeChild(nodeList.item(i));
}
```

To remove all children properly, you can use either of the following code fragments. Both implement the strategy of "remove the first child node until there are no more child nodes."

```
while (node.hasChildNodes()) {
    node.removeChild(node.getFirstChild());
}

NodeList nodeList = node.getChildNodes();
while (nodeList.getLength() > 0) {
    node.removeChild(nodeList.item(0));
}
```

4.2.7 How to Simplify Your Code by Removing Entity References

The second tip concerns entity references. You must take care when an XML document may contain general entity references, such as `&foo;`, which are to be replaced by their definitions. See the example in Table 4.2.

Documents A and B have almost identical meanings. In fact, the validity should be checked after the entity reference `&first;` is replaced by its value, `<first>Ichibanme</first>`. In both cases, the content models of the `root` element are the same and they might look like "`(first, second)`". However, since the XML 1.0 Recommendation requires an XML processor to preserve the entity references in the generated DOM tree, the corresponding DOM trees are different, as shown in Figure 4.10.

TABLE 4.2 A Document without Entity References and a Document with an Entity Reference

DOCUMENT A (document-a.xml)	DOCUMENT B (document-b.xml)
	`<!DOCTYPE root [`
	`  <!ENTITY first "<first>Ichibanme</first>"`
	`]>`
`<root>`	`<root>`
`  <first>Ichibanme</first>`	`  &first;`
`  <second>Nibanme</second>`	`  <second>Nibanme</second>`
`</root>`	`  </root>`

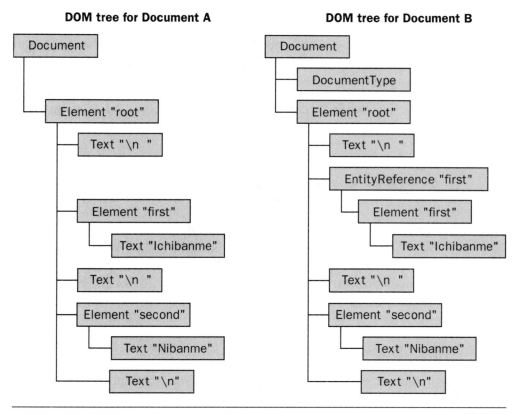

FIGURE 4.10 DOM trees for documents A and B

In the DOM tree for document B, an `EntityReference` node is inserted where an entity reference appeared in the XML document. Therefore if you do not take the possibility of entity references into account you might miss elements. For instance, do not assume, when coding your program, that *the first element in the children of the* `root` *element must be a* `first` *element because it is specified in the content model of the* `root` *element.* The first child element is `second` in the case of document B.

For removing `EntityReference` nodes and replacing them with their contents in a DOM tree, XML for Java provides two methods:

- `Parser#setExpandEntityReferences()`, which tells the parser not to generate `EntityReference` nodes during parsing

- `Parent#expandEntityReferences()`, which removes all of the `EntityReference` nodes beneath the called node

If your application does not need information about whether entity references are used, removing `EntityReference` nodes by using these methods will simplify your code.

In this section, we looked at the details of tree manipulation using the DOM API. In the next section, we tackle a larger, nontrivial, application program.

4.3 LMX: Sample Nontrivial Application

In this section, we develop the *LMX processor* as our sample program. LMX stands for *Language for Mapping XML*, something that we made up for this sample application but which probably will have some practical use. The LMX processor is capable of transforming one XML document into another, and thus it makes heavy use of the DOM API described previously.

4.3.1 Background of LMX

Before defining the LMX language, we will briefly explain why this kind of tool could be helpful. Suppose that company A and company B each have a database that deals with the inventory of its goods. The inventory data is delivered to application programs in the form of XML, so both companies have individually defined their own DTDs. This is depicted in Figure 4.11.

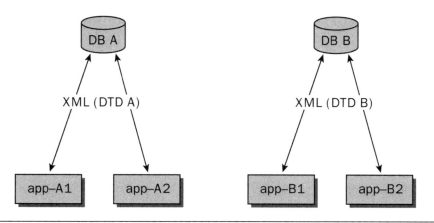

FIGURE 4.11 XML applications in companies A and B

One day, the CEOs of both companies conferred and decided to merge the two. Now the problem is how to make their two inventory systems interoperate. Since both deal with the same subject—inventory—their DTDs logically must be very similar. It would help a lot to have a tool to convert a document in one DTD into another document in another DTD and vice versa. LMX does this.

Figure 4.12 shows a possible configuration of the inventory system after the two companies merge. App-A1 and App-A2 now talk to DB B through LMX. App-B1 is merged into App A-1 and terminated. And App-B2 talks to DB A through LMX.

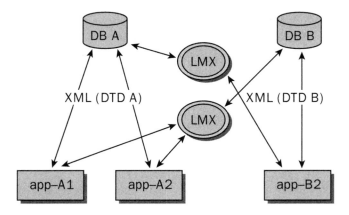

FIGURE 4.12 Possible system configuration after the company merger

In this scenario, all we need are the following two conversions:

- Convert XML documents from DB A (which is based on DTD A) to be valid with DTD B.

- Convert XML documents from DB B (which is based on DTD B) to be valid with DTD A.

The task is to design LMX as a simple but effective tool for doing this.

4.3.2 LMX Defined

LMX is an XML transformation language we designed as a working sample of DOM-tree manipulation. It is a rule language that describes mapping between two sets of documents in logically similar but syntactically different XML documents. It is designed so that the rules can be used bidirectionally. That is, the same rules can be used for mapping from documents with DTD A to documents with DTD B and vice versa. LMX is a very primitive language, so its functionality is limited, but it has proved to be useful in many situations.

In the LMX processor, XML for Java is used in three ways:

- Parsing a rule file

- Parsing a source document

- Generating a target document

For each, DOM is used as the internal structure.

4.3.3 Specification of LMX

In this subsection, we set out the specification of LMX.

Overall Syntax of the LMX Rule File

Following is the general syntax of LMX.

```
<lmx:rules xmlns:lmx="http://www.ibm.com/xml/lmx/">
    <lmx:pattern>
        <lmx:lhs>...<lmx:lhs>      <!-- from-pattern 1 -->
        <lmx:rhs>...<lmx:rhs>      <!-- to-pattern 1 -->
    </lmx:pattern>
```

```
<lmx:pattern>
    <lmx:lhs>...<lmx:lhs>     <!-- from-pattern 2 -->
    <lmx:rhs>...<lmx:rhs>     <!-- to-pattern 2 -->
</lmx:pattern>
    :
    :
<lmx:pattern>
    <lmx:lhs>...<lmx:lhs>     <!-- from-pattern n -->
    <lmx:rhs>...<lmx:rhs>     <!-- to-pattern n -->
</lmx:pattern>
</lmx:rules>
```

The root element of an LMX rule file is `lmx:rules`. This root element has one or more `lmx:pattern` elements as its children. An `lmx:pattern` element represents a single rule and must have two child elements: `lmx:lhs` and `lmx:rhs`, as the left-hand side and the right-hand side of the rule, respectively. Hereafter, we call the `lmx:lhs` element a *from-pattern* and the `lmx:rhs` element a *to-pattern*. A from-pattern is used to match with a part of the source document, while a to-pattern is used to construct the target document. Note that when transforming in the opposite direction, the roles of from-pattern and to-pattern are reversed.

In the root element `lmx` is declared as a namespace prefix for `http://www.ibm.com/xml/lmx/` by `xmlns:lmx` attribute.

Pattern Description

A from-pattern or to-pattern has a document substructure that should be matched with a part of the source document. A variable, designated by $number;, can appear if that part of the pattern can match any constituent. The number in a variable should begin from 1 in a single pattern, and no two variables in a single pattern can have the same number. Following is an example rule.

```
<lmx:lhs>
    <keyval>
        $1;
    </keyval>
</lmx:lhs>
<lmx:rhs>
    <list>$1;</list>
</lmx:rhs>
```

This rule says that

- all of the `keyval` elements in the source document should be translated into `list` elements in the target document and

- all of the child elements of the `keyval` elements in the source document should be translated with the same set of the rule and the translation results should be inserted into corresponding `list` elements in the target document.

Consider the following rule file, `keyval.lmx`.

```
<?xml version="1.0"?>
<lmx:rules xmlns:lmx="http://www.ibm.com/xml/lmx/">
    <lmx:pattern>
        <lmx:lhs>
            <keyval>
                $1;
            </keyval>
        </lmx:lhs>
        <lmx:rhs>
            <list>$1;</list>
        </lmx:rhs>
    </lmx:pattern>

    <lmx:pattern>
        <lmx:lhs>
            <key>$1;</key>
        </lmx:lhs>
        <lmx:rhs>
            <name>$1;</name>
        </lmx:rhs>
    </lmx:pattern>

    <lmx:pattern>
        <lmx:lhs>
            <value>$1;</value>
        </lmx:lhs>
        <lmx:rhs>
            <val>$1;</val>
        </lmx:rhs>
    </lmx:pattern>
</lmx:rules>
```

This rule file defines the translation between `<keyval>` and `<list>` tags, `<key>` and `<name>` tags, and `<value>` and `<val>` tags. We apply this rule file to the following source document, `keyval.xml`.

```
<keyval>
    <key>URL</key>
    <value>http://www.ibm.com/xml</value>
    <key>Owner</key>
    <value>IBM</value>
</keyval>
```

The following target document, `list.xml`, results.

```
<list>
    <name>URL</name>
    <val>http://www.ibm.com/xml</val>
    <name>Owner</name>
    <val>IBM</val>
</list>
```

The same rule file can be used in the reverse direction; that is, applying it to `list.xml` will produce `keyval.xml`.

This example shows simple substitutions of element names. Next, we consider a more complex conversion, that between the following two documents, `stock-a.xml` and `stock-b.xml`, shown in Table 4.3.

In this case, we need not only to substitute the element name, but also to reorder the elements, as well as add and remove additional levels of tags

TABLE 4.3 Two Documents to Compare

stock-a.xml	stock-b.xml
```<list>```	```<stock>```
``` <item>```	``` <fruit>```
``` <name>apple</name>```	``` <type><color>Red</color> <name>```
``` <color>Red</color>```	``` apple</name></type>```
``` <amount>14</amount>```	``` <location>Warehouse-A</location>```
``` <place>Warehouse-A</place>```	``` <left>14</left>```
``` </item>```	``` </fruit>```
``` <item>```	``` <fruit>```
``` <name>lemon</name>```	``` <type><color>Yellow</color> <name>```
``` <color>Yellow</color>```	``` lemon</name></type>```
``` <amount>20</amount>```	``` <location>Warehouse-C</location>```
``` <place>Warehouse-C</place>```	``` <left>20</left>```
``` </item>```	``` </fruit>```
```</list>```	```</stock>```

(`<type>` tag in the second document). The following rule file, `stock.lmx`, can be used to convert between these two XML documents.

```
<?xml version="1.0"?>
<lmx:rules xmlns:lmx="http://www.ibm.com/xml/lmx/">
    <lmx:pattern>
        <lmx:lhs>
            <list>$1;</list>
        </lmx:lhs>
        <lmx:rhs>
            <stock>$1;</stock>
        </lmx:rhs>
    </lmx:pattern>

    <lmx:pattern>
        <lmx:lhs>
            <item>
                <name>$1;</name>
                <color>$2;</color>
                <amount>$3;</amount>
                <place>$4;</place>
            </item>
        </lmx:lhs>
        <lmx:rhs>
            <fruit>
                <type><color>$1;</color> <name>$2;</name></type>
                <location>$4;</location>
                <left>$3;</left>
            </fruit>
        </lmx:rhs>
    </lmx:pattern>
</lmx:rules>
```

Limitations of the LMX Pattern

Although LMX strives for bidirectional conversion, certain conversions cannot be performed. Also, in the simple implementation shown in this book, the following restrictions apply to make the program as simple as possible.

• Elements `lmx:lhs` and `lmx:rhs` each can have exactly one child element.

• A variable may appear only as a single child of some element. For instance, the following Pattern A is okay, while both Pattern B and Pattern C are not.

Pattern A

```
<lmx:lhs>
    <item>
        <name>
            $1;
        </name>
    </item>
</lmx:lhs>
```

Pattern B

```
<lmx:lhs>
    <item>
        $1;
        <name/>
    </item>
</lmx:lhs>
```

Pattern C

```
<lmx:lhs>
    <item>
        <name/>
        $1;
        <address/>
    </item>
</lmx:lhs>
```

The next subsection shows the implementation of the LMX processor.

> **NOTE:** The CD-ROM contains two versions of LMX processor:
>
> - `\samples\chap4\LMXConverter.java`
>
>   This is exactly what is described in this section for illustrating the use of the DOM API and is limited in functionality.
>
> - `\lmx\src\com\ibm\xml\lmx\Converter.java`
>
>   This is a full-functionality version and is used in later chapters in the book.
>
> See the documentation on the CD-ROM for details.

4.3.4 Implementation of the LMX Processor

The overall flow of the LMX processor is as follows.

1. Preparation

   Read a rule file and store it in a form that is convenient for later processes. This is done in the constructor of `LMXConverter`.

2. Conversion

   a. Find a rule that matches the root element. During matching, keep track of nodes that matched a variable (text in the form of `$n;`).

   b. Copy the to-pattern of the rule to the target document. For each variable in the to-pattern, perform matching on the node that matched with the corresponding variable in the from-pattern and replace the to-pattern variable with the result. Thus this matching process will be recursively executed.

This sample LMX processor consists of one class (`LMXConverter`), which has one constructor and nine methods:

- `public LMXConverter(Source src);`

- `public boolean isValid();`

- `public Document convert(Document doc, boolean reverse);`

- `public Element convert(Element element, boolean reverse);`

- `private boolean matching(Vector matched, Element real, Node pattern);`

- `private void substitute(Node node, Vector matched, boolean reverse);`

- `private static Node getFirstElement(Node node);`

- `private static int getVariable(Node node);`

- `private static Node skipIgnorables(Node node);`

- `public static void main(String[] argv);`

Each is explained in the following subsections.

public LMXConverter(Source src)

This constructor creates an LMXConverter object with com.ibm.xml.parser. Source as a parameter. com.ibm.xml.parser.Source is an InputStream or a Reader that represents the input from the rule file.

After the rule file is read and the DOM tree in the variable document is obtained, the child lmx:pattern elements of the root element are scanned and children of lmx:pattern (lmx:lhs and lmx:rhs are stored) in the variable patterns (Vector consisted of Node [2]). If there are no errors during these operations, the variable valid is set to true.

In this operation, two methods—Node#getFirstChild() and Node#getNextSibling()—are used in the for loop as follows.

```
for (Node node = document.getDocumentElement().getFirstChild();
    node != null;
    node = node.getNextSibling()) {
       :
       :
}
```

public boolean isValid()

This method returns false if there is any problem within the constructor. (Most likely, false means a syntax error in the rule file.)

public Document convert(Document doc, boolean reverse)

This top-level method for conversion creates an empty document and then adds as the root element the conversion result of the root element of the source document, as follows.

```
public Document convert(Document doc, boolean reverse) {
    Document resultdoc = new TXDocument(); // @XML4J.
    resultdoc.appendChild(convert(doc.getDocumentElement(),
    reverse));
    return resultdoc;
}
```

public Element convert(Element element, boolean reverse)

This method and the following two (matching() and substitute()) are the heart of this program. This method has one loop, which iterates on the rules (that is, this.patterns.elements()).

```
Enumeration en = this.patterns.elements();
while (en.hasMoreElements()) {
    Node[] pair = (Node[])en.nextElement();
    if (matching(matched, element, pair[from])) {
        :
        :
    }
}
```

For each from-pattern, this method tries to match it with the current element. If a match succeeds, the variable matched will have values that are matched with variables. The method clones the corresponding to-pattern and substitutes the variables in it with the bindings in matched by calling the substitute() method.

```
result = (Element)pair[to].cloneNode(true);
substitute(result, matched, reverse);
    :
    :
```

private boolean matching(Vector matched, Element real,
Node pattern)

This method performs matching. During the matching, variable bindings are recorded in the vector matched.

```
if (pattern.getNodeType() != Node.ELEMENT
    || !real.getNodeName().equals(pattern.getNodeName()))
    return false;
```

First, it checks whether the pattern's type and name match the source element (in variable real). Note that Node#getNodeName() returns the element name if the node type is Element.

```
NamedNodeMap realNamedNodeMap = real.getAttributes();
NamedNodeMap patternNamedNodeMap = pattern.getAttributes();
// patternNamedNodeMap isn't null because pattern is Element.
if (realNamedNodeMap.getLength() != patternNamedNodeMap.getLength())
    return false;
for (int i = 0; i < realNamedNodeMap.getLength(); i ++) {
    Attr realattr = (Attr)realNamedNodeMap.item(i);
    Attr patattr = (Attr)patternNamedNodeMap.getNamedItem(realattr.
    getNodeName());
    if (patattr == null)
        return false;
```

```
        if (!realattr.getValue().equals(patattr.getValue()))
            return false;
    }
```

Next, the method checks whether all of the attributes match. Here, `Node#getAttributes()` is used to obtain all of the attributes from the element. The return value of this method is a `NamedNodeMap` object.

The number of attributes can be obtained by calling `NamedNodeMap#getLength()`. Matching should compare attributes as a set, not as a sequence, so the program enumerates the source attributes using an index and checks whether the same attribute is in the pattern.

```
    Node realch = skipIgnorables(real.getFirstChild());
    Node patch = skipIgnorables(pattern.getFirstChild());
    if (patch != null && patch instanceof Text
        && patch.getNextSibling() == null) {
        int number = getVariable(patch);
        if (0 < number ) {
            :
            :
            matched.addElement(realch);
            return true;
        }
    }
```

Next, this method checks whether the pattern is a variable. If it is, the method makes a note in the variable `matched`.

```
    boolean match = true;
    while (match && realch != null && patch != null) {
        switch (realch.getNodeType()) {
            case Node.ELEMENT_NODE:
                                    // Checks recursively.
                match = matching(matched, (Element)realch, patch);
                break;
            case Node.TEXT_NODE:
                if (patch.getNodeType() == Node.TEXT_NODE) {
                    match = realch.getNodeValue().equals(patch.
                    getNodeValue());
                }
                break;
            default:
                // Comment and ProcessingInstruction don't appear here.
        }
```

```
        realch = skipIgnorables(realch.getNextSibling());
        patch = skipIgnorables(patch.getNextSibling());
    }
    return match && realch == null && patch == null;
```

Finally, for each child in the source and the pattern, this method recursively calls `matching()` to see if the pattern matches the source document.

**private void substitute(Node node, Vector matched,
boolean reverse)**

This method substitutes the variables in the target pattern with the converted result of the matched source. The variable `node` contains a clone of the to-pattern, and the variable `matched` contains bindings of the variables. After locating a variable in the to-pattern, this method is at the following code fragment. At this point, `node` contains a variable and `replace` contains a value to replace the variable. Note that `replace` may have multiple nodes that are to be inserted at this position.

```
//node includes $n;; replace is the first node of nodes matched to $n;.
Node parent = node.getParentNode();
Node prev = node.getPreviousSibling();
parent.removeChild(node);
for (; replace != null; replace = replace.getNextSibling()) {
    Node cloned;
    if (replace .getNodeType() == Node.ELEMENT_NODE) {
        cloned = convert((Element)replace, reverse);
    } else {
        cloned = replace.cloneNode(true);
    }
    if (cloned != null) {
        ((Parent)parent).insertAfter(cloned, prev);
        prev = cloned;
    }
}
```

First, so that the program can remember the insertion point, the parent node and the previous node of `node` are saved. Then the `node` is removed. The `for` loop iterates on the nodes in `replace`. Note that the replace value is further converted by recursive calls to `convert()`.

private static Node getFirstElement(Node node)

This method returns the first `Element` object among the children of `node`.

```
private static Node getFirstElement(Node node) {
    if (node.getNodeType() != Node.ELEMENT_NODE) return null;
    for (node = node.getFirstChild();
        node != null;
        node = node.getNextSibling())
        if (node .getNodeType() == Node.ELEMENT_NODE) return node;
    return null;
}
```

private static int getVariable(Node node)

This method checks whether a node represents a variable in the LMX syntax. That is, it returns the variable number of the node as a `Text` object and its content as a `$number;`. Otherwise, it returns `-1`.

No DOM API is used in this method.

private static Node skipIgnorables(Node node)

During matching, the nodes `Comment` and `ProcessingInstruction` (as well as ignorable whitespaces) are ignored. This method is designed to skip such nodes. Since we use the "ignorable" flag provided by XML for Java, we need to cast `node` when we call the method for accessing it.

```
private static Node skipIgnorables(Node node) {
    while (node != null
        && (node instanceof TXText
            && ((TXText)node).getIsIgnorableWhitespace()
            || node .getNodeType() == Node.PROCESSING_INSTRUCTION_NODE
            || node .getNodeType() == Node.COMMENT_NODE)
        node = node.getNextSibling();
    return node;
}
```

public static void main(String[] argv)

This method prepares a pattern DOM tree and a source DOM tree and then calls the `convert()` method.

In this LMX processor, we assume that no `EntityReference` is in any DOM tree. Therefore we call `Parser#setExpandEntityReferences(true)` to instruct the parser to expand entity references.

Listing 4.2 is the complete listing of the LMX processor. It consists of a single class named `LMXConverter`. This program is written with the DOM API as much as possible, but a few lines are dependent on XML for Java—these are marked with @XML4J.

Listing 4.2 `LMXConverter.java`: LMX processor

```java
import com.ibm.xml.parser.Child;
import com.ibm.xml.parser.Parent;
import com.ibm.xml.parser.Parser;
import com.ibm.xml.parser.Source;
import com.ibm.xml.parser.TXDocument;
import com.ibm.xml.parser.TXText;
import java.io.FileInputStream;
import java.io.OutputStreamWriter;
import java.util.Enumeration;
import java.util.Vector;
import org.w3c.dom.Attr;
import org.w3c.dom.Comment;
import org.w3c.dom.Document;
import org.w3c.dom.Element;
import org.w3c.dom.NamedNodeMap;
import org.w3c.dom.Node;
import org.w3c.dom.ProcessingInstruction;
import org.w3c.dom.Text;

public class LMXConverter {

    boolean valid = false;
                            // A Vector consists of Node[2].
                            // Node[2] has a pair of "lmx:pattern"
                            // elements.
    Vector patterns = new Vector();

    /**
     *
     * @param src Stream of LMX document.
     */
    public LMXConverter(Source src) {
        try {
            // Parse an LMX document
            Parser parser = new Parser("lmx"); // @XML4J
                            // Uses a pseudo name "lmx" because
                            // the constructor doesn't know URL of
                            // src.
```

```
        // Instruct XML4J to use no EntityReference.
        parser.setExpandEntityReferences(true);      // @XML4J
        Document document = parser.readStream(src); // @XML4J
        if (parser.getNumberOfErrors() > 0)           // @XML4J
            return;

    for (Node node = document.getDocumentElement().
      getFirstChild();
        node != null; node = node.getNextSibling()) {
        if (node.getNodeType() == Node.ELEMENT_NODE
                    // Checks whether the element name is
                    // "lmx:pattern".
                    // But this is the wrong way because "lmx:"
                    // is a
                    // namespace prefix.
        && node.getNodeName().equals("lmx:pattern")) {
            Node[] pair = new Node[2];
            for (Node node2 = node.getFirstChild();
                node2 != null; node2 = node2.getNextSibling()) {
                if (node2.getNodeType() == Node.ELEMENT_NODE) {
                    if (node2.getNodeName().equals("lmx:lhs")) {
                            pair[0] = getFirstElement(node2);
                    } else if (node2.getNodeName().equals("lmx:rhs"))
                    {
                            pair[1] = getFirstElement(node2);
                    }
                }
        }
            if (pair[0] == null || pair[1] == null) {
                    System.err.println("A pattern has no proper pair.");
            } else {
                    this.patterns.addElement(pair);
            }

        }
    if (this.patterns.size() == 0) {
        System.err.println("No pattern");
        return;
    }
    this.valid = true;
} catch (Exception e) {
    e.printStackTrace();
}
}
```

```java
/**
 * Returns the first child element of node.
 * When node has no child elements, it returns null.
 */
private static Node getFirstElement(Node node) {
    if (node.getNodeType() != Node.ELEMENT_NODE) return null;
    for (node = node.getFirstChild();
         node != null;
         node = node.getNextSibling())
        if (node.getNodeType() == Node.ELEMENT_NODE) return node;
        return null;
}


/**
 * This method returns <VAR>false</VAR> when the LMX document is
   invalid.
 */
public boolean isValid() {
    return this.valid;
}


/**
 * Convert <VAR>doc</VAR>.
 *
 * @param doc <STRONG>Entity references in <VAR>doc</VAR>
 *            must be expanded</STRONG>.
 * @param reverse Reverse conversion or not.
 * @see com.ibm.xml.parser.Parser#setExpandEntityReferences
 * @see com.ibm.xml.parser.Parent#expandEntityReferences
 */
public Document convert(Document doc, boolean reverse) {
    Document resultdoc = new TXDocument(); // @XML4J
    resultdoc.appendChild(convert(doc.getDocumentElement(),
    reverse));
    return resultdoc;
}


/**
 * Convert <VAR>element</VAR>.
 *
 * @param element <STRONG>Entity references in <VAR>doc</VAR>
 *                must be expanded</STRONG>.
 * @param reverse Reverse conversion or not.
 * @see com.ibm.xml.parser.Parser#setExpandEntityReferences
```

```
    * @see com.ibm.xml.parser.Parent#expandEntityReferences
    */
public Element convert(Element element, boolean reverse) {
    int from = 0, to = 1;
    if (reverse) {
        from = 1;
        to = 0;
    }

                                // A Vector catch matches nodes.
    Vector matched = new Vector();
    boolean isMatched = false;
    Element result = null;
                                // Tries to match to all patterns.
    Enumeration en = this.patterns.elements();
    while (en.hasMoreElements()) {
        Node[] pair = (Node[])en.nextElement();
        if (matching(matched, element, pair[from])) {
                                // When an element matches to
                                // pair[from],
                                // copies a to-pattern.
            result = (Element)pair[to].cloneNode(true);
                                // Searches the result for $n;,
                                // and replaces $n; to matched nodes
            substitute(result, matched, reverse);
            isMatched = true;
            break;
        }
    }
    if (!isMatched) {
        System.err.println("No matched patterns for Element \""
                        +element.getNodeName()+"\".");
    }
    return result;
}

/**
 * @param node Text node.
 * @return Variable number; -1 when <VAR>node</VAR> includes no
   variable.
 */
private static int getVariable(Node node) {
    int number = -1;
    String data = TXText.trim(node.getNodeValue()); // @XML4J
```

```
        if (data.length() >= 2 && data.charAt(0) == '$'
            && data.charAt(data.length()-1) == ';') {
            try {
                number = Integer.parseInt(data.substring(1,
                    data.length()-1));
            } catch (NumberFormatException nfe) {
            }
        }
        return number;
}


/**
 * Check whether <VAR>real</VAR> matches to <VAR>pattern</VAR>.
 * When it matches, nodes matching to variables($n;) are added
 * to <VAR>matched</VAR>.
 */
private boolean matching(Vector matched, Element real, Node
    pattern) {
    if (pattern.getNodeType() != Node.ELEMENT_NODE
        || !real.getNodeName().equals(pattern.getNodeName()))
        return false;

                            // Checks attributes.
    NamedNodeMap realNamedNodeMap = real.getAttributes();
    NamedNodeMap patternNamedNodeMap = pattern.getAttributes();
                            // patternNamedNodeMap isn't null
                            // because pattern is Element.
    if (realNamedNodeMap.getLength() != patternNamedNodeMap.
      getLength())
        return false;
    for (int i = 0; i < realNamedNodeMap.getLength(); i ++) {
        Attr realattr = (Attr)realNamedNodeMap.item(i);
        Attr patattr = (Attr)patternNamedNodeMap.
          getNamedItem(realattr.getNodeName());
        if (patattr == null)
            return false;
        if (!realattr.getValue().equals(patattr.getValue()))
            return false;
    }

                            // Checks the children.
    Node realch = skipIgnorables(real.getFirstChild());
    Node patch = skipIgnorables(pattern.getFirstChild());
```

```
                                    // If the first child includes a
                                    // variable,
                                    // substitutes source nodes to the
                                    // variable.
        if (patch != null && patch instanceof Text
            && patch.getNextSibling() == null) {
            int number = getVariable(patch);
            if (number > 0) {
                if (matched.size() > number) {
                    matched.setElementAt(realch, number);
                } else if (matched.size () == number) {
                    matched.addElement(realch);
                } else {
                    for (int i = matched.size(); i < number; i ++)
                        matched.addElement(null);
                    matched.addElement(realch);
                }
                return true;
            }
        }
        boolean match = true;
        while (match && realch != null && patch != null) {
            switch (realch.getNodeType()) {
                case Node.ELEMENT_NODE:
                                    // Check recursively
                    match = matching(matched, (Element)realch, patch);
                    break;
                case Node.TEXT_NODE:
                    if (patch.getNodeType() == Node.TEXT_NODE) {
                        match = realch.getNodeValue().equals(patch.
                        getNodeValue());
                    }
                    break;
                default:
                                    // Comment and ProcessingInstruction
                                    // don't appear here.
            }
            realch = skipIgnorables(realch.getNextSibling());
            patch = skipIgnorables(patch.getNextSibling());
        }
        return match && realch == null && patch == null;
}
```

```
/**
 * Search for $n; in a tree, and replace it with matched.
   elementAt(n).
 */
private void substitute(Node node, Vector matched, boolean
reverse) {
    if (node.getNodeType() == Node.TEXT_NODE) {
        int number = getVariable(node);
                            // When node includes $n;, number is
                            // greater than 0.
        if (number > 0) {
            Node replace = null;
            if (matched.size() <= number) {
                System.err.println("substitute(): too big number:
                  $"+number);
            } else if ((replace = (Node)matched.elementAt(number))
              == null) {
                            // There is no matched node for this
                            // variable.
                Node parent = node.getParentNode();
                parent.replaceChild(new TXText("null"), node); //
                  @XML4J
            } else {
                Node parent = node.getParentNode();
                Node prev = node.getPreviousSibling();
                            // Removes a node including $n; from
                            // the tree
                parent.removeChild(node);
                            // Inserts clones of matched nodes.
                for (; replace != null; replace = replace.
                  getNextSibling()) {
                    Node cloned;
                            // If replace is Element, it must be
                            // converted.
                    if (replace.getNodeType() == Node.ELEMENT_NODE) {
                        cloned = convert((Element)replace, reverse);
                    } else {   // Clone it if not Element
                        cloned = replace.cloneNode(true);
                    }
                    if (cloned != null) {
                        ((Parent)parent).insertAfter(cloned, prev);
                        prev = cloned;
                    }
                }
            }
        }
    }
}
```

```
            } else {
                            // Converts $$ to $.
            String text = ((Text)node).getData();
            StringBuffer sb = new StringBuffer(text.length());
            for (int i = 0; i < text.length(); i ++) {
                if (text.charAt(i) == '$'
                    && i+1 < text.length()
                    && text.charAt(i+1) == '$') {
                    sb.append((char)'$');
                    i ++;
                } else
                    sb.append((char)text.charAt(i));
            }
            ((Text)node).setData(sb.toString());
        }

    } else if (node.getNodeType() == Node.ELEMENT_NODE) {
        for (Node child = node.getFirstChild(); child != null;
                child = child.getNextSibling())
            substitute(child, matched, reverse);
    }
}


/**
 * @return null or Element or nonignorable Text.
 */
private static Node skipIgnorables(Node node) {
    while (node != null
        && (node instanceof TXText
            && ((TXText)node).getIsIgnorableWhitespace() // @XML4J
            || node.getNodeType() ==
              Node.PROCESSING_INSTRUCTION_NODE
            || node.getNodeType() == Node.COMMENT_NODE))
        node = node.getNextSibling();
    return node;
}


public static void main(String[] argv) {
    try {
        String lmxfile = null, docfile = null;
        boolean reverse = false;

                        // Analyzes command line parameters.
        for (int i = 0; i < argv.length; i ++) {
```

```
            if ('-' != argv[i].charAt(0)) {
                if (lmxfile == null)
                    lmxfile = argv[i];
                else
                    docfile = argv[i];
            } else if ("-r".equals(argv[i]))
                reverse = true;
        }
        if (docfile == null) {
            System.err.println("Require 2 filenames.");
            System.err.println("\tConverter [-r] <lmx-doc>
              <xml-doc>");
            System.exit(1);
        }

                            // Reads an LMX file, and makes an
                            // instance.
        LMXConverter conv = new LMXConverter(new Source(new
          FileInputStream(lmxfile)));
                            // Checks the result of parsing the
                            // lmx file.
        if (!conv.isValid()) {
            System.err.println("Couldn't make converter");
            System.exit(1);
        }
                            // Parses the target XML document
        Parser p = new Parser(docfile);          // @XML4J
        p.setExpandEntityReferences(true);       // @XML4J
        Document doc = p.readStream(new FileInputStream(docfile));
          // @XML4J
        if (p.getNumberOfErrors() > 0) {         // @XML4J
            System.err.println("Specified document has error(s).");
            System.exit(1);
        }
                            // Starts matching and conversion.
        TXDocument outdoc = (TXDocument)conv.convert(doc,
          reverse);// @XML4J
                            // Prints the result.
        outdoc.printWithFormat(new OutputStreamWriter(System.
          out));// @XML4J
    } catch (Exception ex) {
        ex.printStackTrace();
    }
  }
}
```

4.4 Rendering with LMX

LMX has many other applications in addition to converting messages. One is to convert an XML document into an HTML document. Since HTML documents are universally viewable by browsers, converting a document to HTML effectively means *rendering* it. Thus an XML document can be browsed by browsers that have no native XML support. For example, we can browse the following `result.xml` document, shown in Figure 4.13, by converting it to HTML using LMX.

```
<?xml version="1.0"?>
<resultset>
    <result>
        <name>John Doe</name>
        <age>34</age>
        <email>John.Doe@foo.com</email>
    </result>
    <result>
        <name>Bob Smith</name>
        <age>29</age>
        <email>Bob.Smith@foo.com</email>
    </result>
    <result>
        <name>Alice Miller</name>
        <age>26</age>
        <email>Alice.Miller@foo.com</email>
    </result>
</resultset>
```

To do rendering with our LMX, we must take into account the following.

- Use HTML tag names in the target pattern.

- Output the conversion result using `com.ibm.xml.parser.util.HTMLPrintVisitor`, which writes a DOM tree in the HTML syntax. With this method, no XML declaration (`<?xml version="1.0" ...?>`) is generated and any element with no children is written as a single start tag, as in (`<BR>`), not as an empty tag (`</BR><BR/>`).

As an example, we convert `result.xml` into HTML. Since this XML document essentially represents a table of data, we convert it using HTML's `<table>` tag. The rule file, `result.lmx`, should look like the following.

```
<?xml version="1.0" encoding="UTF-8"?>
```

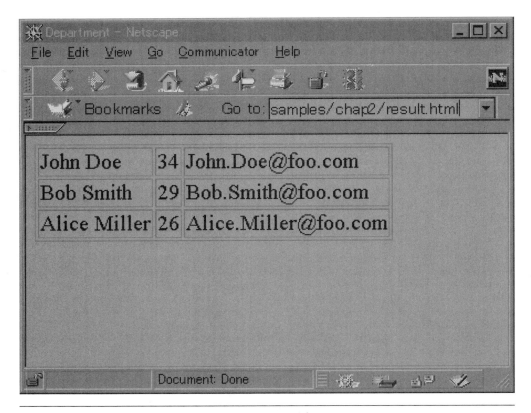

FIGURE 4.13 Displaying `result.html`, converted from `result.xml`

```
<lmx:rules xmlns:lmx="http://www.ibm.com/xml/lmx/">
    <lmx:pattern>
        <lmx:lhs>
        <resultset>$1;</resultset>
    </lmx:lhs>

    <lmx:rhs>
        <html>
            <head><title>Department</title></head>
            <body>
                <table border="1">$1;</table>
            </body>
        </html>
    </lmx:rhs>
    </lmx:pattern>

    <lmx:pattern>
        <lmx:lhs>
```

```
                        <result>
                            <name>$1;</name>
                            <age>$2;</age>
                            <email>$3;</email>
                        </result>
                    </lmx:lhs>

                    <lmx:rhs>
                        <tr><td>$1;</td><td>$2;</td><td>$3;</td></tr>
                    </lmx:rhs>
                </lmx:pattern>
            </lmx:rules>
```

As mentioned earlier in this discussion, we need to make a small modification to LMXConverter using HTMLPrintVisitor so that it generates a proper HTML document. The modified code is on the CD-ROM and has the filename LMXConverter2.java.

First, we need import declarations at the top of the code.

```
import com.ibm.xml.parser.NonRecursivePreorderTreeTraversal;
import com.ibm.xml.parser.Visitor;
import com.ibm.xml.parser.util.HTMLPrintVisitor;
```

Then we change the call of printWithFormat() to a call of HTMLPrintVisitor as follows.

Before:

```
outdoc.printWithFormat(new OutputStreamWriter(System.out));
```

After:

```
    Visitor visitor = new HTMLPrintVisitor(new
OutputStreamWriter(System.out));
    new NonRecursivePreorderTreeTraversal(visitor).traverse(outdoc);
```

With LMXConverter2.java, the previous file, result.xml, is converted into the following HTML file, result.html.

```
<html>
    <head>
        <title>Department</title>
    </head>
    <body>
        <table border="1">
            <tr>
```

```
            <td>John Doe</td>
            <td>34</td>
            <td>John.Doe@foo.com</td>
        </tr>
        <tr>
            <td>Bob Smith</td>
            <td>29</td>
            <td>Bob.Smith@foo.com</td>
        </tr>
        <tr>
            <td>Alice Miller</td>
            <td>26</td>
            <td>Alice.Miller@foo.com</td>
        </tr>
    </table>
  </body>
</html>
```

NOTE: The rendering specification being discussed at W3C is the Extensible Stylesheet Language (XSL). We could not use XSL examples because the XSL Working Draft was not stable enough at the time of this writing. LMX borrowed the idea of "rule-based translation" from XSL, but the syntax is radically different. Although LMX has limited capability, its rules are bidirectional. LMX can be a powerful tool. We use it for rendering and other purposes in Part 2 of this book.

4.5 Summary

In this chapter, we explained in detail the use of the `Node` interface, the most important interface for dealing with a DOM structure, and showed several ways to use it. As a nontrivial XML application, we developed a XML-tree conversion tool, the LMX processor. The code of the LMX processor contains a lot of techniques described so far. In addition, we showed that with the LMX processor, you can render an XML document into an HTML document.

This chapter concludes Part 1. In it, we discussed

- the basics of Web applications along with two enabling technologies, XML and Java,

- the basics of XML processors and their primary functions,

- the generation of an XML document by building an internal DOM tree from scratch, optionally a valid one, and the significance of this in Web applications, and

- the techniques for manipulating DOM trees through the DOM API and the design and implementation of the LMX processor.

Part 2 discusses the use of XML and Java in the context of more-practical Web application scenarios.

CHAPTER 5

Managing Documents and Working with Metacontent

5.1 Introduction

In Chapter 1, we mentioned several different aspects of XML-based applications: document management, metacontent, databases, and messaging. In this first chapter of Part 2, we discuss the document management and metacontent aspects of XML-based Web applications. We also cover the basics of servlets, the central mechanism that allows you to create a Web application using Java.

A common question is how XML can be applied to SGML-based document applications. If you already have an SGML application that works reasonably well, you probably do not want to redesign the system for XML. This is because XML is a relatively small subset of SGML, and hence its representational capacity is limited compared to SGML. However, if you are designing a new system, the simplicity of XML could outweigh this limitation. XML is 20 percent of SGML in complexity, but it can be used in 80 percent of SGML systems.

In many document processing applications, the abilities for example to create stylesheets and to print are among their major features. However, such applications are out of the scope of this book; we focus instead on documents that are primarily displayed on Web browsers. We begin by discussing the basics of Java servlets and give a simple servlet as an example. So that you can try the sample code in this chapter, we include on the accompanying CD-ROM an evaluation copy of IBM's WebSphere Application Server, which provides full support of servlets. Check the documentation on the CD-ROM to see how to install and use it.

Then we create *DocMan,* a Web-based document management system that can create, browse, and search simple documents from Web browsers. Two topics covered in detail are *content search* based on the structure of a document (such as, locate string "XYZ" in element FOO) and the use of *metacontent* for efficient indexing, browsing, and searching.

5.2 Servlet Basics

A *servlet* is a Java program (class) that runs on a Web server and resembles a conventional CGI program. In Chapter 1, we discussed the evolution of server-side application programming from CGI to native API to servlets. Following is a review of the merits of servlets.

- Servlets are more efficient than CGI processes.

  CGI, or **Common Gateway Interface**, is a specification for transferring information between a Web server and a CGI program. CGI programs run on the server and are one of the most common ways to provide dynamic interaction between server and user (browser). One problem with using CGI is that each time a CGI program is executed, a new process must be started. Once the program has executed a request, it disappears. This all results in high overhead and can appreciably slow down servers. The servlet is an increasingly popular alternative to CGI programs. One of its biggest advantages is that it is persistent; that is, once it is started, it remains in memory and can therefore be used to fill multiple requests. Thus servlets are faster and result in much lower overhead.

- Servlets are safe.

  Servlets run in the same address space as the server. Thus the server is potentially vulnerable to attack by unstable or even malicious servlets. However, Java has a protection mechanism that prevents such attacks, thereby making it safe to run servlets in the server's address space.

- Servlets are written in Java.

  Java is a general-purpose programming language and one of the most productive for any kind of task. It has many features that make it well suited for use on the Web. Servlets, as small Java applications, embody the features and advantages of Java.

To work with servlets, we need a Web server software that supports them. The most well-known such software is Java Web Server, developed by Sun Micro-systems. However, there are several plug-in modules for popular Web servers such as Apache that add the servlet capability to servers. In writing this chapter, we used Java Web Server 1.1, but other servlet-enabled Web servers can be used.

The Java Web Server architecture is a general one that can be used for many differ-ent Internet servers (FTP, Telnet, and so on). However, it has specific support for HTTP servers. Generally, an HTTP server processes an HTTP request as follows:

1. Receives the request, GET or POST, from a client.

2. Processes the request, and generates a result.

3. Forms an HTTP response, and sends it back to the client.

The servlet architecture does most of steps 1 and 3 for you. So you can concen-trate on the application logic to process the request without worrying about the details of HTTP (such as parsing a header and calculating content length).

A HTTP servlet is a subclass of the superclass `javax.servlet.http.HttpServlet`. For each request method defined in HTTP—GET or POST—there is a corresponding method—`doGet()` or `doPost()`—defined in this superclass. To implement your own algorithm to fulfill requests, you need to override these methods. For example, to implement a GET method you need to override the following method:

```
public void doGet(HttpServletRequest req, HttpServletResponse res);
```

All of the information concerning the request is passed in the first argument, `req`, including HTTP header information, user authentication information, and param-

> **NOTE:** Every servlet is loaded and its only instance is created either when the server is started or when the servlet is called for the first time. All requests associated with this servlet are processed with this single instance; thus expen-sive object creation and destruction on each request is avoided. However, since Web servers usually have multiple threads running simultaneously, your method (for example, `doGet()`) must be thread-safe. The easiest way to accomplish this is to implement the `javax.servlet.SingleThreadModel` interface, although you might have to forfeit maximum efficiency by using it.

eter values, as well as the body of the request if any. All information about the result of the request should be directed to the other argument, `res`. For each GET method with a URL associated with this servlet, the server would call this method.

To return a response, you need to create a `PrintWriter` by calling `getWriter()` on the second argument `res`. You can use the standard I/O (input/output) methods, such as `println()`, with the `PrintWriter` object for returning the result.

Depending on which request method is used—GET or POST—there are two ways to send variables to a Web server:

- GET method: Encode parameters within a URL. However, because parameters are enclosed in URLs, they must be short.

- POST method: Use the `<FORM>` tag in your HTML form. This method is more flexible because there are no limitations about parameter format and length, so you can send a longer value more safely than can be done with the GET method.

In either case, the values should be encoded using *URL Encoding*, in which every whitespace is replaced by a + and some other special characters are replaced by an escaped hexadecimal notation such as %2E. Fortunately, however, you need not be concerned with these details because they are automatically handled by the server and the servlet libraries.

You can retrieve the parameter values by using `getParameterValues()`. An enumeration of all available parameters is returned by `getParameterNames()`.

For compiling a servlet, you need to include `jws.jar` in your CLASSPATH. It is normally located in the `/lib` directory under the server's root directory. For example, if you set your CLASSPATH in the `autoexec.bat` file, as follows:

```
set CLASSPATH=.;c:\xml4j\xml4j_1_1_9.jar;c:\xml4j\
xml4jSamples_1_1_9.jar
```

and you have `jws.jar` in `c:\JavaWebServer1.1\lib`, change this line to

```
set CLASSPATH=.;c:\xml4j\xml4j_1_1_9.jar;
c:\xml4j\xml4jSamples_1_1_9.jar;c:\JavaWebServer1.1\lib\jws.jar
```

Note that if you use IBM's WebSphere, you have to use the path `jsdk.jar` instead of `jws.jar`.

You also need to register the servlet on the server. How to register a servlet depends on the Web server software used. In the case of the Java Web Server 1.1, you run the Administration Tool. Once the servlet is registered, it can be invoked as if it is a normal Web page. See Section 5.3 for more details.

5.3 A Simple Servlet

A simple servlet is shown in Listing 5.1. This servlet, `MyServlet.java`, receives a GET request and returns two types of information, as shown in Figure 5.1:

- User-Agent (name and version of the browser)

- Parameters on the URL (such as `URL?foo=bar`)

The output of the servlet is shown in Figure 5.1.

Listing 5.1 `MyServlet.java`: A simple servlet

```
import java.io.IOException;
import java.io.PrintWriter;
import javax.servlet.ServletException;
import javax.servlet.ServletOutputStream;
import javax.servlet.http.HttpServlet;
import javax.servlet.http.HttpServletRequest;
import javax.servlet.http.HttpServletResponse;

public class MyServlet extends HttpServlet {

    /**
      * Handle the GET request.
      */
    public void doGet (HttpServletRequest req, HttpServletResponse
      res)
          throws ServletException, IOException {

            // Sets the content type and other response header
            // fields first.
          res.setContentType("text/html");

            // Then writes the data of the response.
          PrintWriter out = res.getWriter();
          out.println("<HEAD><TITLE> My First Servlet Output
            </TITLE></HEAD><BODY>");
          out.println("<h1> My First Servlet Output </h1>");
          out.println("<P>This is output from MyServlet.");

              // Accesses the header information.
          out.println("<P>User-Agent: "+req.getHeader
            ("User-Agent"));
```

```
                // Accesses the parameter information.
        for (java.util.Enumeration e = req.getParameterNames();
            e.hasMoreElements(); ) {
            String name = (String)e.nextElement();
            String vals[] = (String[]) req.
            getParameterValues(name);
            if (vals != null) {
                out.print("<p> " + name + " = ");
                for (int i = 0; i<vals.length; i++)
                        out.println(vals[i]+",");
            }
            out.println("</p>");
        }
        out.println("</BODY>");
        out.close();
    }

    public String getServletInfo() {
        return "A simple servlet";
    }
}
```

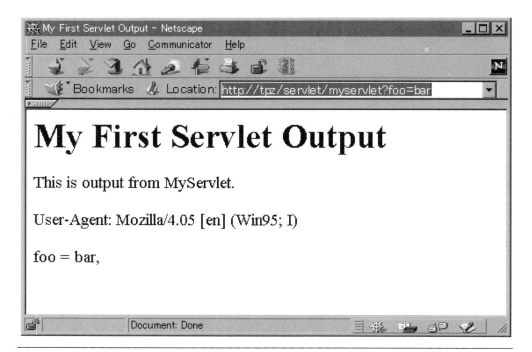

FIGURE 5.1 Output of `MyServlet`

5.3.1 Designing a Servlet

Here, we have developed a very simple servlet, one that did not require a lot of thought prior to its design. However, generally a servlet should be designed and developed by following these steps.

1. Design the program interface.

   * What is the URL of this servlet?

   * What request method is used? Usually GET or POST are used. The GET method does not require a separate HTML page for sending a request (because everything is in a URL), but the POST method is more flexible, as mentioned in Section 5.2.

   * What parameters are to be received? What are appropriate behaviors if one or more parameters are missing?

   * What is the content type of the result? How will the result be computed?

2. Create a servlet class (a subclass of `HttpServlet`).

   * Override the appropriate method, `doGet()` or `doPost()`.

   * If there is any initialization before the first request is processed, override `init()`.

   * Write the body of the process.
     Within `doGet()` or `doPost()`:

     a. Obtain parameters through the `getParameterValues()` or `getParameterNames()` methods of the `HttpServletRequest` class.

     b. Set the content type (such as `text/html`) of the result by using `HttpServletRespose#setContentType()`.

     c. Obtain the output stream by using `HttpServletResponse#getWriter()`, write the result to this stream, and close the stream by calling `close()`.

3. Register the servlet with the pertinent URL.

   As mentioned earlier, how to do this depends on the Web server that you are using. In the case of Java Web Server 1.1, you need to run the Administration Tool. Figure 5.2 shows an example registration panel. Note that "myservlet" highlighted in the left pane is the URL of this servlet.

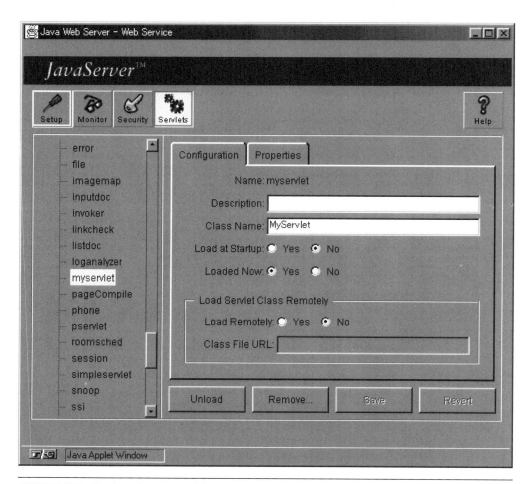

FIGURE 5.2 Registering a servlet

We have covered the basics of servlets, just about enough for you to understand and write the sample programs in this section. Refer to the following material for more details.

- Java Web Server Developer Documentation: http://jeeves.javasoft.com/products/java-server/documentation/webserver1.1/index_developer.html

- Jason Hunter and William Crawford, Java Servlet Programming, O'Reilly: Sebastopol, CA, 1998, ISBN:1-56592-391-X.

In the next section, we start developing our document management application, DocMan.

5.4 Overview of the DocMan System

Our first XML-based Web application is a document management system, called DocMan, for storing and sharing documents, such as schedules. This sample application shows how XML can be effectively used for document management.

1. The user can compose a document from a browser. The document is stored in a Web server (Web application).

2. The user can browse the contents of the stored documents.

3. The user can browse the list of the documents as well as search the documents by title or contents.

You will see how XML enables a simple implementation of this third feature.

First, we define the specification of documents that are handled by DocMan. It is very simple.

```
<doc>
    <title>Any title</title>
    <date>Date of creation</date>
    <body>...Text body...</body>
</doc>
```

All documents are stored in this XML form. However, since the user interface is through a browser, that is, through HTTP/HTML, end users will never see the XML documents directly. The title and the body are entered by the user, the creation date is automatically generated by DocMan.

Based on the three features of this system, the user interface has the following three different views, each of which is implemented as a servlet:

1. *Input* view (`inputdoc` servlet), to create and store a document

2. *Browse* view (`viewdoc` servlet), to display a document

3. *List* view (`listdoc` servlet), to list all documents retrieved by a search

Figure 5.3 depicts the basic structure of DocMan.

The DocMan system requires a number of files. Table 5.1 lists all but the HTML files. All of the class files should be located in the servlet directory of the Web server (in the case of Java Web Server 1.1, it is normally

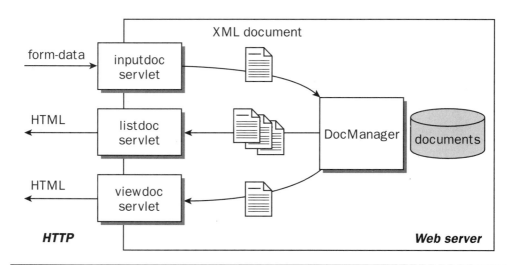

FIGURE 5.3 DocMan system structure

\JavaWebServer1.1\servlets). docman.properties has locale-specific resources (that is, error messages) used in this program and should be in the same directory that contains the class files. The location of the LMX rule file doc.lmx is specified in this resource file. Of course, you need XML for Java and the LMXConverter (described in Chapter 4), which are accessible from the Web server. See your Web server's documentation for the details of how to make these files visible from the server's Java Virtual Machine (JVM).

This program is designed so that it can be used from a simple HTML browser; no applets are used. Everything going between the server and browser is HTML/HTTP; no XML is sent to the client. This is sometimes called the *thin-client* model because the client is only required to do HTML rendering. It is

TABLE 5.1 Programs and Files in DocMan

LISTING NO.	CLASS NAME (FILENAME)	SERVLET NAME
Listing 5.2	DocInput.java, DocInput.class	/servlet/inputdoc
Listing 5.3	DocManager.java, DocManager.class	N/A
Listing 5.4	docman.properties	N/A
Listing 5.5	DocView.java, DocView.class	/servlet/viewdoc
Listing 5.6	doc.lmx	N/A
Listing 5.7	DocList.java, DocList.class	/servlet/listdoc
Listing 5.8	MakeCDF.java, MakeCDF.class	/servlet/all.cdf

> **NOTE:** DocMan does not provide any facilities for distributed authoring, such as versioning, locking, and checking-out/checking-in. The Web Distributed Authoring and Versioning (WebDAV) working group of the Internet Engineering Task Force (IETF) is working on these issues. Once it is completed, document management will be more standardized and more interoperable.

also possible to design using the *fat-client* model, whereby XML documents are sent to the client and rendering is done on the client side.

In the following subsections, we discuss the servlets and class of the system.

5.4.1 `inputdoc` Servlet

The servlet `inputdoc` receives a newly composed document from a browser, converts it to XML, and stores it in the document file.

Since the text body of our document is fairly large, we use the POST method to send document contents to the server. Thus, we need an HTML file that has a `<FORM>` element, as shown next.

```
<FORM action="/servlet/inputdoc" method="POST">
    <DIV>Title:
        <INPUT type="TEXT" name="title" size="80">
    </DIV>

    <TEXTAREA name="body" cols="64" cols="25">
    </TEXTAREA>

    <DIV>
        <INPUT type="SUBMIT">
        <INPUT type="RESET">
    </DIV>
</FORM>
```

This file will be displayed by a browser as in Figure 5.4.

When the Submit Query button is clicked, a POST request is sent to the URL `/servlet/inputdoc`, which corresponds to the `DocInput` class. The value of the title field is passed as the value of the variable `title`, while the value of the body field is in the variable body. The `inputdoc` servlet should retrieve these values and create an appropriate XML document.

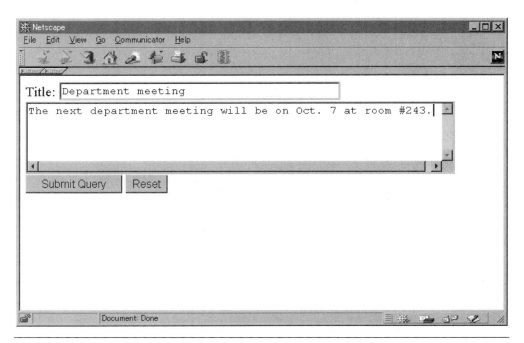

FIGURE 5.4 Input HTML file

Implementation

This servlet accepts only POST methods; sending a GET method to it results in an error message being returned. In doPost(), first the parameters are checked. The HTTP specification does not prohibit the same parameter from appearing multiple times in a single request, so the getParameterValues() method returns an array of character strings. In our application, however, multiple occurrences of the same parameter are treated as errors.

Then, once data is ready, a DOM structure for the XML document is created. As discussed in Chapter 3, this structure is built by creating a Document object (more precisely, an implementation of Document, which is TXDocument in our sample) and creating Element nodes and Text nodes using the factory method.

Storing the created document is done by calling the class DocManager, which is explained later in this section.

Finally, the response is created. In this case, the response is an HTTP redirect response that instructs the client to access another URL as the result of the original request. The user is redirected to a page that shows the contents of the document.

Listing 5.2 shows the entire listing of this servlet.

Listing 5.2 `DocInput.java:inputdoc` **servlet**

```
import org.w3c.dom.Element;
import com.ibm.xml.parser.TXDocument;
import java.io.IOException;
import java.io.PrintWriter;
import java.io.Writer;
import java.net.MalformedURLException;
import java.net.URL;
import javax.servlet.ServletException;
import javax.servlet.http.HttpServlet;
import javax.servlet.http.HttpServletRequest;
import javax.servlet.http.HttpServletResponse;
import javax.servlet.http.HttpUtils;

public class DocInput extends HttpServlet {
    DocManager docman = DocManager.getInstance();

    /**
      * GET method is not used.
      */
    public void doGet(HttpServletRequest req, HttpServletResponse
      res)
        throws ServletException, IOException {
        res.setContentType("text/plain");
        PrintWriter writer = res.getWriter();
        writer.print(this.docman.getString("docman.input.get"));
        writer.close();
    }

    /**
      * Return an error message to the browser.
      */
    private void parameterError(HttpServletResponse res) throws
      IOException {
        res.setContentType("text/html");
        PrintWriter writer = res.getWriter();
        writer.print(this.docman.getString("docman.input.error"));
        writer.close();
    }

    /**
      * Handle the POST method.
      * 1. Check the parameters.
```

```
 * 2. Build a DOM tree.
 * 3. Register it through DocManager.
 * 4. Return an HTTP redirect response.
 */
public void doPost(HttpServletRequest req, HttpServletResponse
  res)
    throws ServletException, IOException {
            // Checks the 'title' parameter.
    String[] values = req.getParameterValues("title");
            // If there are no "title=", or
            // if there are two or more "title=", or
            // if "title=" value is empty, show an error
            // message.
    if (values == null || values.length != 1 || values[0].
    trim().length() == 0) {
      this.parameterError(res);
      return;
    }
    String title = values[0].trim();

            // Checks the 'body' parameter.
    values = req.getParameterValues("body");
    if (values == null || values.length != 1 || values[0].length()
      == 0) {
      this.parameterError(res);
      return;
    }
    String body = values[0];

            // Creates the Document node and the root element.
            // <?xml version="1.0" encoding="UTF-8"?>
            // <doc/>
    TXDocument doc = new TXDocument();
    doc.setEncoding("UTF-8");
    Element root = doc.createElement("doc");
    doc.appendChild(root);

            // Creates "<title>value of title=</title>".
    Element el = doc.createElement("title");
    el.appendChild(doc.createTextNode(title));
    root.appendChild(el); // Appends the title element to the root
                          // element.

            // Creates "<date>Current time</date>".
    el = doc.createElement("date");
```

```
      el.appendChild(doc.createTextNode(DocManager.formatDate()));
      root.appendChild(el); // Appends the date element to the root
                            // element.

            // Creates "<body>text</body>".
      el = doc.createElement("body");
      el.appendChild(doc.createTextNode(body));
      root.appendChild(el); // Appends the body element to the root
                            // element.

            // Registers the document to DocManager.
      int id = this.docman.addDocument(doc);

      try {        // Shows users the document.
         URL u = new URL(HttpUtils.getRequestURL(req).toString());
         u = new URL(u, "/servlet/viewdoc?id="+id);
         res.setStatus(HttpServletResponse.SC_MOVED_TEMPORARILY);
         res.sendRedirect(u.toString());
      } catch (MalformedURLException mue) {
            // Ignore.
      }
   }
}
```

5.4.2 DocManager Class

The DocManager class, shown in Listing 5.3, manages the XML documents created by the inputdoc servlet. Only one instance (object) of this class is created; it is responsible for all management tasks. Its main methods are addDocument() for storing a DOM tree as an XML document in a file system and getDocument() for retrieving a stored XML document. This class also provides utility functions that are used by other classes.

Listing 5.3 DocManager.java: Manages XML documents

```
import com.ibm.xml.parser.Parser;
import com.ibm.xml.parser.TXDocument;
import java.io.BufferedReader;
import java.io.File;
import java.io.FileInputStream;
import java.io.FileNotFoundException;
import java.io.FileOutputStream;
import java.io.FileReader;
import java.io.IOException;
```

```java
import java.io.OutputStreamWriter;
import java.io.PrintWriter;
import java.io.Writer;
import java.text.DateFormat;
import java.text.MessageFormat;
import java.text.ParseException;
import java.util.Date;
import java.util.Locale;
import java.util.MissingResourceException;
import java.util.ResourceBundle;

public class DocManager {
    ResourceBundle resource = null;
    String workdir = null;
    String seqfilename = null;
    TXDocument[] docs;
    int next;

    static DocManager theInstance = null;

    /**
      * Return the instance.
      */
    public static DocManager getInstance() {
        if (DocManager.theInstance == null) {
            DocManager.theInstance = new DocManager();
        }
        return DocManager.theInstance;
    }

    /**
      * Load the property file, "docman.properties".
      */
    private DocManager() {
                // Loads "docman*.properties".
                // When the program runs in Japanese environment,
                // it loads "docman_ja.properties".
        try {
            this.resource = ResourceBundle.getBundle("docman");
        } catch (MissingResourceException mre) {
            mre.printStackTrace();
        }
                // The file "seq" contains the number of documents.
        this.seqfilename = this.getWorkDirectory()+"seq";
        this.next = 0;
```

```java
        BufferedReader br = null;
        try {
            br = new BufferedReader(new FileReader(this.seqfilename));
            String line = br.readLine();
            if (null != line) {
                line = line.trim();
                this.next = Integer.parseInt(line);
            }
            br.close();
        } catch (NumberFormatException nfe) {
            try {
                br.close();
            } catch (IOException ioe) {}
        } catch (IOException ioe) {
                // Ignore.
        }
                // Creates an array of TXDocument in which
                // all documents are stored.
        this.docs = new TXDocument[this.next < 20 ? 20 : this.next*2];
}


/**
  * Return a resource.
  * @return found resource; null if not found.
  */
public String getString(String key) {
    return this.resource == null ? null : this.resource.
    getString(key);
}


public String format1(String key, String param1) {
    Object[] ao = new Object[1];
    ao[0] = param1;
    return MessageFormat.format(getString(key), ao);
}


/**
  * Append File.separator to "docman.workdir", and return it.
  */
public String getWorkDirectory() {
    if (this.workdir == null) {
        String workd = getString("docman.workdir");
        if (workd == null)
            workd = File.separator+"docwork";
```

```
            if (workd.charAt(workd.length()-1) != File.separatorChar) {
                workd = workd+File.separator;
            }
            this.workdir = workd;
        }
        return this.workdir;
    }

    /**
     * Save a document to a file and memory.
     * Increase the counter.
     * @return Index number of added document.
     */
    public synchronized int addDocument(TXDocument doc) throws
        IOException {
                    // Puts doc into a document array.
        if (this.next >= this.docs.length) {
            TXDocument[] temp = new TXDocument[this.next*2];
            System.arraycopy(this.docs, 0, temp, 0, this.docs.length);
            this.docs = temp;
        }
        this.docs[this.next] = doc;
                    // Saves doc to disk.
        String fname = this.getWorkDirectory()+Integer.toString(this.
            next)+".xml";
        Writer wr = new OutputStreamWriter(new FileOutputStream(fname),
            "UTF8");
        doc.printWithFormat(wr);
        wr.close();
                    // Increases the counter.
        this.next ++;
        PrintWriter pw = new PrintWriter(new FileOutputStream(this.
            seqfilename));
        pw.println(this.next);
        pw.close();
        return this.next-1;
    }

    /**
     * Return the number of documents.
     */
    public int getNumberOfDocuments() {
        return this.next;
    }
```

```
/**
 * Return a document in specified index.
 */
public TXDocument getDocument(int index) {
            // Out of range?
   if (index >= this.next) return null;
   synchronized (this.docs) {
            // If target document is not on memory,
      if (this.docs[index] == null) {
         String fname = this.getWorkDirectory()+Integer.
            toString(index)+".xml";
            // load from a file
         Parser p = new Parser(fname); // @XML4J
         try {
            this.docs[index] = p.readStream(new
               FileInputStream(fname)); // @XML4J
         } catch (FileNotFoundException fnfe) {
               // Ignore.
         } catch (IOException e) {
            System.err.println("DocManager: "+e);
         }
      }
   }
   return this.docs[index];
}

/**
 * Create a date string.
 */
public static String formatDate() {
   DateFormat df = DateFormat.getDateTimeInstance(DateFormat.LONG,
                                                  DateFormat.LONG,
                                                  new Locale("en",
                                                  "US"));
   return df.format(new Date());
}
}
```

Implementation

The implementation of DocManager.java is rather complex, so we step
through each of the major methods:

- The constructor, getInstance()

- The utility functions, getString(), format1(), and getWorkDirectory()

- `addDocument()`

- `getDocument()`

Constructor: `getInstance()`

In a design pattern called the *Singleton Pattern*, exactly one instance of the class `DocManager` may be created. The static method `getInstance()` always returns the only instance of the class. `DocManager`'s only constructor is made private so that no other class can create additional instances. In the first call of `getInstance()`, the method creates the instance by calling `DocManager`'s constructor and saves the instance in a variable. `getInstance()` is then called many times from other classes. In all such later calls, it will return the instance in the variable, rather than creating new `DocManager` instances.

XML documents managed by this class are stored in a directory specified by the `docman.workdir` property. This directory has a file named `seq` that holds the number of documents in the directory. Each XML file is named as *number*`.xml`, such as `0.xml`, `1.xml`, and so on.

The constructor performs the following tasks.

- Prepares a `java.util.ResourceBundle` object by reading the `docman.properties` file. Its contents are described later in the chapter.

- Reads the `seq` file, and sets the variable `next` that specifies the index of the next new document.

- Allocates an array of `TXDocument` to hold in-memory documents.

`getString()`, `format1()`, `getWorkDirectory()`

These methods provide access to information in the `ResourceBundle` object prepared in the constructor. The object contains name-value pairs extracted from the property file `docman.properties`. Each property can be accessed by calling the `ResourceBundle#getString(`*property-name*`)` method.

The `ResourceBundle` class is Java's standard way to externalize locale-specific information. In fact, depending on the current locale setting, `ResourceBundle#getBundle("docman")` loads the most appropriate property file by trying to append the locale code to the filename. For example, suppose there are two property files present, `docman_fr.properties` and `docman_ja.properties`.

Then `docman_fr.properties` will be loaded if the current environment is French, while `docman_ja.properties` will be loaded for a Japanese environment. In this way, locale-specific data such as message strings in a national language can be stored externally and the program itself can be used universally.[1]

addDocument()

The `addDocument()` method is used to store a DOM tree created by the `input-doc` servlet. It performs the following steps.

1. Stores the DOM tree in the in-memory array.

2. Generates an XML document from the DOM tree, and stores it in the file `number.xml` in the working directory.

3. Updates the `seq` file.

The XML generation part closely follows what we did in Chapter 3, so you should have no problem understanding this part of the code.

getDocument()

The `getDocument()` method returns a DOM tree of the specified index. It checks if the document is in memory and returns the DOM tree if it is. Otherwise, it opens the file and reads it into memory. Therefore parsing is done only once for every document.

5.4.3 Resource File: `docman.properties`

The `docman.properties` file contains resources that are mostly locale-specific, such as message text. In addition, it specifies the working directory in which to store XML documents (`docman.workdir`) and the pathname of the LMX rule file (`docman.rule`). When this program is run on a Windows system, the directory separator should be written as two backslashes, \\. On a UNIX system, the directory separator is a single slash, /.

---

[1]In `DocManager`, the current locale is the environment of the Web server, so it does not adopt messages depending on the client settings. To send messages that are appropriate to the client setting, you need to check the `Accept-Language:` field of the HTTP header.

Listing 5.4 shows the `docman.properties` file.

Listing 5.4 `docman.properties`: Contains resources

```
docman.workdir=C:\\docwork
docman.rule=C:\\docwork\\doc.lmx
docman.list.error=<H1>Parameter Error</H1>\
<P>This servlet requires:</P>\
<UL>\
    <LI>1 'element' parameter and 1 'string' parameter, or\
    <LI>no parameters.\
</UL>\n
docman.list.header=<HTML>\n <HEAD>\n <TITLE>List</TITLE>\n </HEAD>\n
<BODY>\n
docman.list.footer= <HR>\n </BODY>\n</HTML>\n
docman.list.notfound= <P>No matched documents</P>\n
docman.list.headerall= <H1>All Documents</H1>\n
docman.list.headertitle= <H1>Documents containing '{0}'' in
title</H1>\n
docman.list.headerbody= <H1>Documents containing '{0}''</H1>\n
docman.view.error=<H1>Parameter Error</H1>\
<P>This servlet requires one parameter named 'id'.</P>\n
docman.view.cantget=<H1>Can't get document {0}.</H1>\n
docman.input.error=<H1>Parameter Error</H1>\
<P>This servlet requires a 'title' and a 'body' as parameters.\n
docman.input.get=This servlet doesn't support the GET method.\n
docman.cdf.title=All documents
```

5.5 Browsing, Listing, and Searching Documents

Having covered the core of document management functions provided by `DocManager`, in this section we shift the focus to the other user interfaces, those for browsing, and listing and searching: `viewdoc` servlet and `listdoc` servlet.

5.5.1 `viewdoc` Servlet

First, we look at browsing. Since the document itself is in XML and we assume an HTML browser that is capable only of displaying HTML pages, we need to convert the XML documents into HTML. For this purpose, we use the LMX processor developed in Chapter 4. Figure 5.5 shows the appearance of the document that we have entered in Figure 5.4.

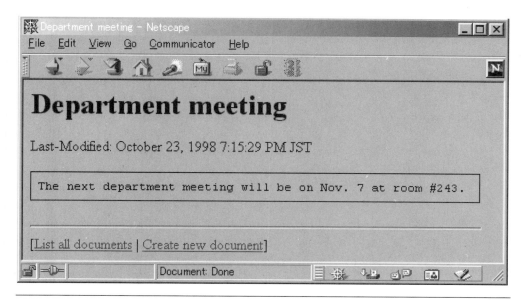

FIGURE 5.5 View document converted to HTML by `viewdoc` servlet

The class `DocView` is a servlet that converts XML documents to HTML documents. It is shown in Listing 5.5.

init()

When this servlet is initialized, it also creates an instance of `LMXConverter`. The rule file specified in `docman.properties` is parsed at the same time, and the rules are kept in memory.

doGet()

This servlet accepts GET requests only. The document index is specified as in `/servlet/viewdoc?id=`*number*. The `doGet` method first checks the parameter and then retrieves the specified DOM tree and converts it into HTML using LMX.

Listing 5.5 `DocView.java`: Converts XML documents to HTML documents

```
import com.ibm.xml.parser.NonRecursivePreorderTreeTraversal;
import com.ibm.xml.parser.Source;
import com.ibm.xml.parser.TXDocument;
import com.ibm.xml.parser.Visitor;
import com.ibm.xml.parser.util.HTMLPrintVisitor;
import java.io.FileInputStream;
```

```
import java.io.IOException;
import java.io.PrintWriter;
import javax.servlet.ServletConfig;
import javax.servlet.ServletException;
import javax.servlet.http.HttpServlet;
import javax.servlet.http.HttpServletRequest;
import javax.servlet.http.HttpServletResponse;

public class DocView extends HttpServlet {
    LMXConverter lmxconv;
    DocManager docman = DocManager.getInstance();

    /**
     * Prepare the servlet by loading the LMX rule file.
     */
    public void init(ServletConfig conf) throws ServletException {
                // Gets a filename of LMX rule document with
                // DocManager.
        String lmxfilename = DocManager.getInstance().
        getString("docman.rule");
        if (lmxfilename == null)
            throw new ServletException("Can't start DocView servlet
              because"
                +" docman.properties has no docman.rules entry.");

        try {  // Creates an LMXConverter instance.
            this.lmxconv = new LMXConverter(new Source(new
            FileInputStream(lmxfilename)));
        } catch (IOException ioe) {
            throw new ServletException("DocView: "+ioe);
        }
        if (!this.lmxconv.isValid()) {
            throw new ServletException("DocView: LMX rule error.");
        }
    }

    /**
     * Return an error message to the browser.
     */
    private void parameterError(HttpServletResponse res) throws
    IOException {
        res.setContentType("text/html");
        PrintWriter writer = res.getWriter();
        writer.print(this.docman.getString("docman.view.error"));
```

```
        writer.close();
}


/**
  * GET method
  * 1. Check the parameters.
  * 2. Retrieve the document.
  * 3. Do the conversion by calling LMX.
  * 4. Generate HTML using a visitor.
  */
public void doGet(HttpServletRequest req, HttpServletResponse res)
    throws ServletException, IOException {
            // 1. Checks parameters.
            // Checks id= parameter in URL.
    String[] values = req.getParameterValues("id");
    if (values == null || values.length != 1 || values[0].trim().
      length() == 0) {
        this.parameterError(res);
        return;
    }
    String numstring = values[0].trim();
            // Is id= parameter number?
    int num = -1;
    try {
        num = Integer.parseInt(numstring);
    } catch (NumberFormatException nfe) {
            // num == -1
    }

    if (num < 0 || num >= this.docman.getNumberOfDocuments()) {
        this.parameterError(res);
        return;
    }
    res.setContentType("text/html");
    PrintWriter pw = res.getWriter();
            // 2. Gets a document.
    TXDocument doc = docman.getDocument(num);
    if (doc == null) {
        pw.print(this.docman.format1("docman.view.cantget",
          Integer.toString(num)));
        pw.close();
        return;
    }
```

```
              doc.expandEntityReferences(); // @XML4J LMX cannot work when
                                        // documents
                     // contain EntityReference nodes.
              // 3. Calls LMX.
         TXDocument outdoc = (TXDocument)this.lmxconv.convert(doc,
           false);
                  // 4. Prints the converted document.
         Visitor visitor = new HTMLPrintVisitor(pw);
         try {
            new NonRecursivePreorderTreeTraversal(visitor).
              traverse(outdoc);
         } catch (Exception e) {
            throw new ServletException("DocView: "+e);
         }
         pw.close();
      }
   }
```

LMX Rule

The LMX, doc.lmx, consists of a single rule that translates the doc element, which has three children, into an HTML page. This rule is used in the viewdoc servlet and is shown in Listing 5.6.

Listing 5.6 doc.lmx: Translates the doc element into an HTML page

```
<?xml version="1.0"?>
<lmx:rules xmlns:lmx="http://www.ibm.com/xml/lmx/">
    <lmx:pattern>
        <lmx:lhs>
            <doc>
                <title>$1;</title>
                <date>$2;</date>
                <body>$3;</body>
            </doc>
        </lmx:lhs>
        <lmx:rhs>
            <HTML>
                <HEAD><TITLE>$1;</TITLE></HEAD>
                <BODY>
                    <H1>$1;</H1>
                    <DIV>Last-Modified: <SPAN>$2;</SPAN></DIV>
                    <PRE style="padding:4px;border-style:solid;
                    border-width:1px;">$3;</PRE>
```

```
                        <HR/>
                        <DIV>[<A href="/servlet/listdoc">List all
                            documents</A>
                               | <A href="/servlet/inputdoc">Create new
                                 document</A>]
                        </DIV>
                    </BODY>
                </HTML>
            </lmx:rhs>
        </lmx:pattern>
    </lmx:rules>
```

5.5.2 `listdoc` **servlet**

The `listdoc` servlet (`DocList` class) deals with outputting the listing and searching results. Given a search criteria, it creates an HTML page that lists all of the matched documents, with the matched string highlighted. If no condition is specified, all documents are listed.

> **NOTE:** During searching, DocMan keeps documents in memory as much as possible so as to reduce the search time. Thus it is not an effective tool for managing thousands of documents. For high-performance document management, it should be combined with one or more backend database systems. We cover such systems in Chapter 6.

This servlet receives a GET request, so its parameters are included in a URL. Two parameters, `element` and `string`, are used to specify the condition, as follows.

- No condition (lists all documents)

  `/servlet/listdoc`

- Documents with *keyword* in the title

  `/servlet/listdoc?element=title&string=keyword`

- Documents with *keyword* in the body

  `/servlet/listdoc?element=body&string=keyword`

To construct these URLs, we use an HTML page, shown next. The screen shot is in Figure 5.6.

```
<HTML><BODY>
<FORM action="/servlet/listdoc" method="GET">
    <DIV>Search
        <SELECT name="element">
            <OPTION selected>title</OPTION>
            <OPTION>body</OPTION>
        </SELECT>
        for
        <INPUT type="TEXT" name="string" size="80">
    </DIV>
    <DIV>
        <INPUT type="SUBMIT" value="Search">
        <INPUT type="RESET" value="Clear">
    </DIV>
</FORM>
</BODY><HTML>
```

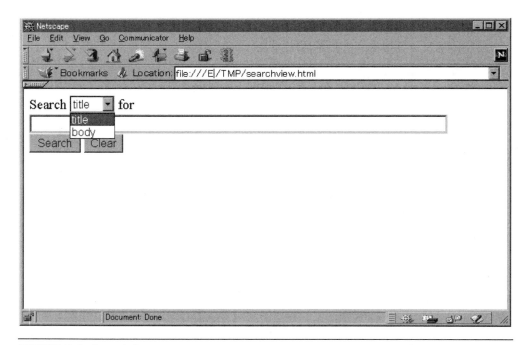

FIGURE 5.6 Search form

Depending on whether the search is on the title or the body, the results might look like either Figure 5.7 or Figure 5.8. Note that the matched string is highlighted.

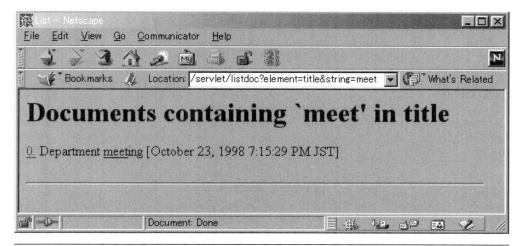

FIGURE 5.7 Result of a search on the title

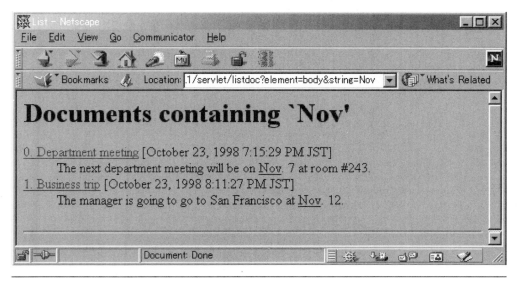

FIGURE 5.8 Result of a search on the body

Implementation

The source `DocList.java`, shown in Listing 5.7, handles the search request. It might look rather long, but its basic structure is the same as that of the previous servlets.

Listing 5.7 `DocList.java`: Handles the search request

```java
import com.ibm.xml.parser.TXDocument;
import com.ibm.xml.parser.TXElement;
import com.ibm.xml.parser.Util;
import java.io.IOException;
import java.io.PrintWriter;
import java.util.StringTokenizer;
import javax.servlet.ServletException;
import javax.servlet.http.HttpServlet;
import javax.servlet.http.HttpServletRequest;
import javax.servlet.http.HttpServletResponse;

public class DocList extends HttpServlet {
    DocManager docman = DocManager.getInstance();

    /**
     * Return an error message to the browser.
     */
    private void parameterError(HttpServletResponse res) throws
    IOException {
        res.setContentType("text/html");
        PrintWriter writer = res.getWriter();
        writer.println(this.docman.getString("docman.list.error"));
        writer.close();
    }

    /**
     * Process a GET request:
     * 1. Check and prepare the parameters.
     * 2. Print the header of HTML.
     * 3. Print the matched documents.
     * 4. Print the footer of HTML.
     */
    public void doGet(HttpServletRequest req, HttpServletResponse res)
        throws ServletException, IOException {
                // 1. Checks the parameters.
        String[] values = req.getParameterValues("element");
```

```
if (values != null && (values.length != 1 || values[0].
  length() == 0)) {
    this.parameterError(res);
    return;
}
          // searchel is null or "title" or "body".
String searchel = values == null ? null : values[0];
String searchstr = null;
values = req.getParameterValues("string");
if (searchel != null) { // searchstr is valid when searchel
                        // isn't null.
    if (values == null || values.length != 1 || values[0].
      length() == 0) {
        this.parameterError(res);
        return;
    }
    searchstr = values[0];
} else {
    if (values != null) {
        this.parameterError(res);
        return;
    }
}


res.setContentType("text/html");
PrintWriter pw = res.getWriter();

          // 2. Prints the header of HTML.
pw.print(this.docman.getString("docman.list.header"));
if (searchel == null) {
    pw.print(this.docman.getString("docman.list.headerall"));
} else if (searchel.equals("title")) {
    pw.print(this.docman.format1("docman.list.headertitle",
        Util.backReference(searchstr, "<&", null)));
} else if (searchel.equals("body")) {
    pw.print(this.docman.format1("docman.list.headerbody",
        Util.backReference(searchstr, "<&", null)));
}
pw.println("<DL>");

          // 3. Checks all documents, and prints those that
          //    match.
boolean exist = false;
for (int i = 0; i < this.docman.getNumberOfDocuments(); i ++) {
```

```
        exist = printMatched(pw, i, this.docman.getDocument(i),
                         searchel, searchstr)
        || exist;
    }


            // 4. Prints the footer of HTML.
    pw.println(" </DL>");
    if (!exist)
        pw.print(this.docman.getString("docman.list.notfound"));
    pw.print(this.docman.getString("docman.list.footer"));
    pw.close();
}


private synchronized boolean printMatched(PrintWriter pw, int i,
                                  TXDocument doc,
                                  String element,
                                  String str) {
    if (doc == null) return false; // Invalid structure.
    TXElement txel = (TXElement)doc.getDocumentElement();
    if (txel == null) return false; // Invalid structure.
    TXElement titleel = txel.getElementNamed("title");
    if (titleel == null) return false; // Invalid structure.
    TXElement dateel = txel.getElementNamed("date");
    if (dateel == null) return false; // Invalid structure.

    if (element == null) { // Simple listing.
        pw.print(" <DT>");
        pw.print("<A href=\"/servlet/viewdoc?id="+i+"\">"+i+". ");
        pw.print(Util.backReference(titleel.getText(), "&<", null));
        pw.print("</A> [");
        pw.print(dateel.getText());
        pw.println("]");
        return true;
    } else if (element.equals("title")) { // Searches the title.
        String title = titleel.getText();
        if (match(title, str, false)) {
            pw.print(" <DT>");
            pw.print("<A href=\"/servlet/viewdoc?id=
                "+i+"\">"+i+".</A> ");
            pw.print(title.substring(0, this.matchedoffset));
            pw.print("<U>");
            pw.print(str);
            pw.print("</U>");
            pw.print(title.substring(this.matchedoffset+str.
                length())));
```

```
                    pw.print(" [");
                    pw.print(dateel.getText());
                    pw.println("]");
                    return true;
            }
        } else if (element.equals("body")) { // Searches the body.
            TXElement bodyel = txel.getElementNamed("body");
            if (bodyel == null) return false; // Invalid structure.
            if (match(bodyel.getText(), str, true)) {
                pw.print(" <DT>");
                pw.print("<A href=\"/servlet/viewdoc?id="+i+"\">"+i+". ");
                pw.print(Util.backReference(titleel.getText(), "&<",
                    null));
                pw.print("</A> [");
                pw.print(dateel.getText());
                pw.println("]");
                pw.print(" <DD>");
                String content = this.matchedline.substring(0, this.
                    matchedoffset);
                pw.print(Util.backReference(content, "&<", null));
                pw.print("<U>");
                pw.print(Util.backReference(str, "&<", null));
                pw.print("</U>");
                content = this.matchedline.substring(this.
                    matchedoffset+str.length());
                pw.println(Util.backReference(content, "&<", null));
                return true;
            }
        }
    }
    return false;
}


private String matchedline;
private int matchedoffset;
private synchronized boolean match(String text, String searchfor,
                                   boolean linesep) {
    if (!linesep) {
        this.matchedoffset = text.indexOf(searchfor);
        if (this.matchedoffset >= 0) {
            this.matchedline = text;
            return true;
        }
    } else {
                    // Splits the text into lines.
        StringTokenizer st = new StringTokenizer(text, "\r\n");
```

```
        while (st.hasMoreTokens()) {
            String line = st.nextToken();
            this.matchedoffset = line.indexOf(searchfor);
            if (this.matchedoffset >= 0) {
                this.matchedline = line;
                return true;
            }
        }
    }
    return false;
}
}
```

doGet()

The main entry point of this servlet is the doGet() method. After checking the parameters, this method calls printMatched() for all of the documents.

printMatched()

The printMatched() method receives one DOM tree, and prints it if it matches the given conditions. Its main purpose is to generate HTML; the string matching is done by the match() method described next. The different conditions produce the following different results, but in all cases, an HTML line is produced.

- When making a list of all documents, printMatched() generates the HTML line

    ```
    <DT><A href=". . .">n. title</A> [date].
    ```

- When showing search results with a keyword in the title, printMatched() generates the HTML line

    ```
    <DT><A href=". . .">n</A>. title[date].
    ```

    In addition, the matched keyword is underlined.

- When showing search results with a keyword in the body text, printMatched() generates the HTML line

    ```
    <DT><A href=". . .">n. title</A> [date].
    ```

    In addition, the line containing the matched keyword is shown in a <DD> tag, as in <DD>matched line. Also, the matched keyword is underlined.

`match()`

The `match()` method does the actual string matching. As you might deduce from the description of `printMatched()`, this method should return the following information.

- When searching a keyword in the title, if there is a match
  Return: the position of the match

- When searching a keyword in the body text, if there is a match
  Return: the line containing the match and
  the position of the match in the line

Because Java has no pointers, it is not easy to return multiple values from a method call. An orthodox way is to use a class that combines return values. Here, however, we use member variables to hold some of the return values. When using this technique, we must ensure that this does not cause a race condition. This is why we declare `printMatched()` as *synchronized*—so that no two threads can execute `printMatched()` simultaneously.

String matching is done by Java's built-in matching library, `String#indexOf(String)`.

> **NOTE:** In `DocList.java`, we generated an HTML document on the fly using `println()` because the generated HTML page is relatively simple. However, it is not generally advisable to generate HTML pages with `println()`. See our discussion in Section 3.2.

5.6 Creating Metacontent

Metacontent, also called *metainformation,* is information about other information. Metacontent of a Web page can consist of the following items:

- Author(s) name(s)
- Title
- Keywords
- Creation date
- Last update date
- URL

- Document size in bytes

- Revision history

The `listdoc` servlet deals with exactly this type of information: metacontent.

Metacontent is useful for managing and searching documents. In many cases, managing and searching can be done on metacontents only, with no need to access the contents (documents) themselves.

XML received attention first as a metacontent format for push applications in 1997. **Push** is a marketing concept whereby information is delivered automatically to the receiver without the receiver's having to initiate the delivery. By contrast, **pull** means the receiver triggers the receipt of information. These concepts apply to the Web as well. A **push application** automatically delivers information to browsers, and hence to users. A **pull application** is the browser pulling information from Web servers, in the sense that the operations are always triggered by end users.

Push can be simulated by automatically pulling pages at predetermined intervals, as is done with subscriptions to Web pages. However, a user who subscribes to hundreds of pages might be unable to read all of them. Sending many pages that are not read is a waste of bandwidth and server resources (considering that establishing a TCP/IP connection for each HTTP request is an expensive operation). Some of the **push technologies**, technologies that push information to browsers, address this problem by delivering metacontent only. A metacontent file that is downloaded with a single HTTP connection might contain the titles, keywords, abstracts, and so on of the pages on the server. The user can browse the list of titles and abstracts and, if interested in a particular one, can get the content itself by issuing a normal HTTP request. The metacontent is refreshed by pulling it periodically, so the user sees the latest information on the screen (as far as the title and abstract are concerned). In this way, the total transfer size as well as the number of connections are minimized.

5.6.1 Channel Definition Format

One of the most popular push technologies is *Active Channel,* which is built into Microsoft Internet Explorer 4.0 (MSIE4). This technology uses a metacontent format called **Channel Definition Format** (CDF). MSIE4 has the ability to periodically obtain CDF files from Web servers and display them on the user's screen.

CDF is defined as XML. Therefore you can use any XML tools to generate a CDF file. As long as it is a valid CDF file, it will be recognized and displayed by

MSIE4. The specification of CDF can be accessed at `http://www.w3.org/TR/NOTE-CDFsubmit.html`.

This specification was authored before the XML 1.0 Recommendation was finalized in February 1998, so some of it does not exactly conform to the XML standard. For example, unlike XML the CDF specification says that element names and attribute names are case insensitive.

Following is a sample CDF file.

```
<?xml version="1.0"?>
<CHANNEL>
    <TITLE>IBM page</TITLE>
    <ITEM href="http://www.ibm.com/xml/">
        <TITLE>IBM XML Web Site, Home Page</TITLE>
        <AUTHOR>IBM</AUTHOR>
    </ITEM>
</CHANNEL>
```

5.6.2 Resource Description Framework

Another metacontent format is **Resource Description Framework** (RDF), a general framework for representing metacontents. RDF specifications are being worked on in two W3C working groups:

- RDF Model and Syntax Working Group
- RDF Schema Working Group

Unlike CDF, RDF has no domain-specific tags, such as `<AUTHOR>` and `<TITLE>`. Instead, it defines a framework for representing a sophisticated data structure that is suited for metacontents.

RDF Model and Syntax specification was Recommendation and RDF Schema specification was Working Draft at the time of this writing (February 1998). Following is an example of an RDF document.

```
<?xml version="1.0"?>
<rdf:RDF>
        xmlns:rdf="http://www.w3.org/TR/WD-rdf-syntax#"
        xmlns:dc="http://purl.org/metadata/dublin_core#">
    <rdf:Description about="http://www.ibm.com/xml/">
        <dc:Author>IBM Corporation</dc:Author>
    </rdf:Description>
</rdf:RDF>
```

For more details on RDF, refer to the Web site `http://www.w3.org/RDF/`.

5.6.3 A Redesign of the DocMan Listing Using CDF

In our DocMan example, we used HTML to show the metacontent. Here, we redesign that part by using CDF. We write a servlet, `MakeCDF.java`, which generates a CDF document from our document database. Once a CDF is generated, it can be downloaded into MSIE4 and displayed. Our example is shown in Figure 5.9 as `all.cdf`.

Implementation

The body of this servlet is class `MakeCDF`, shown in Listing 5.8.

The basic structure is very similar to that of `DocList`. However, instead of generating an HTML page, this servlet creates a DOM tree and then generates it as a CDF file.

Listing 5.8 `MakeCDF.java`: Creates a DOM tree, generating it as a CDF file

```
import com.ibm.xml.parser.TXDocument;
import com.ibm.xml.parser.TXElement;
import java.io.IOException;
import java.io.PrintWriter;
import javax.servlet.ServletException;
import javax.servlet.http.HttpServlet;
```

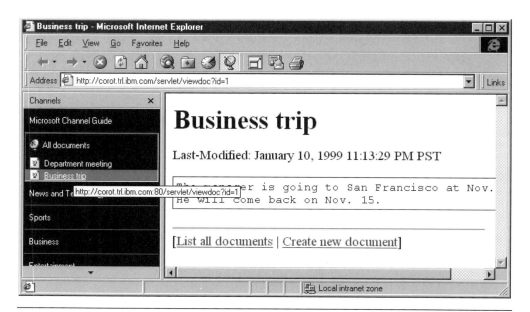

FIGURE 5.9 MSIE4 showing `all.cdf`

```java
import javax.servlet.http.HttpServletRequest;
import javax.servlet.http.HttpServletResponse;
import org.w3c.dom.Document;
import org.w3c.dom.Element;

public class MakeCDF extends HttpServlet {
    static final String S_CHANNEL = "CHANNEL";
    static final String S_ITEM = "ITEM";
    static final String S_TITLE = "TITLE";
    static final String S_HREF = "href";

    DocManager docman = DocManager.getInstance();
    String servername;

    /**
     * Handle the HTTP GET request.
     * Builds a CDF DOM tree from the contents of DocManager.
     */
    public void doGet(HttpServletRequest req, HttpServletResponse res)
        throws ServletException, IOException {

                // Creates the name of this server.
        StringBuffer sb = new StringBuffer();
        sb.append(req.getScheme());
        sb.append("://");
        sb.append(req.getServerName());
        if (req.getServerPort() > 0)
            sb.append(":"+req.getServerPort());
        this.servername = sb.toString(); // "http://foo.bar.com:8888"

                // Content-Type should be application/x-cdf.
        res.setContentType("application/x-cdf");
        PrintWriter pw = res.getWriter();

                // Creates CDF document.
        Document doc = new TXDocument();// @XML4J
                // The root element is <CHANNEL>
        Element channel = doc.createElement(S_CHANNEL);
        doc.appendChild(channel);
        Element title = doc.createElement(S_TITLE);
        channel.appendChild(title);
        title.appendChild(doc.createTextNode(docman.getString
          ("docman.cdf.title")));
                // <CHANNEL>
                //   <TITLE>....</TITLE>
```

```
                    //  :
                    //  :
                    // </CHANNEL>

                    // Creates ITEM elements for all documents.
        for (int i = 0; i < this.docman.getNumberOfDocuments(); i ++) {
            Element item = createItem(doc, i);
            if (item != null)
                channel.appendChild(item);
        }
                    // Prints the CDF document to the stream.
        ((TXDocument)doc).printWithFormat(pw);// @XML4J
        pw.close();
    }


    /**
      * Build an ITEM element from a document.
      */
    private Element createItem(Document doc, int i) {
                    // Gets information of the specified document
                    // while checking structure of the document.
        Document d = this.docman.getDocument(i);
        if (d == null) return null;
        Element el = d.getDocumentElement();
        if (el == null) return null;
        el = ((TXElement)el).getElementNamed("title");
        if (el == null) return null;
        String title = ((TXElement)el).getText();
        String uri = this.servername+"/servlet/viewdoc?id="+i;

        // <ITEM href="uri">
        // <TITLE>title</TITLE>
        // </ITEM>
        Element item = doc.createElement(S_ITEM);
        item.setAttribute(S_HREF, uri);
        el = doc.createElement(S_TITLE);
        el.appendChild(doc.createTextNode(title));
        item.appendChild(el);

        return item;
    }
}
```

doGet()

doGet() first creates the top element of a CDF, as follows.

```
<CHANNEL>
    <TITLE>content of docman.cdf.title</TITLE>
</CHANNEL>
```

After that, for each document in DocManager, createItem() is called to add each entry as ITEM elements to this root element. Finally, the content type is set to application/x-cdf and the generated CDF file is written to the result stream.[2]

createItem()

Given a document tree, this method creates the following structure and returns it.

```
<ITEM href="url">
    <TITLE>title</TITLE>
</ITEM>
```

5.7 Summary

In this chapter, we designed and implemented a simple document management system, DocMan, as a Web application. Java servlets play the central role in such a web application. We also looked at techniques for using and searching metacontent.

---

[2]MSIE4 does not recognize the content type, so the URL of this servlet should end with .cdf.

CHAPTER 6

Interfacing Databases and XML

6.1 Introduction

In Chapter 5, we discussed the basics of servlets and how to use XML to represent metacontent of structured documents. In this chapter, we focus on how to represent structured data using XML.

The three-tier model of application development discussed in Chapter 1 consists of Web browsers as tier 1, HTTP servers as tier 2, and database systems or transaction systems as tier 3. Relational database management systems (RDBMSs) are the most common type of backend system in three-tier systems (see Figure 6.1)

How can Java and XML contribute to the database world in terms of Web applications? Java has a common API for accessing database systems called

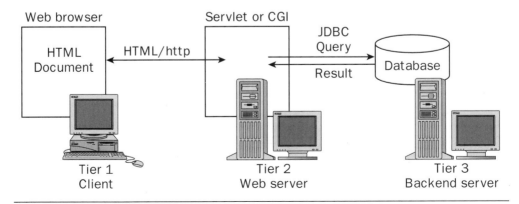

FIGURE 6.1 Current Web application architecture for accessing databases

Java Database Connectivity (JDBC). JDBC is a part of the standard JDK 1.1. Database vendors supply JDBC drivers that implement this API for accessing their own implementations of a database. Thus JDBC provides Java programmers with a high-level interface and relieves them from dealing with low-level details of database access. Section 6.2 presents the basics of JDBC, when we describe a small program for accessing a database and printing the result.

RDBMSs are very efficient in dealing with large amounts of data as well as providing the essential characteristics of mission-critical applications such as robustness, integrity, consistency, and availability. However, when it comes to transmitting data between different RDBMSs, no established standard exists for a common data exchange format. Here is where XML comes in. XML is not particularly efficient compared to other compact binary formats, but it is easy and well understood. Whenever interoperability is more important than anything else, there is nothing like XML. It is widely supported by vendors as a standard data format. However, to connect a database system to XML-based application programs, you need some kind of "bridge" between the two. Section 6.3 gives you a complete subsystem, called *SQLX*, that does exactly this for you.

Figure 6.2 shows the architecture of a possible XML-enabled Web application that accesses a backend database system via JDBC. It would handle queries like this.

1. A query expressed in XML comes in as an HTTP request, is analyzed, and is converted to a JDBC query.

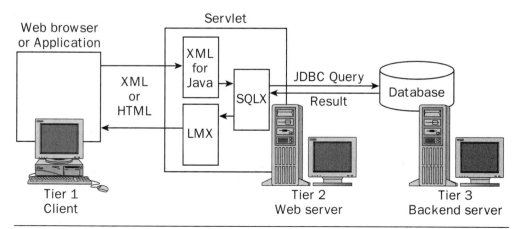

FIGURE 6.2 XML-enabled Web application architecture for accessing databases

2. The database is consulted.

3. The result is converted to a presentation-neutral XML document and then converted into either HTML or another XML form and sent back to the client.

This chapter shows techniques to realize this architecture.

6.2 JDBC Primer

JDBC is a standard SQL (Standard Query Language) database access API. It provides programmers with a uniform interface to various databases regardless of differences in implementation. JDBC, as a part of JDK 1.1, is in the `java.sql` package. As mentioned in Section 6.1, database vendors ship JDBC drivers that enable access to their databases from Java programs. For example, DB2, IBM's RDBMs, provides a JDBC driver class, `COM.ibm.db2.jdbc.app.DB2Driver`, that translates JDBC calls into native DB2 calls as well as converts the DB2 results into JDBC data structure. The class `"COM.ibm.db2.jdbc.net.DB2Driver"` is used for remote access of the database. Thus application programs that use JDBC can run with different RDBMSs without modification. JavaSoft maintains a list of more than 40 JDBC drivers supplied by database vendors at its Web page, `http://www.javasoft.com/products/jdbc/jdbc.drivers.html`.

In this chapter, we use DB2 Universal Database (UDB), which we call DB2 in this section, as the RDBMS implementation, but the example programs included on the CD-ROM should run with any other implementation as well, provided it includes a JDBC driver. The CD-ROM that accompanies this book contains a trial version of DB2 you can use. Or you can download a trial version from the Web at `http://www.software.ibm.com/data/`. See the documentation on-line for details about using it.

In the database we use in this section, there is an instance `sample` that contains a table named `employee`, which has the schema shown in Table 6.1.

Entries such as CHARACTER and DATE are the SQL data type of data given in a column. For example, `CHARACTER(6)` represents the data type of a 6-letter character string, while `VARCHAR(12)` represents the data type of a character string that is at most 12 characters long.

TABLE 6.1 Schema of Employee Table

COLUMN NAME	DATA TYPE
EMPNO	CHARACTER(6)
FIRSTNAME	VARCHAR(12)
LASTNAME	VARCHAR(15)
PHONENO	CHARACTER(4)
JOB	CHARACTER(8)
SEX	CHARACTER(1)
BIRTHDATE	DATE
SALARY	DECIMAL
BONUS	DECIMAL

We use the data in Table 6.1 as shown in Table 6.2, which is based on the schema in Table 6.1.

TABLE 6.2 Employee Table

EMPNO	FIRSTNAME	LASTNAME	PHONE NO	JOB	SEX	BIRTHDATE	SALARY	BONUS
000010	SHILI	HAAS	3978	PRES	F	1933-08-24	52750.00	1000.00
000020	MICHAEL	THOMPSON	3476	MANAGER	M	1948-02-02	41250.00	800.00
000030	SALLY	KWAN	4738	MANAGER	F	1941-05-11	38250.00	800.00
000050	JOHN	GEYER	6789	MANAGER	M	1925-09-15	40175.00	800.00
000060	IRVING	STERN	6423	MANAGER	M	1945-07-07	32250.00	500.00
000070	EVA	PULASKI	7831	MANAGER	F	1953-05-26	36170.00	700.00
000090	EILEEN	HENDERSON	5498	MANAGER	F	1941-05-15	29750.00	600.00
000100	THEODORE	SPENSER	0972	MANAGER	M	1956-12-18	26150.00	500.00
000110	VINCENZO	LUCCHESSI	3490	SALESREP	M	1929-11-05	46500.00	900.00
000120	SEAN	O'CONNELL	2167	CLERK	M	1942-10-18	29250.00	600.00

6.2.1 Importing the JDBC Package

Next, we write a simple program that accesses the employee table in Table 6.2 using JDBC. First, we need to import the JDBC package, as follows.

```
import java.sql.*;
```

This package defines the classes listed in Table 6.3 and the interfaces in Table 6.4.

TABLE 6.3 Classes Defined in the JDBC

CLASS NAME	DESCRIPTION
DriverManager	A class that provides basic services for managing multiple JDBC drivers, such as loading drivers and logging on.
Types	A class that defines SQL data types such as INTEGER and VARCHAR.
Date	A subclass of java.util.Date and a thin wrapper of the SQL DATE data type.
Time	A subclass of java.util.Date and a thin wrapper of the SQL TIME data type.
Timestamp	A subclass of java.util.Date and a thin wrapper of the SQL TIMESTAMP data type.
DriverPropertyInfo	A class for accessing properties of loading drivers. Only for advanced programmers.

TABLE 6.4 Interfaces Defined in the JDBC

INTERFACE NAME	DESCRIPTION
Driver	The main body of a JDBC driver. A driver must implement this interface.
Connection	An interface that represents a session with a specific database. Created by calling the Driver#connection() method.
Statement	An interface used to execute an SQL statement.
PreparedStatement	A subinterface of Statement that represents a compiled query for efficiently executing the same query multiple times.
ResultSet	An interface that provides access to a table of data generated by executing an SQL query using a Statement object.
ResultSetMetaData	An interface that is used to access the properties of query results, such as data types and column names.
CallableStatement	An interface used for executing a stored procedure of SQL.
DatabaseMetaData	An interface used for accessing properties of a database as a whole.

6.2.2 Loading a JDBC Driver

The second step in writing our simple program is to load a JDBC driver. We do this by telling DriverManager to do so. There are several ways to achieve this, but the simplest is to use the Class.forName() method as follows:

```
Class.forName("COM.ibm.db2.jdbc.app.DB2Driver");
```

In this case, we used the JDBC driver for DB2 (http://www.software.ibm.com/data/db2/java/). The class name must be replaced according to the JDBC driver that is being used.

NOTE: Note that the static method `forName()` defined in the class `Class` generates a class object of the specified class. How is the JDBC driver registered to the `DriverManager` by simply creating a class object? Any JDBC driver must have a static initialization part that is executed when the class is loaded, as shown next. As soon as the class loader loads this class, the static initialization is executed—this automatically registers it as a JDBC driver to the `DriverManager`.

```
public class DB2Driver {
    public DB2Driver() {
    ...
    }
    static {
        try {
            DriverManager.registerDriver(new DB2Driver());
            return;
        } catch(SQLException sqlexception)
    }
}
```

Some drivers do not automatically create an instance when the class is loaded. If `forName()` alone does not create a driver instance for you, you might need to explicitly create an instance as follows:

```
Class.forName("COM.ibm.db2.jdbc.app.DB2Driver").newInstance();
```

6.2.3 Connecting to a Database

With the driver in place, we next need to specify the data source we want to access. In JDBC, a data source is specified by a URL with the protocol prefix `jdbc:`. The syntax of the URL is as follows:

```
jdbc:<subprotocol>:<subname>
```

`subprotocol` represents the type of the data source, normally the name of the database system, such as `db2` or `oracle`. `subname` specifies information for the database. The content and syntax of `subname` depend on `subprotocol`. For example, to access a table named `sample` stored in a local DB2, we would create a URL as follows:

```
String url = "jdbc:db2:sample";
```

If the database is on a remote machine, the URL would look like this:

```
String url = "jdbc:db2:monet.trl.ibm.com/sample";
```

> **NOTE:** If you want to use Open Database Connectivity (ODBC), a standard API for accessing a database, to connect Java applications to Microsoft Access or Excel, you can use the JDBC-ODBC bridge. However, describing the details of doing that exceeds the scope of this book. See Appendix C for some resources.

We connect the database using this URL by calling the `getConnection()` method:

```
Connection con = DriverManager.getConnection(url);
```

Often, databases are protected by user ids and passwords for proper access control. With JDBC, you specify your user id and password when connecting to a database, as follows.

```
String uid = "user";
String passwd = "password";
Connection con = DriverManager.getConnection(url, uid, passwd);
```

6.2.4 Submitting a Query

Once a connection is established, we can submit queries to the database. However, we first need to create a `Statement` object by calling the `createStatement()` method of `Connection` object:

```
Statement stmt = con.createStatement();
```

Now we are ready to submit an SQL query to obtain all information from the `employee` table.

> **NOTE:** We call the `executeQuery()` method with an SQL statement as its only argument. The results will be set to a `ResultSet` object.

```
String SQLQuery = "select * from employee"
// Get result of the query
ResultSet rs = stmt.executeQuery(SQLquery);
```

The class `ResultSet` defines a number of methods for accessing the result. The result set is basically a sequence of rows, over which we can iterate using the `next()` method. The result of a query maintains a `cursor` to remember the current row in the result set. Repetitive calls to `next()` advance this cursor to the next row until the end of data, where `next()` returns `null`. Within the cursor row, we can access the value of each column by specifying either the index number of the column or the name of the column. The get*XX* method, where *XX* represents data types such as `Int` and `String`, can be used to access each column.[1] The following code fragment shows how to retrieve the first and second columns of the result set.

```
while (rs.next()) {
    String firstColumn = rs.getString(1);
    String secondColumn = rs.getString(2);

    System.out.print("1st="+firstColumn);
    System.out.print("2nd="+secondColumn);
    System.out.print("\n");
}
```

JDBCSample.java

`IDBCSample.java`, given in Listing 6.1, accesses a database and prints the first and second columns of every row.

Listing 6.1 `JDBCSample.java`: Accesses a database using JDBC

```
import java.sql.*;

class JDBCSample {
    static {
        try {
            // Registers the driver with DriverManager.
            Class.forName("COM.ibm.db2.jdbc.app.DB2Driver");
        } catch (Exception e) {
            e.printStackTrace();
        }
    }

    public static void main(String args[]) {
        try {

            // The URL is jdbc:db2:dbname.
            String url = "jdbc:db2:sample";

            // Connects using the default userid and password.
            Connection con = DriverManager.getConnection(url);
```

---

[1]Java uses naming convention such as "Int" (first letter is capitalized), while usually all capitalized in SQL data types.

```
            Statement stmt = con.createStatement();

            // A SQL query is given as an argument of this program
            String SQLquery = "select * from employee";

            // Get result of the query
            ResultSet rs = stmt.executeQuery(SQLquery);

            // Display Result
            while (rs.next()) {
                String firstColumn = rs.getString(1);
                String secondColumn = rs.getString(2);

                System.out.print(firstColumn);
                System.out.print(" " + secondColumn);
                System.out.print("\n");
            }
            rs.close();
            stmt.close();

        } catch( Exception e ) {
            e.printStackTrace();
        }
    }
}
```

Executing this program generates the following output.

```
R:\samples\chap6>java JDBCSample
000010 SHILI
000020 MICHAEL
000030 SALLY
000050 JOHN
000060 IRVING
000070 EVA
000090 EILEEN
000100 THEODORE
000110 VINCENZO
000120 SEAN
```

6.3 SQL Embedded in XML: SQLX

In this section, we develop a program called *SQLX* that bridges the worlds of XML and RDBMSs.

Recall the input and output of the executeQuery() method in Listing 6.1. An SQL query was passed to this method as a string parameter, while the result of the database retrieval was returned in a ResultSet object. In addition, you had to supply the name of database, the driver to be used, and optionally the user id and password to authenticate yourself. It might be natural to represent these input and output as XML documents. You might construct a query XML document that contains a database name, an SQL query, and so on, and send it to an XML-enabled database system. The result would also be expressed as an XML document, which can be processed or rendered by other XML-enabled application programs. This idea leads to a flexible architecture in which queries are dynamically produced by manipulating a DOM structure and the retrieval results are embedded in a larger DOM structure and combined with other data expressed as XML.

6.3.1 What Is SQLX

SQLX, meaning "SQL embedded in XML," is a front end of a relational database that provides XML-based input and output. It receives a query description in XML and translates it into a sequence of JDBC calls. Then the query result is converted to a DOM structure and returned. As an XML-JDBC bridge example, we show in this section the details of SQLX step-by-step. At the end of this section, we will have a complete implementation of SQLX.

To describe the external functionality of SQLX, we begin with the following XML document, sample.xml. This document contains both an SQL query to be submitted to the database and the necessary settings for making a connection to the database using JDBC.

```
<?xml version="1.0"?>
<sqlx>
    <inputSpec>
        <param name=":salary" default="40000"/>
    </inputSpec>
    <execute url="jdbc:db2://monet.trl.ibm.com/sample"
            driver="COM.ibm.db2.jdbc.net.DB2Driver"
            user="userid"
```

```
                  password="secret"
                  sql="select lastname,salary from employee where salary >=
                  :salary order by salary"/>
      </sqlx>
```

This document, marked up with the **sqlx** tag, consists of the following sub-elements:

- `inputSpec`. defines runtime variables and their default values used in the query.

- `execute`. gives the parameters of the query and the query string itself.

The `sql` attribute contains the SQL statement, which may contain embedded variables. These variables will be replaced with specific values if they are specified in the command line argument before the query statement is submitted to JDBC. This document retrieves high-salaried employees from the employee database in Table 6.2, with the salary threshold determined by the variable `:salary`. We call this type of document a *query document.*

The query result is also represented as an XML document. The following example, `result.xml`, shows the query result that is obtained by applying the query document `sample.xml` to the employee database shown in Table 6.2. As you can see, last names and salaries for all of the employees were extracted.

```
<?xml version="1.0"?>
<!DOCTYPE results [
<!ELEMENT results (row)>
<!ELEMENT row (LASTNAME,SALARY)>
<!ELEMENT LASTNAME EMPTY>
<!ATTLIST LASTNAME value CDATA #IMPLIED
                type CDATA #FIXED "12">
<!ELEMENT SALARY EMPTY>
<!ATTLIST SALARY value CDATA #IMPLIED
          type CDATA #FIXED "3">
]>
<results>
    <row>
        <LASTNAME value="HASS    "/>
        <SALARY value="52750.00"/>
    </row>
    <row>
        <LASTNAME value="THOMPSON "/>
        <SALARY value="41250.00"/>
    </row>
    <row>
```

```
        <LASTNAME value="GEYER    "/>
        <SALARY value="40175.00"/>
    </row>
    <row>
        <LASTNAME value="LUCCHESSI "/>
        <SALARY value="46500.00"/>
    </row>
  </results>
```

The result is represented by the `results` element that contains multiple `row` elements, each of which corresponds to a record.

Note that each column of a database table is data-typed. However, XML 1.0 has no notion of data type. Yet, data types are sometimes very important in database applications. In SQLX, they are encoded in the `type` attribute of each value. However, adding a `type` attribute to every column value is space-consuming, as well as redundant (notice that all of the values of the `value` attribute in the `SALARY` elements are integers), so this information is represented as a fixed attribute of these elements. This is why we need a DTD embedded in this XML document. In the previous example, each data type is represented as an integer (such as 3 and 12) whose value is defined in the JDBC `Types` class. We call this result document an *SQL document.*

6.3.2 Implementing SQLX

Next, we implement SQLX. SQLX will consist of the seven classes listed in Table 6.5.

Figures 6.3 and 6.4 show the relationships between the SQLX classes and the elements in both the query and SQL documents.

TABLE 6.5 The Seven Classes of SQLX

CLASS NAME	DESCRIPTION
SQLX	The main program.
SQLXParser	Parses query documents.
SQLXDocument	An SQL document (an XML document that contains the retrieval result and its DTD.)
InputSpecElement	A query condition when a query is being executed.
InputSpecElements	A collection of InputSpecElements.
ExecuteElement	A parameter that is passed to an SQL query or to a database.
SQLXResults	The query results.

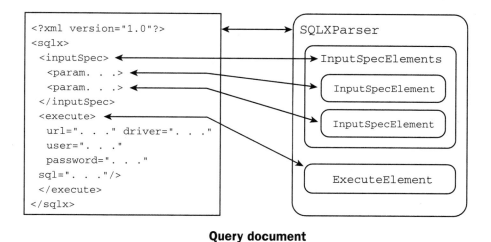

Query document

FIGURE 6.3 Relationships between elements in the query document and the classes

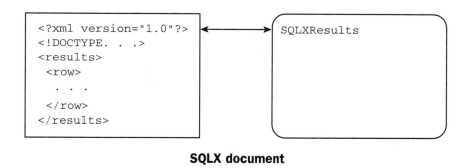

SQLX document

FIGURE 6.4 Relationships between the elements in the SQLX document and the classes

The main program is provided to run SQLX from the command line. The command line syntax is as follows:

```
SQLX input-filename {variable1=value1} ... {variablen=valuen}
```

The `input-filename` argument is the filename of a query document. The rest of the line is zero or more variable-value parameter pairs used to dynamically substitute values into the SQL statement. For example, the command

```
R:\samples\chap6>java SQLX sample.xml :salary=30000
```

uses the SQL XML file named `sample.xml`, substituting the variable `:salary` with the value `30000`.

Recall that in `sample.xml`, the variable is embedded in the SQL query:

```
"select lastname,salary from employee where salary >= :salary order
by salary"
```

The variable is replaced before it is submitted, by using the input parameter:

```
"select lastname,salary from employee where salary >= 30000 order by
salary"
```

If there is no variable in the command line, the default value defined in the query document (`40000`, in this case) is used.

In the following subsections, we discuss the SQLX classes, beginning with the main program, `SQLX.java`, which is shown in Listing 6.2.

Class `SQLX`

Listing 6.2 `SQLX.java`: SQLX main program

```java
import com.ibm.xml.parser.FormatPrintVisitor;
import com.ibm.xml.parser.NonRecursivePreorderTreeTraversal;
import com.ibm.xml.parser.Visitor;
import java.io.DataOutputStream;
import java.io.File;
import java.io.FileOutputStream;
import java.io.OutputStream;
import java.io.PrintWriter;

/**
 * This is a sample program that shows how to parse a SQLX file,
   execute the SQL statement,
 * and display the results
 */
public class SQLX {
    public static void main(String argv[]) {
        // Initializes the filename.
        String xmlin = null;
        // If parameters are passed in
        if (argv.length > 0)
            // Uses the 1st parameter as the filename.
            xmlin = argv[0];

        // If no filename, shows instructions.
        if (xmlin == null) {
            System.out.println("SQLX {input filename}
            {variable1=value1} ... {variablenn=valuenn}");
```

```
                System.out.println(" where {input filename}
                  is the filename of a SQL XML file [required]");
                System.out.println(" where {variablenn=valuenn} is a
                  variable=value param pair used to dynamically
                  substitute values into the SQL statement [optional]");
                System.out.println("\nExample: SQLX sample.xml
                  :salary=40000");
                System.out.println(" would use the SQL XML file
                  named 'sample.xml', substituting the variable
                  named ':salary' with a value of '40000'");
                System.out.println("\nSQLX resultset is written to:
                  {input filename}.out");
                return;
            }

[33]        try {
                // parses the SQLX file.
                SQLXParser parser = new SQLXParser(xmlin);

                // Overrides "inputSpec" param attribute's default value.
                parser.getInputSpecElements().override(argv);

                // Execute the SQL statement.
                SQLXResults results = new SQLXResults(parser);

                // Prints the results to System.out.
[44]            Visitor visitor = new FormatPrintVisitor(new
                  PrintWriter(System.out));
                NonRecursivePreorderTreeTraversal tree = new
                  NonRecursivePreorderTreeTraversal(visitor);
                tree.traverse(results.getDoc());

                // Save the results to {input filename}.out.
[49]            visitor = new FormatPrintVisitor(new
                  PrintWriter(openFile(xmlin+".out")));
                    tree = new NonRecursivePreorderTreeTraversal(visitor);
                    tree.traverse(results.getDoc());
            }
            // Displays any error messages.
            catch(Exception exc) {
                System.out.println(exc.toString());
            }
        }
```

```
/**
 * This is the method used to open a file output stream.
 */
public static OutputStream openFile(String filename) throws java.
  io.IOException {
    File file = new File(filename);
    FileOutputStream fos = new FileOutputStream(file);
    return new DataOutputStream(fos);
}
}
```

After checking the input arguments, the program is into its center, which is enclosed in the `try` clause (line [33]). From there, the program creates an instance of `SQLParser`. The parser immediately parses the input file specified in the argument `xmlin`. An `InputSpecElements` object and an `ExecuteElement` object are created.

```
SQLXParser parser = new SQLXParser(xmlin);
```

Next, the variables in the query document are substituted. The `getInputSpecElements` method returns the `InputSpecElements` object, which receives the `override()` method to substitute the variables in it. This method is explained in detail later in the chapter.

```
parser.getInputSpecElements().override(argv);
```

All of the parameters that need to be passed to JDBC are already in the query document, so we execute the query and obtain the results. Creating a `results` object with the parsed query document as an argument means the SQL query is executed through the JDBC interface and the query results are converted into a DOM tree and represented and held in the `results` object.

```
SQLXResults results = new SQLXResults(parser);
```

The `SQLX` class, which is a command line program, outputs the results to the standard output. We use the `FormatPrintVisitor` class that is a part of XML for Java. Since it is a visitor, we create a traversal object (`NonRecursivePreorderTreeTraversal` class in this case) and let this object take care of the traversal strategy.

```
[44] Visitor visitor = new FormatPrintVisitor(new
     PrintWriter(System.out));
     NonRecursivePreorderTreeTraversal tree = new
     NonRecursivePreorderTreeTraversal(visitor);
     tree.traverse(results.getDoc());
```

The same results are also written to a `"filename.out"` (filename is the name of the input file) file using the same technique.

```
[49] visitor = new FormatPrintVisitor(new
     PrintWriter(openFile(xmlin+".out")));
     tree = new NonRecursivePreorderTreeTraversal(visitor);
     tree.traverse(results.getDoc());
```

Class `SQLXParser`

The `SQLXParser` class, shown in Listing 6.3, analyzes a query document using XML for Java. As the class definition shows, this class has two instance variables that are used to hold an `InputSpecElements` object and an `ExecuteElement` object. These are used to analyze the structure of the corresponding elements (that is, `inputSpec` elements and `execute` elements in query document).

Listing 6.3 `SQLXParser.java`: Analyzes a query document

```
import com.ibm.xml.parser.Parser;
import java.io.FileInputStream;
import java.io.InputStream;
import org.w3c.dom.Document;
import org.w3c.dom.Element;
import org.w3c.dom.Node;
import org.w3c.dom.NodeList;

/**
 * This class is used for parsing the SQLX XML file.
 */
public class SQLXParser {
    // Instance of inputSpecElements.
    private InputSpecElements inputSpecElements
                                  = new InputSpecElements();
    // Instance of execute.
    private ExecuteElement    executeElement
                                  = new ExecuteElement();

    /**
     * Constructor method used to create an instance of this class.
     */
    public SQLXParser(String filename) throws java.io.IOException {
        // Opens the input stream for the named file.
        InputStream is = new FileInputStream(filename);
        // Parses the file.
```

```
              Document doc = new Parser(filename).readStream(is);
                  // Closes the input stream.
                  is.close();

                  // Gets the root most element of the document.
[30]              Element root = (Element)doc.getDocumentElement();
                  // Creates an iterator of the child nodes.
[32]              NodeList nl = root.getChildNodes();
                  // Loops through the child nodes.
[34]              for(int i = 0; i < nl.getLength(); i++) {
                      Node ch = nl.item(i);
[36]                  if (ch instanceof Element) {
                          Element el = (Element)ch;
                          if (el.getNodeName().equals(InputSpecElement.
                            INPUTSPEC))
                              // Processes the "inputSpec" elements.
                              getInputSpecElements().process(el);
                          else
                              if (el.getNodeName().equals(ExecuteElement.
                                EXECUTE))
                                  // Processes the "execute" elements.
                                  getExecuteElement().process(el);
                      }
                  }
          }

          /**
           * Method to get the instances of inputSpec.
           */
          public InputSpecElements getInputSpecElements() {
              return inputSpecElements;
          }

          /**
           * Method to set the instances of inputSpec.
           */
          public void setInputSpecElements(InputSpecElements param) {
              inputSpecElements = param;
          }

          /**
           * Method to get the instance of execute.
           */
          public ExecuteElement getExecuteElement() {
              return executeElement;
          }
```

```
    /**
     * Method to set the instance of execute.
     */
    public void setExecuteElement(ExecuteElement param) {
        executeElement = param;
    }
}
```

After the parsing of the query document is done and the DOM tree is set to the variable `doc`, the root element and the list of its children are set to the variables `root` and `nl`, respectively.

```
[30] Element root = doc.getDocumentElement();    // Gets the root element of
                                                 // the document.

[32] NodeList nl = root.getChildNodes();         // Creates an iterator of
                                                 // the child nodes.
```

Then, each child is visited using one of the standard techniques described in Chapter 4.

```
[34] for(int i=0; i<:nl.getLength(); i++) {
         Node ch = nl.item(i);
         ...
     }
```

Depending on the element name of the child (either `inputSpec` or `execute`), the corresponding object is called with the `process()` method.

```
[36] if (ch instanceof Element) {
         Element el = (Element)ch;
         if (el.getNodeName().equals(InputSpecElement.INPUTSPEC))
         // Processes the "inputSpec" elements.
            getInputSpecElements().process(el);
         else if (el.getName().equals(ExecuteElement.EXECUTE))
         // Process the "execute" elements.
            getExecuteElement().process(el);
     }
```

Class `InputSpecElement`

An `InputSpecElement` object represents a variable-value variable pair. An object may have a default value, so it has three member variables—`name`, `value`, and `defaultvalue`—that are accessed through the `getXX()` methods and `putXX()` methods (XX is `name`, `value`, or `defaultvalue`). The listing for the class is given in Listing 6.4.

Listing 6.4 `InputSpecElement.java`: Holds a variable-value pair

```java
import org.w3c.dom.Element;

/**
 * This class is an instance of an "inputSpec" param.
 */
public class InputSpecElement {
    // The name of inputSpec param (default: null).
    private String         name              = null;
    // The value for inputSpec param provided at SQLX exection;
    // if specified, overrides defaultValue (optional) (default:
    // null).
    private String         value             = null;
    // The default value for inputSpec param provided at SQLX
    // exection (optional) (default: null).
    private String         defaultValue      = null;
    public static final String INPUTSPEC      = "inputSpec";
    public static final String NAME           = "name";
    public static final String VALUE          = "value";
    public static final String DEFAULTVALUE   = "default";

    /**
     * Constructor method used to create an instance of this class.
     */
    public InputSpecElement(Element root) {
        setName(root.getAttribute(NAME));
        setValue(root.getAttribute(VALUE));
        setDefaultValue(root.getAttribute(DEFAULTVALUE));
    }

    /**
     * Method to get runtime values for the element. If value !=
       null,
     * it returns value. Otherwise, it returns the default value.
     */
    public String getRuntimeValue() {
        if (getValue() != null)
            return getValue();
        return getDefaultValue();
    }

    /**
     * Method to get the name of inputSpec param (default: null).
     */
    public String getName() {
```

```
        return name;
    }

    /**
     * Method to set the name of inputSpec param (default: null).
     */
    public void setName(String param) {
        name = param;
    }

    /**
     * Method to get the value for inputSpec param provided at SQLX
       exection;
     * if specified, overrides defaultValue (optional) (default: null).
     */
    public String getValue() {
        return(value);
    }

    /**
     * Method to set the value for inputSpec param provided at SQLX
       exection;
     * if specified, overrides defaultValue (optional) (default: null).
     */
    public void setValue(String param) {
        value = param;
    }

    /**
     * Method to get the default value for inputSpec param provided
       at SQLX
     * exection (optional) (default: null).
     */
    public String getDefaultValue() {
        return defaultValue;
    }

    /**
     * Method to set the default value for inputSpec param provided
       at SQLX
     * exection (optional) (default: null).
     */
    public void setDefaultValue(String param) {
        defaultValue = param;
    }
}
```

The `getRuntimeValue()` method returns the value to be substituted (`:salary`, for example) in the SQL statement. It is the default value when no value is specified in the command line.

Class `InputSpecElements`

`InputSpecElements` is a subclass of `Vector` and holds multiple `InputSpecElement` objects. An `inputSpec` element has zero or more variable definitions, as shown in the following example.

```
<inputSpec>
    <param name=":salary" default="25000"/>
    <param name=":bonus" default="500"/>
</inputSpec>
```

Each `param` line defines a variable and is represented by an `InputSpecElement` object. `InputSpecElement.java`, shown in Listing 6.5, scans the children of the `inputSpec` element and creates `InputSpecElement` objects.

Listing 6.5 `InputSpecElements.java`: Inputs parameters to a database

```java
import java.util.Vector;
import org.w3c.dom.Element;
import org.w3c.dom.Node;
import org.w3c.dom.NodeList;

/**
 * This class represents a vector containing instances of inputSpec.
 */
public class InputSpecElements extends Vector {
    public static final String PARAM          = "param";

    /**
     * Constructor method used to create an instance of this class.
     */
    public InputSpecElements() {
    }

    /**
     * Method used to process an "inputSpec" node.
     */
    public void process(Element root) {
        NodeList nl = root.getChildNodes();
        for (int i = 0; i < nl.getLength(); i++) {
            Node ch = nl.item(i);
```

```
            if (ch instanceof Element) {
                Element el = (Element)ch;
                if (el.getNodeName().equals(PARAM))
                    // Adds inputSpec.
                    this.addElement(new InputSpecElement(el));
            }
        }
    }

    /**
     * Method used to override inputSpec default values with those
     * defined in String[].
     */
    public void override(String[] array) {
            // See the source code in the CD-ROM.
    }

    /**
     * Method used to replace all inputSpec elements in the text.
     */
    public String substitute(String text) {
        // Loops through all inputSpec.
        for(int i = 0; i < this.size(); i++) {
            InputSpecElement inputSpec = (InputSpecElement)this.
              elementAt(i);
            // Loops while text is found; if found, replaces.
            while(text.indexOf(inputSpec.getName()) > -1) {
                text = text.substring(0, text.indexOf(inputSpec.
                  getName()))
                    + inputSpec.getRuntimeValue()
                    + text.substring(text.indexOf(inputSpec.getName())
                    + inputSpec.getName().length());
            }
        }
        // Return the substituted text.
        return text;
    }
}
```

An instance of the `InputSpecElements` class is created by an `SQLXParser` object and referred to by the member variable `inputSpecElements`. The `process()` method is called by the `SQLXParser` object when it sees an `inputSpec` element in the query document (see `SQLX.java`, Listing 6.2).

```
public void process(Element root) {
    NodeList nl = root.getChildNodes();
    for (int i=0; i<nl.getLength(); i++)
    {
        Node ch = nl.item(i);
        if (ch instance of Element)
        {
            Element el = (Element)ch;
            if (((TXElement)el).getName().equals(PARAM))
            // Add inputSpec.
            this.addElement(new InputSpecElement(el));
        }
    }
}
```

process() scans the children of the given node and for each param element, creates an InputSpecElement object.

The InputSpecElements class also is responsible for substituting the values of the variables if they are specified in the command line arguments.

Another important method in this class is override(), which is called in the main function. This method takes command line arguments (argv) and search variables. If a variable is found, the value from the query document is updated.

Suppose that the command line argument is given as follows:

```
R:\samples\chap6>java SQLX sample.xml :salary=40000"
```

and the inputSpec element in sample.xml is as follows:

```
<inputSpec>
<param name=":salary" default="25000"/>
</inputSpec>
```

The override() method separates the argument ":salary=40000" into the name and value and substitutes the value of the corresponding InputSpecElement for this value. Please see the source code in R:\samples\chap6\InputSpecElements.java.

Class ExecuteElement

The ExecuteElement class represents the other component of a query document, that is, the execute element. It has the following member variables:

- driver. The JDBC driver (fully qualified class name)

- url. The URL for specifying the database to be accessed

- `user`. The user id for user authentication

- `password`. The password for user authentication

- `sql`. The SQL statement

Like an `InputElements` object, an `ExecuteElement` object is created in the `SQLXParser` class when an `execute` element is encountered. The `process()` method is then called.

Listing 6.6 `ExecuteElement.java`: Represents the `execute` element

```java
import org.w3c.dom.Element;

/**
 * This class represents an "execute" object.
 */
public class ExecuteElement {
    // The JDBC driver; must be in a form appropriate for the
    // resource,
    // e.g., a JDBC driver such as "sun.jdbc.odbc.JdbcOdbcDriver".
     private String       driver        = null;
    // The JDBC database name; must be in a form appropriate for the
    // resource,
    // e.g., a JDBC url such as "jdbc:odbc:sample" for databases that
    // support JDBC.
    private String         url           = null;
    // The userid (login) for the database; if not specified, the
    // current user,
    // as defined by the operating environment, is assumed.
    private String         user          = null;
    // The password for the specified user; if not specified,
    // the current password for the user, as defined by the operating
    // environment, is assumed.
    private String         password      = null;
    // The SQL statement to execute against the specified driver,
    // URL, user, and password.
    private String         sql           = null;
    public static final String EXECUTE     = "execute";
    public static final String DRIVER      = "driver";
    public static final String URL         = "url";
    public static final String USER        = "user";
    public static final String PASSWORD    = "password";
    public static final String SQL         = "sql";
```

```java
/**
 * Constructor method used to create an instance of this
   class.
 */
public ExecuteElement() {
}

/**
 * Method to process an execute element.
 */
public void process(Element root) {
    setDriver(root.getAttribute(DRIVER));
    setUrl(root.getAttribute(URL));
    setUser(root.getAttribute(USER));
    setPassword(root.getAttribute(PASSWORD));
    setSql(root.getAttribute(SQL));
}

/**
 * Method to get the JDBC driver this must be in a form
   appropriate
 * for the resource, e.g., a JDBC driver such as
 * "sun.jdbc.odbc.JdbcOdbcDriver".
 */
public String getDriver() {
    return driver;
}

/**
 * Method to set the JDBC driver; must be in a form
   appropriate for the
 * resource, e.g., a JDBC driver such as "sun.jdbc.odbc.
   JdbcOdbcDriver".
 */
public void setDriver(String param) {
    driver = param;
}

/**
 * Method to get the JDBC database name; must be in a form
   appropriate for
 * the resource, e.g., a JDBC url such as "jdbc:odbc:sample"
   for databases
 * that support JDBC.
 */
```

```java
public String getUrl() {
    return url;
}

/**
 * Method to set the JDBC database name; must be in a form
   appropriate for
 * the resource, e.g., a JDBC url such as "jdbc:odbc:sample"
   for databases
 * that support JDBC.
 */
public void setUrl(String param) {
    url = param;
}

/**
 * Method to get the userid (login) for the database; if not
   specified,
 * the current user, as defined by the operating environment,
   is assumed.
 */
public String getUser() {
    return user;
}

/**
 * Method to set the userid (login) for the database; if not
   specified,
 * the current user, as defined by the operating environment,
   is assumed.
 */
public void setUser(String param) {
    user = param;
}

/**
 * Method to get the password for the specified user; if not
   specified,
 * the current password for the user, as defined by the
   operating environment,
 * is assumed.
 */
public String getPassword() {
    return password;
}
```

```
/**
 * Method to set the password for the specified user; if not
   specified,
 * the current password for the user, as defined by the
   operating environment,
 * is assumed.
 */
public void setPassword(String param) {
    password = param;
}

/**
 * Method to get the SQL statement to execute against the
   specified driver,
 * URL, user, and password.
 */
public String getSql() {
    return sql;
}

/**
 * Method to set the SQL statement to execute against the
   specified driver,
 * URL, user, and password
 */
public void setSql(String param) {
    sql = param;
}
}
```

By now, we have defined the internal structure of a query document. Next, we define a class for submitting a query and generating a result structure.

Class SQLXResults

The SQLXResults class is used to access a database using JDBC and returns the results. The complete code for class SQLXresults is shown in Listing 6.7.

Listing 6.7 SQLXResults.java: Represents the results of the query

```java
import java.sql.Connection;
import java.sql.DriverManager;
import java.sql.ResultSet;
import java.sql.Statement;
```

```
      /**
       * This class represents the execution of a SQLX "execute" element.
       */
      public class SQLXResults {
          // A result set containing the results of the execute()'ed query.
          private ResultSet          resultSet          = null;
          // An instance of the result set as a SQLXXMLDocument.
          private SQLXDocument       doc                = null;

          /**
           * Constructor method used to create an instance of this class.
           */
[18]      public SQLXResults(SQLXParser parser)
              throws java.sql.SQLException, ClassNotFoundException {
              // Gets SQL statement.
              String sql = parser.getExecuteElement().getSql();
              // If "inputSpec" are defined
              if (parser.getInputSpecElements() != null)
                 // Substitutes names with values.
                 sql = parser.getInputSpecElements().substitute(sql);
              // Executes the SQL statement.
              execute(parser.getExecuteElement().getDriver(),
                      parser.getExecuteElement().getUrl(),
                      parser.getExecuteElement().getUser(),
                      parser.getExecuteElement().getPassword(),
                      sql);
[32]      }

          /**
           * Constructor method to create an instance of this class.
           */
          public SQLXResults(String aDriver, String aUrl, String aUser,
                             String aPassword, String aSql)
              throws java.sql.SQLException, ClassNotFoundException {
              // Executes the SQL statement.
              execute(aDriver, aUrl, aUser, aPassword, aSql);
          }

          /**
           * Method to execute an SQL statement and generate an
             SQLXDocument
           * instance of the results.
           */
[50]      private void execute(String aDriver, String aUrl, String aUser,
                             String aPassword, String aSql)
              throws java.sql.SQLException, ClassNotFoundException {
```

```
                   // Loads the datasource driver, and establishes the
                   // connection.
                   Class.forName(aDriver);
                   Connection connection = DriverManager.getConnection(aUrl,
                   aUser, aPassword);
                   Statement statement = connection.createStatement();
                   statement.execute(aSql);
                   // Saves the resultset.
                   setResultSet(statement.getResultSet());
                   // Creates Document based on the resultset.
                   getDoc();
[63]           }

               /**
                * Method to get an instance of the result set as an
                  SQLXDocument.
                */
[69]           public SQLXDocument getDoc() throws java.sql.SQLException {
                   if (doc == null)
                       doc = new SQLXDocument(this);
                   return doc;
[73]           }

               /**
                * Method to get the result set containing the results of the
                  execute()'ed query.
                */
               public ResultSet getResultSet() {
                   return resultSet;
               }

               /**
                * Method to set the result set containing the results of the
                  execute()'ed query.
                */
               public void setResultSet(ResultSet param) {
                   resultSet = param;
               }
           }
```

Recall that this class is used in SQLX.java (Listing 6.2) as follows.

```
// Parses the SQLX file.
SQLXParser parser = new SQLXParser(xmlin);
...
SQLXResults results = new SQLXResults(parser);
```

As shown, the constructor of this class takes an `SQLParser` object as input. Everything important happens in this constructor, including calls to JDBC to fetch the database contents. The constructor is shown next (lines [18] through [32] in Listing 6.7).

```
[18] public SQLXResults(SQLXParser parser) throws java.sql.SQLException,
     java.lang.ClassNotFoundException {
         // Gets the SQL statement.
         String sql = parser.getExecuteElement().getSql();
         // If "inputSpec"s is defined
         if (parser.getInputSpecElements() != null)
         // substitutes names with values.
         sql = parser.getInputSpecElements().substitute(sql);
         // Executes the SQL statement.
         execute(parser.getExecuteElement().getDriver(),
             parser.getExecuteElement().getUrl(),
             parser.getExecuteElement().getUser(),
             parser.getExecuteElement().getPassword(),
             sql);
[32] }
```

The `substitute()` method is defined in the `InputSpecElements` class and does substitution of variables specified in the `inputSpec` element.

Then the `execute()` method is called. This method takes a JDBC driver name, a URL, a user id and a password, and an SQL statement. `execute()` is defined as follows (lines [50] through [63] in the listing).

```
[50] private void execute(String aDriver, String aUrl, String aUser,
     String aPassword, String aSql)
         throws java.sql.SQLException, java.lang.ClassNotFoundException {
         // Loads the datasource driver, and establishes the connection.
         Class.forName(aDriver);
         Connection connection = DriverManager.getConnection(aUrl, aUser,
         aPassword);
         Statement statement = connection.createStatement();
         statement.execute(aSql);
         // Saves the result set.
         setResultSet(statement.getResultSet());
         // Creates TXDocument based on the result set.
         getDoc();
[63] }
```

The first part of this method follows the standard pattern of accessing a JDBC database that is described in Section 6.2. Then the result set is stored in a member variable (`resultSet`) and transformed into a DOM structure by a call to the `getDoc()` method. `getDoc()` in turn calls the constructor of class `SQLXDocument`.

```
[69] public SQLXDocument getDoc() throws java.sql.SQLException {
         if (doc == null)
             doc = new SQLXDocument(this);
         return(doc);
[73] }
```

Class `SQLXDocument`

The last, and largest, class in our SQLX program is `SQLXDocument`. The results of a JDBC query are returned in a `ResultSet` object that is defined by JDBC. `SQLXDocument` converts this object into a DOM structure. The complete listing is given in Listing 6.8.

Listing 6.8 `SQLXDocument.java`: Represents the query results as a DOM tree

```
import com.ibm.xml.parser.Attlist;
import com.ibm.xml.parser.AttDef;
import com.ibm.xml.parser.CMLeaf;
import com.ibm.xml.parser.CMNode;
import com.ibm.xml.parser.CM1op;
import com.ibm.xml.parser.CM2op;
import com.ibm.xml.parser.ContentModel;
import com.ibm.xml.parser.DTD;
import com.ibm.xml.parser.ElementDecl;
import com.ibm.xml.parser.TXDocument;

import org.w3c.dom.Document;
import org.w3c.dom.Element;
import org.w3c.dom.Node;

// This class depends on XML for Java.

/**
  * This class is used to represent the results of a query as an XML
    parsable document document.
  */
public class SQLXDocument extends com.ibm.xml.parser.TXDocument {
    // The results of a SQLX function.
    private SQLXResults    results           = null;
    public static final String ROWSET          = "rowset";
```

```
       public static final String ROW              = "row";
       public static final String VALUE            = "value";
       public static final String TYPE             = "type";


       /**
        * Base constructor.
        */
[33]   public SQLXDocument(SQLXResults aSQLXResults) throws java.sql.
       SQLException {
           super();
           setResults(aSQLXResults);
           // If there is a resultset
           if (getResults().getResultSet() != null)
               // Builds the XML row elements.
               buildXML();
[40]   }


       /**
        * Method to build the DTD based on column resultset metadata.
        */
[45]   private void buildDTD() throws java.sql.SQLException {
           // Initializes the DTD.
[47]       DTD dtd = this.createDTD();
           dtd.setName(ROWSET);

           // Constructs rowset node.
           CMNode cmNode = new CM1op('*', new CMLeaf(ROW));
           ContentModel contentModel = this.
           createContentModel(ElementDecl.MODEL_GROUP);
           contentModel.setContentModelNode(cmNode);
[55]       ElementDecl rowset = this.createElementDecl(ROWSET,
             contentModel);
[56]       dtd.appendChild(rowset);

           // Constructs the node containing all column names.
[59]       cmNode = new CMLeaf(getResults().getResultSet().getMetaData().
             getColumnName(1));
           for(int i = 2; i <= getResults().getResultSet().getMetaData().
           getColumnCount(); i++) {
               cmNode = new CM2op(',', cmNode, new CMLeaf(getResults().
                 getResultSet().getMetaData().getColumnName(i)));
           }
           contentModel = this.createContentModel(ElementDecl.
             MODEL_GROUP);
```

```
                  contentModel.setContentModelNode(cmNode);
                  ElementDecl row = this.createElementDecl(ROW, contentModel);
                  dtd.appendChild(row);

                  // Adds the attributes for the columns.
                  for(int i = 1; i <= getResults().getResultSet().getMetaData().
                    getColumnCount(); i++) {
                      ElementDecl column = this.createElementDecl(getResults().
                        getResultSet().getMetaData().getColumnName(i), this.
                        createContentModel(Node.ELEMENT_NODE));
                      column.setContentType(ElementDecl.EMPTY);
                      dtd.appendChild(column);

[76]                  Attlist attlist = this.createAttlist(getResults().
                        getResultSet().getMetaData().getColumnName(i));
                      AttDef value = this.createAttDef(VALUE);
                      value.setDeclaredType(AttDef.CDATA);
                      value.setDefaultType(AttDef.IMPLIED);
                      attlist.addElement(value);
                      AttDef type = this.createAttDef(TYPE);
                      type.setDeclaredType(AttDef.CDATA);
                      type.setDefaultType(AttDef.FIXED);
                      type.setDefaultStringValue(""+getResults().getResultSet().
                        getMetaData().getColumnType(i));
                      attlist.addElement(type);
[86]                  dtd.appendChild(attlist);
                  }
                  this.appendChild(dtd);
[89]          }


          /**
           * Method to build the resultset row data.
           */
[94]      private void buildXML() throws java.sql.SQLException {
              // Initializes rows added switch.
[96]          boolean rowsAdded = false;
              // Initializes rowset.
[98]          Element rowset = this.createElement(ROWSET);
              // Loops while rows exist in the resultset.
[100]         while (getResults().getResultSet().next()) {
                  rowsAdded = true;
                  Element row = this.createElement(ROW);
                  rowset.appendChild(row);
                  // Adds the row named "column" with the "value" attribute.
```

```
[105]              for(int i = 1; i <= getResults().getResultSet().
                     getMetaData().getColumnCount(); i++) {
                      String colName = getResults().getResultSet().
                        getMetaData().getColumnName(i);
                      Element col = this.createElement(colName);
                      col.setAttribute(VALUE, getResults().getResultSet().
                        getString(i));
                      row.appendChild(col);
[110]              }
[111]          }
               // If at least one row was added
[113]          if (rowsAdded == true) {
                  // Builds the DTD, and adds rows.
                  this.setVersion("1.0");
                  buildDTD();
                  this.appendChild(rowset);
[118]          }
[119]      }

        /**
         * Method to get the results of an SQLX function.
         */
        public SQLXResults getResults() {
            return results;
        }

        /**
         * Method to set the results of an SQLX function.
         */
        public void setResults(SQLXResults param) {
            results = param;
        }
    }
```

Since XML has no data types either in element contents or in attribute values, we explicitly add a data type attribute called type to every element that corresponds to a column value. To do this, we need to dynamically generate a DTD. Although we showed in Chapter 3 how to generate an XML document through the standard DOM API, DOM does not specify the standard data structure for a DTD. So we are forced to use the native API of XML for Java for dealing with DTD structures.

We start with the constructor of SQLDocument. This is called inside the SQLResult.getDoc() method (lines [69] through [73] in Listing 6.7), shown in lines [33] through [40] in Listing 6.8.

```
[30] public SQLXDocument(SQLXResults aSQLXResults) throws java.sql.
     SQLException {
         super();
         setResults(aSQLXResults);
         // If there is a result set
         if (getResults().getResultSet() != null)
             // Builds the XML row elements.
             buildXML();
[40] }
```

The `SQLResult.getDoc()` method in turn calls the `buildXML()` method (lines [94] through [119]).

Now we can look into the method.

```
[96] boolean rowsAdded = false;                      // Initializes the
                                                     // rows-added switch.
```

The variable `rowsAdded` is set to `true` if the query returned at least one record. When it is `true`, then we can go forward with building a DTD, which we do in the next subsection.

```
[98] Element rowset = this.create.Element (ROWSET) ; // Initializes the
                                                     // rowset.
```

Then we create a `rowset` element to hold the set of records. Remember that `createElement()` is a DOM API. ROWSET is the constant variable ("rowset") that is defined by `SQLXDocument.java` (Listing 6.8).

```
[100] while (getResults().getResultSet().next() ) { // Loops while rows
                                                     // exist
                                                     // in the result set.
          rowsAdded = true;
          Element row = this.createElement(ROW);
          rowset.appendChild(row);
          ...
[111] }
```

This loop iterates on each record returned by the JDBC call. For each record, a `row` element is created and added to the parent node (the `rowset` element).

```
[105]   for (int i=1; i<=getResults().getResultSet().getMetaData().
            getColumnCount(); i++) {
            String colName = getResults().getResultSet().getMetaData().
            getColumnName(i);
```

```
        Element col = this.createElement(colName);
        col.setAttribute(VALUE, getResults().getResultSet().
        getString(i));
        row.appendChild(col);
[110] }
```

The expression `getResults().getResultSet()` refers to an instance of
`ResultSet`. Calling the `getMetaData()` method returns a `ResultSetMetaData`
object that contains various useful information on the table, such as the
number of columns (accessed by `getColumnCount()`), column names
(accessed by `getColumnName()`), and column type name (accessed by
`getColumnTypeName()`). See the `java.sql` package for more details. In the
previous code fragment, the column names are used as the element names and
the values are set to the attribute "value," which is represented by the constant
`VALUE`. By this point, the JDBC `ResultSet` data structure has been successfully
converted to a DOM structure.

Building a DTD

Next, we need to create a DTD so that the data types can be specified. This is
done by calling the `buildDTD()` method (lines [45] through [89]) in the
`buildXML()` method.

```
[113] if (rowsAdded == true) {
        // build DTD, add rows
        this.setVersion("1.0");
        buildDTD();
        this.appendChild(rowset);
[118]   }
```

The rest of this section describes how to build a DTD within the `buildDTD()`
method.

XML for Java provides a set of classes and methods for building an internal
representation of DTD. We use the following code to illustrate how these APIs
can be used.

```
[45] private void buildDTD() throws java.sql.SQLException {
        // Initializes the DTD.
[47]    DTD dtd = this.createDTD();
        dtd.setName(ROWSET);
```

```
            // Constructs the rowset node.
            CMNode cmNode = new CM1op('*', new CMLeaf(ROW));
            ContentModel contentModel = this.createContentModel(ElementDecl.
            MODEL_GROUP);
            contentModel.setContentModelNode(cmNode);
[55]        ElementDecl rowset = this.createElementDecl(ROWSET,
            contentModel);
[56]        dtd.appendChild(rowset);

            // Constructs the node containing all column names.
[59]        cmNode = new CMLeaf(getResults().getResultSet().getMetaData().
            getColumnName(1));
            for(int i=2; i<=getResults().getResultSet().getMetaData().
            getColumnCount(); i++) {
                cmNode = new CM2op(',', cmNode, new CMLeaf(getResults().
                  getResultSet().getMetaData().getColumnName(i)));
                }
            contentModel = this.createContentModel(ElementDecl.MODEL_GROUP);
            contentModel.setContentModelNode(cmNode);
            ElementDecl row = this.createElementDecl(ROW, contentModel);
            dtd.appendChild(row);

            // Adds attributes for columns.
            for(int i=1; i<=getResults().getResultSet().getMetaData().
              getColumnCount(); i++) {
                ElementDecl column = this.createElementDecl(getResults().
                  getResultSet().getMetaData().getColumnName(i),
        this.createContentModel(Node.ELEMENT_NODE));
                column.setContentType(ElementDecl.EMPTY);
                dtd.appendChild(column);

[76]            Attlist attlist = this.createAttlist(getResults().
                  getResultSet().getMetaData().getColumnName(i));
                AttDef value = this.createAttDef(VALUE);
                value.setDeclaredType(AttDef.CDATA);
                value.setDefaultType(AttDef.IMPLIED);
                attlist.addElement(value);
                AttDef type = this.createAttDef(TYPE);
                type.setDeclaredType(AttDef.CDATA);
                type.setDefaultType(AttDef.FIXED);
                type.setDefaultStringValue(""+getResults().getResultSet().
                getMetaData().getColumnType(i));
                attlist.addElement(type);
```

```
[86]        dtd.appendChild(attlist);
        }
    this.appendChild(dtd);
[89] }
```

Recall the DTD that this code is supposed to produce. It must define two
database-independent elements (that is, `rowset` and `row`) and one element for
every column in the result table. The following example DTD shows the idea.

```
<!ELEMENT rowset (row*)>
<!ELEMENT row (LASTNAME,SALARY)>
<!ELEMENT LASTNAME EMPTY>
<!ATTLIST LASTNAME value CDATA #IMPLIED type CDATA #FIXED "12">
<!ELEMENT SALARY EMPTY>
<!ATTLIST SALARY value CDATA #IMPLIED type CDATA #FIXED "3">
```

The first element declaration (element `rowset`) is produced by the following
lines.

```
[47] DTD dtd = this.createDTD();
     dtd.setName(ROWSET);
     // constructs rowset node
     CMNode cmNode = new CM1op('*', new CMLeaf(ROW));
     ContentModel contentModel = this.createContentModel
     (ElementDecl.MODEL_GROUP);
     contentModel.setContentModelNode(cmNode);
[55] ElementDecl rowset = this.createElementDecl(ROWSET,
     contentModel);
[56] dtd.appendChild(rowset);
```

First, a DTD object must be created. Its name is set to `rowset`. The first element
declaration, `rowset`, is created in line [55]. To have this done, you need to create a content model structure using `CM1op` and set it to a `ContentModel` object.
Then you must create an `ElementDecl` object. See the following note for the
details of the content model. Other constituents used in a DTD have the corresponding classes in XML for Java given in Table 6.6.

The content model of the declaration of the row element should be dynamically constructed depending on the query results, as shown next.

```
<!ELEMENT row (LASTNAME,SALARY)>
```

Line [59] uses the `java.sql.ResultSetMetaData.getColumnName()` method
to extract the column names from the result set and create a content model.
Here, we need to use the `CM2op` class to represent the comma operator.

TABLE 6.6 Corresponding Classes of DTD Constituents

CONSTITUENT IN DTD	CLASS IN XML FOR JAVA
DTD	DTD
Element declaration	ElementDecl
Content model	ContentModel
Leaf node in a content model	CMLeaf
Unary operator (* or ?) in a content model	CM1op
Binary operator (, or |) in a content model	CM2op

NOTE: Class CMNode is a building block for representing a content model and a parent class of the following three classes:

- CMLeaf. Leaf node

- CM1op. Unary operators (* and ?)

- CM2op. Binary operators (, and \|)

A content model is built using the CMLeaf, CM1op, and CM2op nodes. For example, the element declaration for the following element foo is constructed as shown in Figure 6.5.

```
<ELEMENT foo (title, chapter*, reference)>
```

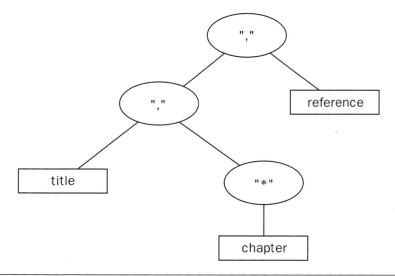

FIGURE 6.5 Content model tree for `<ELEMENT foo (title, chapter*, reference)>`

Finally, element declarations corresponding to the columns need to be generated. Since we need to express the value and data type of the element, attribute declarations are also necessary. Classes used in attribute declarations are shown in Table 6.7.

TABLE 6.7 Classes Used in Attribute Declarations

CONSTITUENT IN DTD	CLASS IN XML FOR JAVA
Attribute declaration	`Attlist`
One attribute in an attribute declaration	`AttDef`

Class `AttDef` has attribute properties such as declaration type and default type. These properties can be accessed through a set of methods, such as `setDeclareType()` and `getDefaultType()`. Lines [76] through [86] generate the following attribute declaration.

```
<!ATTLIST SALARY value CDATA #IMPLIED type CDATA #FIXED "3">
```

As we have shown in this SQLX implementation, it is possible to convert database query results into a DOM tree along with an appropriate DTD. SQLX can be used as a reusable software component that provides easy access to RDBMSs from DOM-based application programs. Although we used the JDBC driver for DB2, this program should work with any other JDBC driver without modification.

6.4 Web Application with a Database

In the previous sections, we showed two essential software components, JDBC and SQLX, for DOM-based application programs to access DBMSs. How can these components be used to build an end-to-end application?

Figure 6.2 showed an example of such applications. In this case, the client is a normal HTML browser. The user's input is received by a servlet, which generates a query document using XML for Java. This query document is processed by SQLX and JDBC and fed to the backend database as an SQL query. The retrieval results go through these two components in the reverse order to form a DOM tree. This DOM tree is converted to an HTML page using the LMX processor described in Chapter 4. Of course, the same scenario can be realized with existing "publisher" or "connector" middleware as well, provided the application is simple and deals only with a browser client. However, if the application logic becomes complex and involves accessing other Web applications through XML, having a DOM as the central data structure will offer a lot of benefits.

Listing 6.9 is a sample LMX rule set for converting a DOM tree that is obtained through SQL into an HTML document.

Listing 6.9 toHTML.lmx: Converts SQLX output into HTML

```
<?xml version="1.0"?>
<lmx:rule xmlns:lmx="http://www.ibm.com/xml/lmx/">
    <lmx:pattern>
        <lmx:lhs>
            <results>$1;</results>
        </lmx:lhs>
        <lmx:rhs>
            <html>
        <head/head>
        <body>
            <h2>Result</h2>
            <table border="1">$1;</table>
        </body>
        </html>
        </lmx:rhs>
    </lmx:pattern>

    <lmx:pattern>
        <lmx:lhs>
        <row>
            <LASTNAME value="$1;" type="$2;"/>
            <SALARY value="$3;" type="$4;"/>
        </row>
        </lmx:lhs>
        <lmx:rhs>
        <tr>
            <td>$1;</td>
            <td>$3;</td>
        </tr>
        </lmx:rhs>
    </lmx:pattern>
</lmx:rule>
```

Applying this rule set to the XML document produced by the SQLX creates the following HTML document.

```
R:\samples\chap6>java com.ibm.xml.lmx.Main -html toHTML.lmx
result.xml
<html>
<head>
</head>
<body>
   <table border="1">
      <tr><td>HAAS       </tdtd>52750.00</td></tr>
      <tr><td>THOMPSON   </tdtd>41250.00</td></tr>
      <tr><td>GEYER      </tdtd>40175.00</td></tr>
      <tr><td>LUCCHESSI  </tdtd>46500.00</td></tr>
   </table>
</body>
</html>
```

This will display on a browser as shown in Figure 6.6.

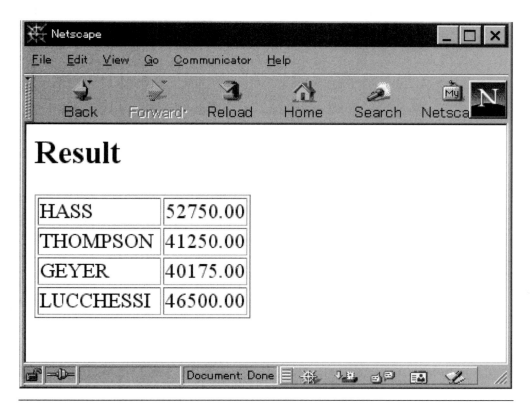

FIGURE 6.6 Rendering results

```
Note that variables appear as values of attributes. LMXConverter
described in Chapter 4 cannot handle this, since it was used to
represent the basic concept of the converter. An enhanced version of
LMXConverter, with the source code, is included on the accompanying
CD-ROM. You can study the details about it and use it to convert a
SQL document to a HTML file by using table tags.
```

6.5 Summary

In this chapter, we shed light on XML from the database point of view. We discussed how the XML world and the database world can be bridged. Databases are good for efficiently storing a large volume of data, while XML is good for exchanging data among different applications and different organizations. Although quite simple and primitive, SQLX is effective as an XML frontend of RDBMSs. Combining DOM-centric middlewares such as XML for Java, LMX, and SQLX should make application development much easier. The next chapter deals with another aspect of XML, that of the communication message format.

CHAPTER **7**

Exchanging Messages Securely on the Internet

7.1 Introduction

In Chapter 1, we indicated that application areas of XML are the following:

1. document markup

2. metacontent

3. databases

4. messaging

We covered document markup and metacontent in Chapter 5 and databases in Chapter 6. In this chapter, we cover the last area, *messaging*.

Today, many new computer applications are built on top of other existing applications. A typical example is the so-called *e-Business* application, a new Web-based application built by leveraging the data stored in enterprise systems. The heart of this type of application is glue code that interfaces with the existing applications. Since existing applications are typically running on different hosts and platforms, the glue code is built on top of distributed computing middleware such as CORBA and MQSeries (IBM's product for asynchronous messaging).

In this book, we call exchanging data between computer application programs *messaging.* In the narrow sense, this term refers to asynchronous communication such as e-mail and MQSeries. But we use this term in the wider sense to include synchronous communication as well.

XML is expected to play an important role in messaging because of its openness, simplicity, and internationalization. In this chapter, we explore the possibilities and design considerations in using XML for messaging. In particular, we address the security issue, the biggest stumbling block to applying the Internet technology to business-to-business (B2B) communication.

First, we discuss several different alternatives for transport and for message formats, the two important aspects of messaging. Then, we build the Power-Warning application introduced in Chapter 1 as a concrete example of messaging based on HTTP and XML. We discuss how to design a good message format using XML and show that the public-key infrastructure and secure sockets layer (SSL) that are rapidly being deployed can be used to secure end-to-end communication even through the Internet. We end with a discussion on a digital signature for XML documents that can be used as nonrepudiatable evidence of a business transaction.

7.2 Transport and Message Formats

Suppose that there is an existing application A and you want to build a new application B using the functionality provided by that application. From various system and operational considerations, you do not want to modify application A, including the platform on which it is running, so you decide to build application B on a separate machine. Therefore application A and application B must interact through a network.

Messaging between these applications requires that they agree on two important things:

1. The *transport* for conveying messages

2. The *format* of the message contents

For the two application programs to communicate with each other, the specifications of these must be unambiguously defined.

7.2.1 Transports

Transport refers to a protocol, an agreed-upon format for transmitting data between two devices. The protocol is usually defined independently of the message content. Several reasonable choices as transport exist, including asynchronous transports such as e-mail and MQSeries and synchronous transports such as sockets, HTTP, and CORBA/IIOP. We look at these alternatives briefly next.

Asynchronous Transport

With asynchronous transport, the message sender does not wait for the reply from the message receiver. The sender can immediately proceed to the next task after sending a message. Thus asynchronous transport is useful, for example, when the recipient is not always available; for instance, your business partner operates Mondays through Thursdays and you send a message to it on Friday. It also is useful when time is required to process the message; for instance, your order must be approved by a human supervisor.

Electronic Mail

The most well-known asynchronous messaging transport is *electronic mail,* or *e-mail.* This is a pervasive infrastructure. Virtually every corporation and institution has an e-mail facility in some form, and these systems are interconnected through gateways even if they are completely different systems from Internet's SMTP standard (Simple Mail Transfer Protocol, RFC-821). Unfortunately, however, the current systems based on SMTP lack functionality, such as reliable delivery and delivery confirmation, that are essential for B2B communication and so SMTP is not suitable as a messaging transport in many cases.

MQSeries

IBM's MQSeries is an asynchronous messaging transport that is being widely used in enterprise systems. Unlike e-mail, it supports guaranteed message delivery, message confirmation, and so on. It runs on a broad spectrum of different platforms, from big mainframe computers to UNIX workstations to PCs. It is very likely that an existing application that you want to utilize in developing a new application already has an MQ interface. In such a case, it is quite natural to use MQSeries as the message transport in your system. The downside of MQSeries is its high cost.

Synchronous Transport

In synchronous messaging, the sender waits for a reply from the recipient. Since the sender does not proceed to the next task until it receives the reply, synchronous messaging should be used for short turnaround interactions.

Today, many applications ultimately used by human users are interactive. For these, synchronous messaging is better suited because the user's input error and processing results can be immediately fed back to the user. Synchronous transport protocols usually implement acknowledgement-based reliability, so no additional confirmation of message delivery is necessary.

Sockets

Probably the most primitive synchronous transport of interest is the bare TCP/IP (transmission control protocol/Internet protocol), or its programming interface *socket*. It provides only a basic bidirectional stream transport on top of which many other protocols such as HTTP and FTP are implemented. It is theoretically possible to use the socket interface to implement your own proprietary transport protocol, but it is not recommended unless you have very unusual requirements that can never be satisfied with existing transports.

HTTP

The most widely used synchronous transport today is *hypertext transfer protocol* (HTTP). When using HTTP, the client sends a request prepended by a header consisting of one or more *tag:value* pairs. The header and the request body are separated by a blank line. The server's reply also has a header. A number of header tags are defined, such as `Content-Length` (length of the message body), `Content-Type` (MIME type of the message body), and `User-Agent` (type and version of the client software). The latest HTTP specification is HTTP 1.1 (RFC 2068) published January 1997 by the IETF. One merit of using HTTP is that it can pass through firewalls. This is because the firewalls of most corporations are configured to allow outbound HTTP connections so that their employees can access Web sites outside of the company. Another merit of HTTP is that its secure version, HTTP-SSL, known as HTTPS, is readily available, so little cost is involved in incorporating security. We discuss SSL in Section 7.5.

CORBA/IIOP

Common Object Request Broker Architecture, or CORBA, is a set of specifications of common middleware for object-to-object communication. It is defined by the OMG (Object Management Group `http://www.omg.org/`). It is supported by over 700 companies in the information technology industry, but excluding Microsoft.

CORBA has a long history. The CORBA 1.1 Specification was published in 1991. As is always true with a standard activity involving many vendors, CORBA was huge and took a long time to implement. It started to gain popularity in 1995 when the OMG released CORBA 2.0, which specified the **Internet Inter-ORB Protocol** (IIOP). This protocol enables interoperating CORBA implementations of different vendors using the Internet infrastructure. The central part of CORBA is an API specification for distributed objects whereby a requesting object calls a method of a remote object through an *object request broker* (ORB). This is shown in Figure 7.1.

CORBA is not exactly a transport. Rather, it is an architecture that includes an API, protocol, message format, and much more. Any CORBA implementation has a binding to programming languages such as C, Smalltalk, and Java, so application programs are supposed to use CORBA's messaging mechanism via library routines that are provided by the ORB of some CORBA vendor. Thus, any host participating in CORBA communication should have an ORB installed.

CORBA is a huge and complex architecture. It is impossible to explain the whole picture here because of space limitations. The latest CORBA Specification is CORBA 2.2, published July 1997, and consists of almost 1,000 pages. We think the learning curve associated with CORBA-based programming is the biggest obstacle to its adoption.

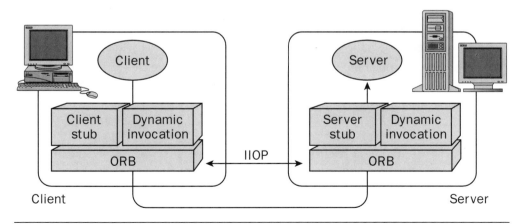

FIGURE 7.1 CORBA Architecture

What Transport to Pick?

Table 7.1 summarizes the pros and cons of the transport alternatives.

TABLE 7.1 Comparison of Transports

TRANSPORT	SYNCHRONOUS/ ASYNCHRONOUS	PROS	CONS
SMTP	Async	Simple, pervasive (you can send messages to virtually any computer in the world, even if it is not IP-reachable)	Unreliable (no guarantee of delivery and no acknowledgment)
MQ Series	Async	Guaranteed delivery, cross-platform, proven in enterprise systems	Proprietary, high cost
Socket	Sync	Allows low-level protocol design for specific needs	Requires low-level programming
HTTP	Sync	Widely used, can connect through a firewall, can be secured by using SSL	Inefficient, sessionless (a special treatment is necessary if multiple connections need to share a common session's information)
CORBA/IIOP	Sync	Efficient, rich functionality, common API available for many programming languages and platforms	Complex, ORB required for all participating hosts

> **NOTE:** One merit of using sockets or HTTP as a transport is that you can use Telnet, one of the common tools that comes with most TCP/IP implementations, for trying the protocol to see what it looks like. For example, if you need to learn about the HTTP protocol, you can connect to a Web server using Telnet and type in several lines manually as if you were a program communicating with the server through HTTP. As shown in the following sample session, after connecting to the server's port 80, you type `GET / HTTP/1.0` and press the Enter key twice to see the text returned by the Web server. Similar things can be done for any TCP/IP or HTTP-based protocol. (We often use this technique for debugging our programs.) *(continued)*

```
R:\samples\chap7>telnet www.xweather.com 80
GET / HTTP/1.0

HTTP/1.1 200 OK
Server: JavaWebServer/1.1
Content-Length: 1999
Content-Type: text/html
Last-Modified: Wed, 10 Dec 1997 12:09:14 GMT
```

7.2.2 Message Formats

A *message format* defines the syntax of messages that are to be transferred by an underlying transport. Of course, we will discuss XML as the preferred message format, but first we take a look at other alternatives:

- Text-based, such as EDI, an RFC822 derivative, and SGML

- Binary, such as ASN.1 and CORBA/IIOP

Text-Based Formats

Text-based format alternatives include EDI, an RFC822 derivation, and SGML. These are discussed in the following subsections.

Electronic Data Exchange

When considering B2B message exchange, the first thing that comes to mind is Electronic Data Interchange (EDI). In a wide sense, EDI means electronic data exchange in general. Usually, however, it is used to refer to either

- Electronic Data Interchange for Administration, Commerce and Transport (EDIFACT) (http://www.unece.org/trade/untdid/), an international standard defined by the United Nations, or

- ASC X12 (http://polaris.disa.org/index.html), the U.S. domestic standard similar to EDIFACT.

The EDI activities started in the 1970s and focused on standardizing the format of messages exchanged among business partners. It is a text-based format, with dictionaries of globally defined tag sets. An EDI message is layered, including such layers as Data Element, Compound Data Element, Data Segment, Loop, and Business Document. Thus it has some, although limited, capability to represent tree-structured data. However, it is not as flexible as XML. This is because its number of layers is fixed. With XML, by contrast, you can define a data structure that has an arbitrary number of layers.

The following code fragment, delineated in Table 7.2, is an EDT message for a book order defined by *EDI+EUR EDI Implementation Guidelines for Book Trade Distribution*, a specification defined by the European Group for Electronic Commerce in the Book and Serials Sectors (`http://www.editeur.org/`). As you can see, EDT messages are text with special characters (', +, and :) as field separators. The tags, for example, ENH, BGM, and DTM, are defined in the U.N.'s EDIFACT dictionaries. In Table 7.2, the message content is shown line by line in the left column. The right column annotates the content.

This EDI message fragment could be represented in an XML form as follows.

```
<?xml version="1.0"?>
<!DOCTYPE order SYSTEM
        "http://www.myco.org/messages/XML/message1.xml">
<order>
   <order-no type="original">B00002</order-no>
   <date>19940202</date>
   <buyer>
      <name>Stadt- und Universitaetsbibliothek </name>
      <address>
         <street>Frankfurt, Bockenheimer Landstr. 134-13 8</street>
         <city>Frankfurt</city>
         <postcode>60325</postcode>
      </address>
      <Buyer-ID>DE1141110388</Buyer-ID>
   </buyer>
   <supplier>
      <name>DREIER</name>
   </supplier>
   <currency type="order">DEM</currency>
   :
</order>
```

The biggest difference between EDI and XML is that in XML, the element names can be self-descriptive. By contrast, with EDI, unless you are an expert in EDIFACT, you need the U.N.'s EDIFACT dictionaries in order to understand the three-letter mnemonic codes used. With XML, instead of, for example, EDI's obscure NAD code, you can use more meaningful element names such as `name` and `address`. Of course, EDI messages are supposed to be processed by programs, not by human users. However, readability still is crucial, for example for application programmers (who are human) who develop, debug, and

TABLE 7.2 Sample EDI Message

`UNH 000002+ORDERS;DD 96A UN:EAN008`	Header
`BGM+220_B00002-9'`	Order number
`DTM-137-19940202:102'`	Message date
`NAD+BY Stadt-und Universitaetsbibhotbek :`	
`  Frankfurt-Bockenheimer Landstr. 134-13`	
`  8+Frankfurt++60325'`	Buyer name and address
`RFF+API:DE1141110388'`	Buyer ID number
`NAD+SU+++DREIER'`	Supplier name
`CUX+2:DEM:9'`	Order currency: DMark

maintain the programs that process EDI messages. Imagine, for example, that you are the head of a group of programmers but are not fluent in the EDIFACT dictionaries. You have been asked to estimate the development cost of a new application that must talk to another existing application using EDI or XML. Would you estimate the same development cost for both EDI and XML? Probably not.

One common question about EDI and XML concerns efficiency. Does XML-based messaging require much more bandwidth than EDI and therefore is it less efficient? Some people say that XML-based messages are 30 percent to 50 percent longer than the same messages in EDI. In the example in Table 7.2, the EDI fragment is 244 bytes; its XML counterpart is 507 bytes, more than double. Still, we believe that the readability and flexibility of XML more than makes up for the performance loss. EDI was first designed in the late 1970s when a company's typical network connection was a 1,200-bps link to a value added network (VAN). Today, even SOHOs—Small Office/Home Office—often have a permanent ISDN connection to the Internet, which is 100 times faster than speeds available 20 years ago. A 50 percent increase of network traffic is a small penalty to pay for readability. If you are really concerned with bandwidth, you should consider using one of the binary formats described in the next subsection.

Another question is whether it is worth redesigning an existing EDI-based system to use XML. The answer is probably no. This is because the chief advantage of using XML is to lower the barrier for *new* applications to enable them to participate in communication; nothing will be gained for applications that are already communicating with each other. If you need to invite new applications to your EDI environment, the best approach is to develop a *gateway* that translates XML messages to EDI messages and vice versa. One attempt to standardize such transformations between XML and EDI is XMLEDI (http://www.xmledi.net)

RFC-822 Derivative

You can define your own message format by following the convention defined in RFC-822, the Internet Mail Standard. This method involves encoding a *tag:value pair* on each line. This is a very simple method and cannot represent complex data that involves nested structures. If your message consists of a handful of variables whose values are short text strings, this might be a good candidate.

Standard Generalized Markup Language

Standard Generalized Markup Language (SGML, ISO8879) was defined in 1986 as an ISO standard for electronic document exchange, archiving, and processing. It was designed for encoding the structure of complex documents but can also be used as a message format. Because XML, which is a subset of SGML, has enough representational power for even very complex messages, using XML instead of SGML for most cases is advised.

Binary Formats

Text-based formats are inherently redundant—the same amount of information can be encoded more concisely using a *binary format.* If the bandwidth of the communication or the computing overhead for converting between a program's internal binary representation and an external text-based message is a serious concern, consider using a binary format for messages. However, be aware that when developing and debugging systems that use binary messages, you will need special tools to browse and edit the messages because text editors and general-purpose tools (such as Telnet) cannot be used.

Binary formats include ASN.1 and CORBA/IIOP.

ASN.1

Abstract Syntax Notation 1 (ASN.1) is a binary message format for designing efficient protocols. It consists of two related ISO standards:

- ISO 8824/ITU X.208, which specifies the abstract syntax of messages

- ISO 8825/ITU X.209, which specifies the encoding rule (that is, the bit and octet representation of a message)

The abstract syntax of a message is defined using a BNF-like notation. Each element is represented as a binary string consisting of a tag field, a length field, and data field. Low-level bit manipulation is necessary to encode and decode a message. The X.509 digital certificate, discussed later in this chapter, is encoded with ASN.1. Another example is the Simple Network Management Protocol (SNMP), in which the complex data about hosts and routers are expressed in the ASN.1 format. Since the ASN.1 message syntax is defined with BNF-like rules, it can represent nested tree-structured data just as XML can. Unfortunately, general ASN.1 tools are relatively expensive. A tool to convert from XML to ASN.1 messages and vice versa would be very useful.

CORBA/IIOP

CORBA/IIOP enables you to define a data structure, to be sent as a parameter in terms of an IDL. The message is encoded in a platform-neutral binary representation and sent over the network. Thus CORBA/IIOP can be considered a binary message format as well as a message transport protocol.

7.2.3 HTTP+XML

The main point in the previous arguments concerning selecting HTTP as the transport and XML as the message format is that simplicity and flexibility are more important than efficiency. Simplicity and flexibility of your messaging protocol leads to more business partners because it lowers the cost of developing new applications that talk to your messaging protocol. In the past, the major motivation of many companies to introduce an EDI system was because a business partner required it, not because doing so would improve the business process (they also had to subscribe to an expensive VAN connection, install hardware and software designated by the business partner, and so on). Companies that could not afford to develop a customized EDI application could not connect the EDI system to their own business application, so the data was copied among these systems manually.

In contrast to the older technologies such as EDI and SGML, HTTP and XML are *Internet technologies,* technologies that have been cultivated in the Internet culture. It is much easier and less expensive to develop a system based on these technologies than with the older technologies. This is because the practice of publishing source code on the Internet, where skilled programmers can hack on the code, fixing bugs and improving performance, has resulted in a lot of very high-quality software, which has the added advantage of also being free.

Thus there are many more programmers who are familiar with the Internet technologies than with the older ones. This all results in a significantly lower cost to an enterprise to have B2B automation.

Simplicity is most important when programs are developed by independent groups of people such as vendors and those programs need to talk to each other. A complex message format specification means a greater chance of misunderstanding the specification, while a simple format ensures greater opportunity to understand and to communicate effectively.

In the next section, we give a concrete example of HTTP/XML-based messaging using the PowerWarning application described in Chapter 1.

7.3 PowerWarning Application

In this section, we develop the PowerWarning application, described in Chapter 1, as a simple example of HTTP/XML-based messaging. Our application runs on a Web server located at www.powerwarning.com, and our customers will connect to this site using a normal HTML browser. The customer fills in the form specifying the city and the warning conditions and submits it. Our application is responsible for periodically polling the weather information site, www.xweather.com, to fetch the current temperature of the designated city. If the temperature exceeds the warning level for more than the specified number of hours, a warning message is sent to the customer via e-mail or pager. The application is depicted in Figure 7.2.

We assume that the weather information site is XML-enabled, meaning that it accepts an HTTP request and returns an XML document as the reply. Hence, our application and the weather information site perform messaging between themselves.

The system structure of this application is shown in Figure 7.3. This application itself is also a Web application that accepts HTTP requests from browsers, so the front end PowerWarn.java is implemented as a servlet. The user parameters in the form are extracted and stored in a Watcher object, which is registered in a hashtable named userTable. A separate thread implemented as a Scheduler object makes a roll call of these Watcher objects every hour. When a thread is dispatched by the scheduler, a Watcher object makes an HTTP/XML connection to www.xweather.com to look up the current temperature and sends an e-mail warning if necessary.

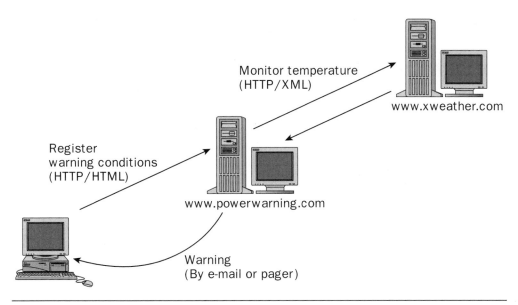

FIGURE 7.2 PowerWarning application

We discuss next the three parts of the PowerWarning application:

1. The `PowerWarn.java` servlet

2. The class `Watcher.java`

3. The class `Scheduler.java`

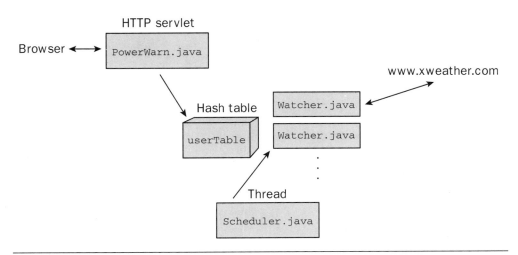

FIGURE 7.3 System structure of the PowerWarning application

TABLE 7.3 HTTP POST Request Parameters

PARAMETER NAME	DESCRIPTION	EXAMPLE
User	E-mail address of the user	User=maruyama@us.ibm.com
State	Two-letter state name	State=NY
City	City name	City=White+Plains
Temperature	Temperature threshold for warning	Temperature=100
Duration	Number of hours the temperature is above the threshold for a warning to be generated	Duration=3

7.3.1 `PowerWarn.java`

`PowerWarn.java` is a servlet that receives an HTTP POST request that has several parameters and registers the request in the user table. We assume that this servlet recognizes the parameters in the POST method listed in Table 7.3.

`PowerWarn.java` extracts the values of these parameters from a POST request, generates a `Watcher` object with the values, and registers the object in the hashtable `userTable`. This is a typical servlet implementation, so the code should be self-explanatory. See Chapter 5 for the details of the servlet API. The class `PowerWarn.java` is shown in Listing 7.1.

Listing 7.1 `PowerWarn.java`: Registers a user for the PowerWarning application

```
import com.ibm.xml.parser.Util;
import java.io.IOException;
import java.io.PrintWriter;
import java.util.Hashtable;
import javax.servlet.ServletConfig;
import javax.servlet.ServletException;
import javax.servlet.http.HttpServlet;
import javax.servlet.http.HttpServletRequest;
import javax.servlet.http.HttpServletResponse;

public class PowerWarn extends HttpServlet {
    static Hashtable userTable;

    public void init(ServletConfig conf) throws ServletException {
        PowerWarn.userTable = new Hashtable();
        Scheduler scheduler = new Scheduler();
        scheduler.start();
    }
```

```java
public void doGet(HttpServletRequest req, HttpServletResponse res)
    throws ServletException, IOException {
    res.setContentType("text/plain");
    PrintWriter writer = res.getWriter();
    writer.print("No support for GET method.\n");
    writer.close();
}


private void parameterError(HttpServletResponse res) throws
IOException {
    res.setContentType("text/plain");
    PrintWriter writer = res.getWriter();
    writer.print("Parameter error.\n");
    writer.close();
}


public void doPost(HttpServletRequest req, HttpServletResponse res)
    throws ServletException, IOException {
                        // Checks the "User" parameter.
    String[] values = req.getParameterValues("User");
    if (values == null || values.length != 1 || values[0].trim().
      length() == 0) {
        this.parameterError(res);
        return;
    }
    String par_user = values[0].trim();
                        // Checks the "State" parameter.
    values = req.getParameterValues("State");
    if (values == null || values.length != 1 || values[0].trim().
      length() == 0) {
        this.parameterError(res);
        return;
    }
    String par_state = values[0].trim();
                        // Check the "City" parameter.
    values = req.getParameterValues("City");
    if (values == null || values.length != 1 || values[0].trim().
      length() == 0) {
        this.parameterError(res);
        return;
    }
    String par_city = values[0].trim();
                        // Checks the "Temperature" parameter.
    values = req.getParameterValues("Temperature");
```

```
if (values == null || values.length != 1 || values[0].trim().
  length() == 0) {
    this.parameterError(res);
    return;
}
int par_temp;
try {
    par_temp = Integer.parseInt(values[0].trim());
} catch (NumberFormatException nfe) {
    this.parameterError(res);
    return;
}

                   // Checks the "Duration" parameter.
values = req.getParameterValues("Duration");
if (values == null || values.length != 1 || values[0].trim().
  length() == 0) {
    this.parameterError(res);
    return;
}
int par_duration;
try {
    par_duration = Integer.parseInt(values[0].trim());
} catch (NumberFormatException nfe) {
    this.parameterError(res);
    return;
}


                   // Creates a Watcher, and records it.
Watcher watcher = new Watcher
  (par_user, par_state, par_city, par_temp, par_duration);
PowerWarn.userTable.put(par_user, watcher);


                   // Outputs recorded values for users.
res.setContentType("text/html");
PrintWriter writer = res.getWriter();
writer.print("<HTML><HEAD><TITLE>Accepted</TITLE></HEAD>\n");
writer.print("<BODY><H1>Accepted your request</H1>\n");
writer.print("<TABLE border=\"1\">\n");
writer.print("<TR><TH>User</TH><TD>"+Util.backReference
  (par_user, "&<")+"</TD></TR>\n"); // @XML4J
writer.print("<TR><TH>State</TH><TD>"+Util.backReference
  (par_state, "&<")+"</TD></TR>\n");
writer.print("<TR><TH>City</TH><TD>"+Util.backReference
  (par_city, "&<")+"</TD></TR>\n");
```

```
writer.print("<TR><TH>Temperature</TH><TD>
  "+par_temp+"</TD></TR>\n");
writer.print("<TR><TH>Duration</TH><TD>
  "+par_duration+"</TD></TR>\n");
writer.print("</TABLE>\n</BODY>\n</HTML>\n");
writer.close();
  }
}
```

7.3.2 `Watcher.java`

A `Watcher` object keeps information pertinent to a particular user. This includes the parameters specified by the user, as well as the current status of how many hours have passed with the temperature above the threshold. The `run()` method is called by the `Scheduler` object each hour. This method connects to the weather reporting site, parses the returned XML, and extracts the current temperature. If the preset warning condition is met, `warning()` is called. This method sends a warning message, for example, by executing an external `sendmail` program to send a canned warning e-mail message to the user.

Following is a sample HTTP interaction between `Watcher` and the weather reporting site.

```
GET /weather?city=White+Plains&state=NY HTTP/1.0
Accept: */*

HTTP/1.1 200 OK
Content-Type: text/xml
Content-Length: 132
Last-Modified: Sat, 25 Jul 1998 14:09:14 GMT

<?xml version="1.0"?>
<!DOCTYPE WeatherReport SYSTEM
        "http://www.xweather.com/WeatherReport.dtd">
<WeatherReport>
    <City>White Plains</City>
    <State>NY</State>
    <Date>Sat Jul 25 1998</Date>
    <Time>11 AM EDT</Time>
    <CurrTemp Unit="Farenheit">70</CurrTemp>
    <High Unit="Farenheit">82</High>
    <Low Unit="Farenheit">62</Low>
</WeatherReport>
```

We are interested in only the `CurrTemp` element in the reply, so we do not need to build a whole DOM tree. Thus instead of the DOM API we use the SAX API to extract the temperature value. Recall from Section 2.5 that the `Parser` interface in the `org.xml.sax` package differs from the `Parser` in `com.ibm.xml.parser`. Its `parse()` method can take a URL as a parameter and access a remote site using the GET method of the HTTP protocol. Thus the details of HTTP are completely hidden in the SAX interface.

The listing for `Watcher.java` is in Listing 7.2.

Listing 7.2 `Watcher.java`: User's agent to watch the power warning condition

```java
import org.xml.sax.AttributeList;
import org.xml.sax.DocumentHandler;
import org.xml.sax.Locator;
import org.xml.sax.Parser;
import org.xml.sax.SAXException;
import org.xml.sax.helpers.ParserFactory;
import java.io.IOException;
import java.net.URLEncoder;
import java.net.URL;
import java.net.MalformedURLException;

/**
 * A Watcher object represents a subscriber.
 * It also implements the listener of SAX events (DocumentHandler).
 */
public class Watcher implements Runnable, DocumentHandler {
    String user;
    String state;
    String city;
    int temp;
    int duration;
    int overTemp;

    /**
     * The constructor initializes the parameters.
     */
    public Watcher(String user, String state, String city, int temp,
    int duration) {
        super();
        this.user = user;
        this.state = state;
        this.city = city;
        this.temp = temp;
```

```
        this.duration = duration;
        this.overTemp = 0;
    }


    /**
     * This method is called each hour.
     * 1. Create a URL for the weather information site.
     * 2. Call SAX to get the URL, and parse the results with the SAX
     *    API.
     * 3. Check the temperature, and send a warning.
     */
    public void run() {
                        // 1. Creates a URL for weather information.
                        //    "http://www.xweather.com/weather?city=
                        // ...&state=.."
        String weatheruri = "http://www.xweather.com/weather?city="
            +URLEncoder.encode(this.city)
            +"&amp;state="+URLEncoder.encode(this.state);

                        // 2. Calls the parser with a SAX event
                        //    handler.
        try {
            Parser parser = ParserFactory.makeParser("com.ibm.xml.
              parser.SAXDriver");
            parser.setDocumentHandler(this);  // Declares self as the
                                              // SAX event handler.
            parser.parse(weatheruri);
        } catch (Exception e) {
            e.printStackTrace();
            systemError();
            return;
        }
                        // 3. Checks the current temperature, and
                        //    send a warning.
        if (this.currentTemp == null) {
            System.err.println("currentTemp==null");
            systemError();
            return;
        }
        int currentTempNumber;
        try {
            currentTempNumber = Integer.parseInt(this.currentTemp.
              trim());
        } catch (NumberFormatException nfe) {
            nfe.printStackTrace();
```

```
            systemError();
            return;
        }
        if (currentTempNumber > this.temp) {
            this.overTemp ++;
            if (this.overTemp >= this.duration) {
                warning();
            }
        } else {
            this.overTemp = 0;
        }
}


/**
 * Send a warning to the subscriber (dummy).
 */
public void warning() {
    System.out.println("Warning to "+this.user+
                       ": Temperature of "+this.city+
                       ", "+this.state+
                       " exceeded "+this.temp+
                       " degrees for "+this.overTemp+
                       " hours.");
    // Sends an e-mail to this.user.
}

/**
 * Send an error message to the system administrator (dummy).
 */
public void systemError() {
    // Sends an e-mail to the system manager.
}



StringBuffer buffer;
String currentTemp;

/***************************************************************
 * The following methods are SAX callback routines. Some of them
   are empty.
  ***************************************************************/
public void setDocumentLocator(Locator locator) {
}
```

```
/**
 * New parsing is started.
 */
public void startDocument() throws SAXException {
    this.currentTemp = null;
}


public void endDocument() throws SAXException {
}


/**
 * Processing a new element is started. If the tag is "CurrTemp",
 *      prepare a buffer to keep the content.
 */
public void startElement(String name, AttributeList atts) throws
SAXException {
    if (name.equals("CurrTemp")) {
        this.buffer = new StringBuffer();
    }
}


/**
 * An element is just closed.  If the element is "CurrTemp",
 *      copy the content to this.currTemp.
 */
public void endElement(String name) throws SAXException {
    if (name.equals("CurrTemp")) {
        this.currentTemp = this.buffer.toString();
        this.buffer = null;
    }
}


/**
 * Accumulate characters if the buffer has been allocated.
 */
public void characters(char ch[], int start, int length) throws
SAXException {
    if (this.buffer != null)
        this.buffer.append(ch, start, length);
}


public void ignorableWhitespace(char ch[], int start, int length)
throws SAXException {
}
```

```
        public void processingInstruction(String target, String data)
        throws SAXException {
        }
    }
```

7.3.3 `Scheduler.java`

The only remaining class is `Scheduler.java`, shown in Listing 7.3. This simple class wakes up every hour and roll calls the `Watcher` objects.

Listing 7.3 `Scheduler.java`: Triggers the `Watcher` objects each hour

```java
import java.util.Enumeration;

/**
 * Trigger all of the Watchers every hour.
 * Runs in a separate thread.
 */
public class Scheduler extends Thread {

    public Scheduler() {
        super();
    }

    public void run() {
        while (true) {
                    // Calls start() methods of Watcher instances.
            Enumeration en = PowerWarn.userTable.elements();
            while (en.hasMoreElements()) {
                Watcher wa = (Watcher)en.nextElement();
                new Thread(wa).start();
            }

            try {
                Thread.sleep(1000*3600); // 1 hour
            } catch (InterruptedException ie) {
                    // Ignore.
            }
        }
    }
}
```

Here, we have developed a simple application that communicates with another application using HTTP as the transport and XML as the message format. You might have noticed that many of the program lines are for extracting and checking user parameters, and the message handling part of the program is surprisingly small, thanks to the high-level SAX API.

7.4 Designing XML Messages

In this section, we discuss how to design a message format based on XML that is specific to B2B messaging. A message is generated at one application, transmitted, and then consumed by another application. These applications are operated by different departments or different companies, so once the message format is fixed, modifying it is not easy. So, it is very important to design the message format carefully from the beginning.[1]

This section considers DTD design from the following points of view:

- Extensibility

- Compatibility

- Messages consisting of multiple resources

- How to represent non-tree-structured data

- Validation of messages

- Character encoding

7.4.1 Extensibility

There is no formal way to describe compatibility between DTDs. Thus it is very difficult to modify a DTD once it is fixed and being used in production systems. A good DTD should be usable for a long time without revisions; a poorly designed DTD might require frequent changes in the participating applications. A viable approach to designing a DTD is to reuse one already known to be good. Thus a good reusable DTD must be readable and maintainable.

---

[1]General tips concerning DTD design for SGML documents also apply to DTDs for XML. The following books contain useful information in this regard.
- Maler, Eve and Jeanne El Andaloussi, *Developing SGML DTDs—From Text to Model to Markup*, Prentice Hall: Upper Saddle River, N.J., 1996. ISBN 0-13-309881-8
- Megginson, David, *Structuring XML Documents*, Prentice Hall: Upper Saddle River, N.J., 1998. ISBN 0-13-642299-3

Improving Readability and Maintainability by Using Entities

One technique to make a DTD readable and maintainable is to use entities wisely. Consider the following order form DTD, `order-orig.dtd`.

```
<!ELEMENT order        (customer, shop, itemlist+)>
<!ATTLIST order        status CDATA #REQUIRED>
<!ELEMENT customer     (name, address)>
<!ELEMENT shop         (name, address)>
<!ELEMENT itemlist     (item)+>
<!ELEMENT item         (name, author*, publisher?, quantity)>
<!ELEMENT name         (#PCDATA)>
<!ELEMENT author       (#PCDATA)>
<!ELEMENT address      (#PCDATA)>
<!ELEMENT publisher    (#PCDATA)>
<!ELEMENT quantity     (#PCDATA)>
```

Customers and shops are both business partners, so they share the same content model. Instead of defining their content models independently, you can use an *entity* to represent the common content model, as in the following revised DTD, `order.dtd`.

```
<!ENTITY  % partner    "name, address">
<!ELEMENT order        (customer, shop, itemlist)>
<!ATTLIST order        status CDATA #REQUIRED>
<!ELEMENT customer     (%partner;)>
<!ELEMENT shop         (%partner;)>
<!ELEMENT itemlist     (item)+>
<!ELEMENT item         (name, author*, publisher?, quantity)>
<!ELEMENT name         (#PCDATA)>
<!ELEMENT address      (#PCDATA)>
<!ELEMENT author       (#PCDATA)>
<!ELEMENT publisher    (#PCDATA)>
<!ELEMENT quantity     (#PCDATA)>
```

Say you need to add a `zipcode` element to the business partner data. Instead of modifying the two declarations of `customer` and `shop`, you can modify the first line as follows:

```
<!ENTITY % partner "name, address, zipcode">
```

This technique is particularly useful when the DTD is large (for example, the DTD for HTML 4.0 has more than 1,000 lines). Be warned, however, that you need to carefully plan the use of entities because poor use of them might destroy the readability.

7.4.2 Compatibility

Even if a DTD is readable and maintainable, you must be careful when updating a DTD. This is because changes to the DTD might require changes in the applications using the DTD. What are the conditions that allow updates of a DTD while preserving the compatibility of the applications? We discuss these next.

Two Types of Compatibility of a Modified DTD

Suppose you own an order processing system for company A and do business with companies X, Y, and Z using XML on the Internet, as depicted in Figure 7.4. You have been using `order.dtd` so far, but recently company X came to you and proposed using a new DTD. But will a change impact your other business partners, companies Y and Z? This will depend on the nature of the change and whether you are the originator of a message using the DTD (case (a) in the figure) or the receiver of such a message (case (b)).

We consider the following three types of modification on a DTD:

- Specialization

- Generalization

- Other

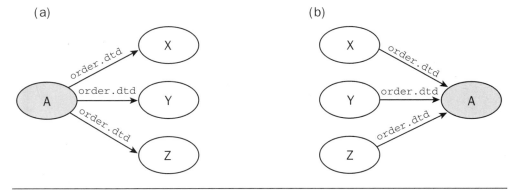

FIGURE 7.4 XML messaging between companies A, X, Y, and Z

Specialization

Specialization means to restrict the content model by allowing fewer choices. Here are some examples.

- Fix the number of repeated elements, for example:

```
<!ELEMENT itemlist    (item)+>
<!ELEMENT itemlist    (item,item)>
```

- Make an optional element a required one, for example:

```
<!ELEMENT item        (name, author*, publisher?, quantity)>
<!ELEMENT item        (name, author*, publisher, quantity)>
```

- Fix the value of an attribute, for example:

```
<!ATTLIST order       status CDATA "closed">
<!ATTLIST order       status CDATA #FIXED "closed">
```

Combining any of these specializing modifications results in a specialized DTD. There is an important property about this operation: *Valid messages with the specialized DTD are always valid with the original DTD.*

Thus, in the case of Figure 7.4(a), companies Y and Z do not need to modify their applications if you and company X decide to use a specialized version of `order.dtd`. On the other hand, in the case of Figure 7.4(b), you must negotiate with companies Y and Z to use the specialized DTD before modifying your own application.

Generalization

Generalization is the reverse of specialization. Here are some examples.

- Loosen the condition on the number of elements allowed, for example:

```
<!ELEMENT order       (customer, shop, itemlist)>
<!ELEMENT order       (customer, shop+, itemlist)>
```

- Add a new optional element, for example:

```
<!ELEMENT item        (name, author*, quantity)>
<!ELEMENT item        (name, author*, quantity, note?)>
```

- Make an attribute optional, for example:

```
<!ATTLIST order       status CDATA #REQUIRED>
<!ATTLIST order       status CDATA #IMPLIED>
```

- Introduce a new optional attribute, for example:

```
                   none
    <!ATTLIST order       id CDATA #IMPLIED>
```

Any combination of these modifications results in a generalized DTD. *Any message valid with the original DTD is valid with the generalized DTD.* Thus, if you are on the receiving side of the message, as in Figure 7.4(b), you do not need to negotiate with companies Y and Z. You just tell them that you are now capable of accepting messages with the generalized DTD. They do not need to modify their existing applications. However, in the case of Figure 7.4(a), companies Y and Z will need to modify their applications to allow generalized messages.

Other Modifications

Some modifications are neither generalized nor specialized. Here are two examples.

- Change element names.

- Delete a mandatory element from a content model.

With these modifications, all parties concerned should first agree on the new DTD before it is deployed.

A technique to minimize DTD changes is to assign generic names as element names, such as DIV, and use attribute values to indicate the *role* of the element. For example, instead of using the element shop, use instead `<DIV role="shop"> ... </DIV>`. The advantage is that introducing a new role does not involve a change in the DTD, so DTD compatibility is not an issue. Note, however, that even though the DTD stays the same, application programs using it still must be modified to process the new role. Further, using generic element names means a validating XML processor will do less validity checking—it will even go so far as to accept nonsense tags such as `<DIV role="hello"> ... </DIV>`. Recall that one of the values of using a validating processor is that it can perform syntax checking based on the DTD. If the DTD is too general so that it passes virtually anything, the application programs using it will need to be responsible for checking whether the input is meaningful. So we suggest you avoid using this technique unless there are compelling reasons to use it.

7.4.3 Working with Messages Consisting of Multiple Resources

A message often consists of multiple resources, such as images, HTML pages, other XML documents, and binary data. How do you send such compound messages? There are two general strategies:

- Put everything in a single large XML document.

- Separate metacontent from resources.

We discuss these in the following two subsections.

Use a Single XML Message

Using the strategy of putting everything in a single XML message, you put everything, including binary data, into a single XML document. In this way, the issue of maintaining the consistency and integrity of the constituent parts does not exist.

There is no official standard for embedding binary data in an XML document. One popular method is to use **Base64 encoding**.

> **NOTE:** Base64 encoding is one method for representing binary data with printable characters. It uses 64 printable characters consisting of alphabets (a–z, A–Z), digits (0–9), and the symbols + and /. With these 64 characters, you represent 3 binary bytes as a four-character string. If the data length is not exactly a multiple of 3, the end of the encoded data is padded with equal signs (=). This is a simple and efficient coding method and is widely used, for example in mail, Web pages, and protocols such as HTTP.

You may want to specify the encoding algorithm in an attribute of the element. The biggest drawback of this method is possible inefficiency if the amount of binary data is very large. However, the ease of implementing a single document that contains everything makes this strategy workable when the message is not too complex or too big.

Separate Metacontent and Resources

Using the strategy of separating metacontent and resources, you have a message represented as a combination XML document (metacontent) and set of resources. The XML metacontent maintains links to the resources. This strategy is further categorized into two substrategies depending on the form of transmission:

- Package the metacontent and all of the resources as a single unit and transmit it.

- Send the metacontent only. The recipient then fetches the resources as needed.

With the first substrategy, to send all resources at once you need a separate "container" format to package the resources, such as ZIP or jar (Java Archive). Since everything is in the package, such problems as missing parts and inconsistency between the versions of the parts do not exist. However, some recipients might not be interested in some of the resources, such as JPEG images, which can be as big as several hundred kilobytes. In this case, communication bandwidth to send the whole package will be wasted.

With the second substrategy, once the metacontent is received only the necessary resources are fetched, so bandwidth is not wasted sending unwanted resources. However, two disadvantages are that the target resource might not be available or might have been modified since the original message was created. The latter problem might be solved by using a message digest to refer to the resource. (We discuss a message digest definition for XML documents later in this chapter.)

7.4.4 Representing Non-Tree-Structured Data

Basically, XML is for representing tree-structured data. However, its flexibility allows it also to be used to represent other data structures. For example, a table can be represented in XML as follows.

```
<row><col1/><col2/>...<coln/></row>
<row><col1/><col2/>...<coln/></row>
<row><col1/><col2/>...<coln/></row>
```

Note that if this table is parsed and internally represented as a DOM tree, iterating on columns of the same row is much faster than iterating on rows of the same column. Thus if you know the standard access pattern in your application, you might need to consider this method when designing the DTD.

7.4.5 Validating Messages

Messaging on the Internet using HTTP means that anybody can connect to your Web site using a Web browser, or even Telnet. To avoid bad effects on your system, your messaging application must thoroughly check the validity of all messages and reject any meaningless ones. Thus when you are messaging using XML, every message received should be validated by a validating XML processor with proper DOCTYPE declarations in the input XML documents.

XML is an extremely flexible format, so even if your application seems to be satisfied with the content of an incoming message, the message could cause problems. For example, suppose your business is to manufacture lawn mowers. You receive an order from a customer, enclosed in the following message.

```
<?xml version="1.0"?>
<!DOCTYPE order SYSTEM "order.dtd">
<order status="final">
    <customer>
        <name>Hiroshi Maruyama</name>
        <address>1623-14, Shimotsuruma, Yamato-shi, Kanagawa Japan
        </address>
    </customer>
    <item>
        <description>Lawn mower model 375</description>
        <part_no>375-74722X</part_no>
        <quantity>1000</quantity>
    </item>
    <DeliveryCondition>This order is not effective unless the
entire volume is delivered by Oct. 10, 1998</DeliveryCondition>
</order>
```

In this message, your customer has taken advantage of the flexibility of XML syntax by adding an extra element, `<DeliveryCondition>` (it and its contents are shown in bold in the message). That is, the order is contingent on the entire order's being delivered by October 10, 1998, a requirement your company cannot meet. Your automated order processing system checks the values of the elements such as "customer" and "item" and finds no problems. So it happily sends the data to the backend production planning system—which would then start production for 1,000 lawn mowers that cannot be delivered by October 10. With an appropriate DTD and a validating processor that returns an error whenever the message cannot be validated, you can avoid this kind of problem.

However, even if the XML processor decided that a message was valid, this would mean nothing to your application if it has no knowledge of the specified DTD. So you need to instruct the XML processor to accept only a fixed set of DTDs. If the DOCTYPE declaration in an incoming message contains something unknown, the message must be rejected at once because further processing makes no sense.[2]

7.4.6 Encoding Characters

Another important issue is agreement on the set of character encodings allowed in messages. Since different companies might have different XML processors running on different platforms, they might also have different sets of supported character encodings.

The XML 1.0 Recommendation stipulates that every conforming XML processor must support both UTF-8 and UTF-16. Thus your message should be encoded in either of the two. Since UTF-8 is compatible with USASCII for the ASCII characters, it is a good choice for messages used mainly in the United States. If the document contains a lot of double-byte characters, UTF-16 might be more efficient. Either way, your message is guaranteed to be accepted by any XML processor.

7.5 Secure Message Exchange with SSL

Security is the largest issue in deploying B2B messaging over the Internet. If your purchase order is monitored, altered, or delivered to a wrong person, you cannot build trusted relationships with your business partners. Historically, Internet technology has been weak in terms of security because in its early days, the Internet was used by a small group of cooperating, trusted people.

In the physical layer, Ethernet packets are visible to anyone who has a locally attached machine because Ethernet is essentially a broadcast media. In the

---

[2] With the current version of XML for Java, one way to achieve this is to subclass `TXDocument` and override `createDTD()` so that it checks the URL passed to this method and throws an exception if the URL is not one of the authorized ones.

network and transport layers, it is easy to modify the packet headers to disguise a sender who is at a different address. And in the application layer, the most often-used protocols such as Telnet and FTP use plain text user ids and passwords for user authentication. Once you log on to your host from the Internet by using Telnet, your password is no longer secret. The same is true for the simple authentication of HTTP. Unless you know that the Web site requesting a password uses SSL for message encryption, it is unwise to type in your password on a Web page because it will travel through the Internet in plain text.

7.5.1 Overview of Current Security Options

The recent development of cryptography technologies is changing this situation. If properly used, these technologies can make your Internet communication secure at any level. Cryptographic protocols can be applied either on the message transport or message format. Several widely accepted security standards to secure communication on the Internet are available, including the following.

- IPSec

  IPSec (RFC 2401-2412, published by the IETF November, 1998), short for IP Security, provides security at the IP level. It is widely used for virtual private networks (VPNs), which connect two intranets by establishing a secure tunnel between firewalls. Users can reach a business partner's intranet as if it is a part of their own.

- Secure Sockets Layer

  SSL is defined by Netscape Communications for securing HTTP connections. Since it implemented SSL in its browser, SSL has become a de facto standard for secure HTTP connection. Today, virtually all browsers and HTTP servers support SSL. SSL is a secure protocol in the session layer, so it can provide end-to-end security even if there are application gateways such as a proxy in between. The current version is SSL v3. The IETF is working on standardizing SSL as the Transport Layer Security (TLS). SSL uses X.509 certificates for authentication. We discuss X.509 certificates later in the chapter.

- S/MIME (PKCS#7)

  Public Key Cryptography Standard (PKCS) is a series of standards concerning security-related data formats, primarily based on public-key cryptography, that are being assembled by RSA Data Security and others. PKCS#7 applies to encryption envelopes and digital signatures and is a basis of S/MIME (Secure / Multipurpose Internet Mail Exchange). S/MIME is gaining popularity as a secure mail standard because Netscape and Microsoft support it in their popular mail products. S/MIME uses X.509 certificates for authentication. We discuss X.509 certificates later in the chapter.

- Pretty Good Privacy (PGP)

  Pretty Good Privacy (PGP) is the most widely used program to secure e-mail over the Internet. Now a de facto standard for e-mail security, it also can be used to send encrypted *digital signatures,* which let receivers verify the senders' identities and be assured that messages were not changed en route. It further can be used to encrypt stored files so that they are unreadable by other users or intruders.

IPSec and SSL provide transport-level security, while S/MIME and PGP provide security for message formats. In this section, we focus on SSL.

7.5.2 Extent of SSL Security

Generally speaking, there are four aspects of secure messaging.

- Confidentiality. Message contents cannot be monitored or copied by an unauthorized entity.

- Integrity. Message contents cannot be altered by an unauthorized entity.

- Authentication. No one can disguise oneself as the legitimate communication party.

- Nonrepudiatability. The message sender cannot deny the fact of sending a message and the contents of the message.

SSL provides the first three protections: confidentiality, integrity, and authentication. Confidentiality is achieved by using a symmetric cryptosystem, such as

- DES (Data Encryption Standard, which has a 56-bit key) and

- RC-4, or Ron's Code, which was developed by the famous cryptographer Ron Rivest. Its key length is variable but normally 40–128 bits.

Integrity is guaranteed by using message authentication code (MAC) based on a secure hash function such as MD5 (Message Digest 5) and SHA 1 (Secure Hash Algorithm 1).

Client authentication is optional in an SSL connection, but server authentication is mandatory. In client authentication, the focus is on identifying the client. In server authentication, the focus is on identifying the server—usually the client knows the server's identity but the server does not know the client's. Client authentication, in the form of digital certificates, is not yet very popular, so most SSL Web sites use server authentication only. We cover both types in more detail in the next several subsections.

Server Authentication

Figure 7.5 depicts how SSL works for server authentication. To use SSL, a Web site must acquire a server's **digital certificate** from a **Certificate Authority** (CA), a third-party organization that issues digital certificates. A digital certificate guarantees that the public key contained in it belongs to its owner so that the receiver of a digitally signed message can verify the identity of the signer. The digital certificate format used in SSL is *X.509*, defined by the ITU-T (International Telecommunications Union-Telecommunication Standardization Sector).

Netscape, in its earlier version of its Navigator browser, used Verisign, Inc.'s certificate. Verisign is the most popular CA in terms of Web site certification. To obtain a server certificate from Verisign, you follow these steps:

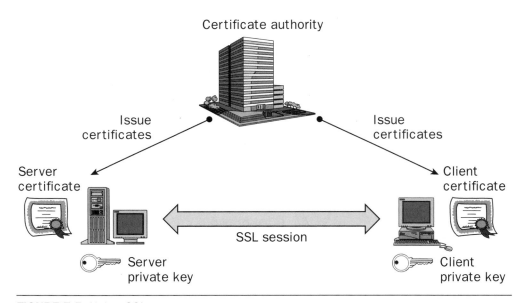

FIGURE 7.5 Using SSL

1. Generate a private key / public key pair in the server's key management software.

2. Send the public key along with the identity information of the server owner (or operator) to Verisign. You might be required to send an official document verifying this identity.

3. Once Verisign is satisfied with the requester's identity and the fact that the key was in fact generated by the requester, it creates a certificate that binds the requester's distinguished name (DN) to the public key by signing the certificate. The signed certificate is sent back to the requester.

4. The server administrator installs the certificate in the server software.

When a client connects to a server using SSL, the client and server first look for the strongest common cryptographic algorithm and agree on it. Then they exchange a symmetric key that is used in the encryption of the message body. The key exchange is done by using public-key cryptography as follows.

1. The server sends its X.509 certificate containing the server's public key.

2. The client generates a 48-byte random number, a *premaster secret,* and encrypts the number using the server's public key. It then sends the encrypted premaster secret to the server.

3. The server decrypts the encrypted premaster secret using its private key.

4. The server and the client, sharing the same premaster secret, which cannot be obtained by anybody else, generate symmetric keys for message encryption from the premaster secret and start communicating using the generated key.

Since only the server that owns the proper private key can decrypt the encrypted premaster secret (and thus generate the proper symmetric key), the client knows, by decrypting the first encrypted message from the server, that it is in fact talking to the correct server.

Client Authentication

Client authentication is particularly helpful in a retail environment, when selling goods or services to customers. For example, with our PowerWarning application, we provide a service to customers, whom we charge for the service, so we must be able to identify our customers. Two client authentication methods are popularly used with HTTP:

1. HTTP basic authentication combined with SSL without client authentication

2. SSL certificate-based client authentication

We discuss both of these in the following two subsections.

HTTP Basic Authentication with SSL

Basic authentication is a part of the HTTP protocol specification and is based on user ids and passwords. Because both are sent without encryption (they are Base64-encoded but are not encrypted), this is not a secure method of authentication. So, it must be combined with SSL, which provides confidentiality.

When basic authentication with SSL occurs, the following takes place:

1. The client connects to the Web site using a URL, for example `https://www.powerwarning.com`, in the case of our PowerWarning application. Note, the protocol used is not http but rather *https,* which as we mentioned earlier in the book, refers to HTTP over SSL.

2. When the SSL connection is established, the client knows the server's identity with confidence because of the server's X.509 certificate. However, the server does not know the client's identity, so it replies with a return code, *401,* thereby requesting that the user authenticate itself.

3. The client sends its Base64-encoded user id and password in the HTTP header.

Now, all of the data is going through the SSL connection, so it cannot be stolen during transmission. Also, no malicious server can successfully pretend to be the original Web server, in an attempt to steal the user's password.

SSL Certificate-Based Client Authentication

Using SSL client authentication requires that a client digital certificate be prepared to prove a client's identity. A client requesting a certificate must generate a public key/private key pair in his or her browser. The private key is kept secret in the browser and is protected by a **passphrase**, a password-like character string of arbitrary length. Then, in the same process for obtaining a server's certificate, the public key part of the key pair is sent to a CA and the certificate is issued.

Obtaining client digital certificates can be done in any of the following ways.

1. Some CAs issue X.509-based client certificates for general use. This is the easiest way to obtain a client certificate. For example, Verisign issues them for

e-mail and software signing purposes and even provides free, 60-day trial certificates for individual users called *Class 1*. Anyone who has access to an Internet e-mail address can obtain a Verisign Class 1 certificate. When using this certificate, however, you must be sure that the level of security it provides is sufficient to meet your needs. A Class 1 certificate guarantees that the e-mail address of the certificate holder is unique. Thus if your security requirement is simply to identify the certificate holder by e-mail address, it might be enough. But it does not guarantee anything about the true identity of the certificate holder. Although this level of security might be enough security for casual e-mail exchange, it certainly is not for serious e-Business users. For them, Verisign offers Class 2 and Class 3 certificates, for a price. For more information, check out Verisign's Web site at `http://digitalid.verisign.com/`.

2. Outsource CA operations to outside vendors (such as Verisign). Operating a CA properly is not easy. It requires a highly secure hardware and software installation that is professionally maintained, as well as security policies and auditing rules, among other requirements. It also is not cheap. Therefore it is reasonable to outsource the CA operation.

3. *Operate one's own CA.*

   It is relatively easy to set up your own Certificate Authority, although as just discussed *operating* one is a different matter. This can be done by using any of the few packaged CA software products available, such as Netscape Certification Server and Entrust/PKI. This might be a good choice for trial purposes because you, for example, can obtain experience issuing and revoking certificates and can apply certificate-based authentication. You also possibly can assess the security risk of your system. It also is a possible choice if your organization is serious about setting up its own public-key infrastructure that will be used across many different applications.

In any case, it is very important that you document your certification policy that dictates the condition of issuing and revoking the certificates.

Comparison of HTTP Basic Authentication with SSL and SSL Certificate-Based Authentication

The advantage of using X.509-based client authentication over the HTTP basic authentication with SSL is that with the former, it is possible to separate the application and the user administration. That is, the application does not need to maintain a user id/password database. It needs only to verify that the certificate presented by the client is indeed signed by a trusted CA.

Consider the following situation. Suppose our power warning service cannot attract enough clients by itself, so we decide to partner with nine other companies that provide similar services on the Internet. As a group of service providers, we offer a package deal to our common customers. A customer pays a fixed monthly fee to a designated billing company for accessing ten different services operated by the ten independent companies.

In this case, HTTP basic authentication with SSL has some drawbacks.

- Each application must maintain its own copy of the user id/password database. This entails associated security risks.

- The billing company must notify each company of the addition and deletion of new customers and changes to customers' payment status. In addition, this communication must be secure.

- The customer must remember ten different passwords (if the same password is used, a dishonest employee of, for example, company A can use your password to access, for example, company B).

By contrast, when X.509-based authentication is used applications do not need to do user administration. Figure 7.6 shows that the user presents its certificate

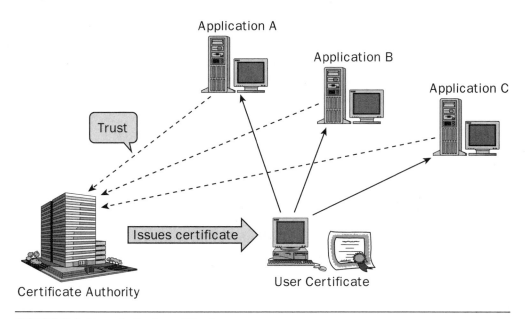

FIGURE 7.6 Use of client certificates

to companies A, B, and C. Since this certificate is issued by the CA, the companies can trust that the user is in fact a legitimate user. Thus they are freed from the burden of the complex and possibly human-intensive task of registering and charging the users.

7.5.3 Implementing SSL-Based Web Applications

Because SSL is supported by most Web browsers and Web servers, the basic mechanisms for making a Web application SSL-enabled are already in place.

Implementing on the Server Side

One advantage of using Java Web Server or other Web servers with SSL support is that the same application can be used for both HTTP (port 80) and HTTPS (port 443) connections. To enable SSL, you need only to reconfigure your Web server. This reconfiguration process includes obtaining and installing a server certificate as described previously. In addition, you need either

- to configure access control based on basic authentication, as in HTTP with SSL, or

- to install the trusted CA's certificate that is used for verifying client certificates, as in X.509-based authentication.

With X.509-based client authentication, the application program can check the contents of the client certificate. Java Web Server 1.1 comes with a sample servlet, SnoopServlet, that shows the contents of the client certificate if it is connected using SSL with client authentication. The portion of the sample code that accesses the client certificate is shown next.

```
javax.security.certX509Certificate certChain [] =
    (javax.security.cert.X509Certificate[])
        req.getAttribute ("javax.net.ssl.peer_certificates");
```

getAttribute("javax.net.ssl.peer_certificates")[3] returns an array of certificates. This is because the client normally sends a chain of certificates, starting with its own client certificate and followed by its signer's (CA's) certificate, and so on, until the chain reaches the trusted root CA.

---

[3] This API has not been standardized, so it might change in the future.

Implementing on the Client Side

If the client is a browser, no additional programming is necessary because popular browsers such as Navigator and IE support SSL. If SSL client authentication is to be used, the client certificate must be installed in the browser. Although no programming is involved, you likely will need to provide very good end-user education and support because average users are not familiar with the notion of public key infrastructure.

By contrast, if the client is an application program, you need to ensure you use a JVM that has HTTPS support, otherwise you cannot use HTTPS. JDK 1.1.6 does not support HTTPS. So if your application is running on the server side, you need to use one of the commercially available SSL implementations in Java. However, the easiest solution is to run your application as an applet in a browser, since in a browser JVM the `URLConnection` class supports HTTPS as a protocol. So, for example, to make an SSL connection, instead of calling

```
URLConnection uc = new URLConnection (new URL("http://www.abc.com/"));
```

you can call

```
URLConnection uc = new URLConnection(new URL("http://www.abc.com/"));
```

The authentication process might require user interaction, to provide either a user id and a password in the case of the basic authentication or a passphrase to enable the private key in the case of X.509-based authentication. In either case, before calling `connect()` you need to call

```
uc.setAllowUserInteraction(true);
```

to allow user interaction.

Since SSL-enabled Web pages are popular these days, firewalls of corporations usually allow outbound HTTPS (port 443) connections in addition to HTTP (80) connections. This means that your application can have an end-to-end secure connection to an external HTTPS server, with nobody in between being able to read the messages. Compared to VPN, in which encryption is done only *between* firewalls, SSL's end-to-end encryption is more secure against insider attacks. It is said that in the United States, more than 50 percent of network crimes are committed from inside a firewall. Given this fact, the end-to-end security achieved by SSL has a large value.

7.6 Hash and Digital Signatures of XML Documents

In the previous section, we discussed how SSL can satisfy three of the four security requirements: confidentiality, integrity, and authentication. What about the last of the four, non-repudiatability? Suppose that you receive a purchase order for a $2,000 PC from company X. This order came via an SSL connection with client authentication, and the client X.509 certificate verified flawlessly according to your trusted CA. Satisfied, you process the order and ship the PC. But you do not receive payment. What can you do? Even if you kept all of the communication logs, including the X.509 certificate itself, you cannot prove that you actually received the order from company X because you cannot deny the possibility that you forged the log.

Here is where digital signatures play a key role. A digitally signed order form can be used as undeniable evidence of the order because only the person who has the private key can create the signature bit string (normally 512 to 2,048 bits). This technology is mature enough that some governments such as those of Singapore and the state of Utah in the United States have passed legislation that gives digitally signed business contracts the same legal standing as contracts signed by humans.

There are several standard digital signature formats. The most widely used is PKCS#7, whose syntax is based on ASN.1. It takes a binary bit string as the data to be signed. The type of the data is irrelevant as far as the signature's validity is concerned. Any signature algorithm is expensive to apply directly to a large amount of data, so first a *hash* (or *digest*) value (typically 128 bits or 160 bits) is calculated for all of the data and then the hash value is signed. Even a single bit change in the bit string always results in a completely different hash value, so any modification of the data invalidates the signature.

7.6.1 Digitally Signing XML Documents

To digitally sign an XML document, you first must calculate the hash value of the document. It is possible to take an XML document as a character string (and thus a bit string) and compute its hash value. The problem with this approach is that logically the same XML document can be represented in many different ways because of XML's flexibility regarding character encoding, whitespace handling, and so on. If a purchase order signed by one company is processed through several applications equipped with different implementations of XML processor, the surface string might be changed during the process without the logical content being changed, thereby resulting in an invalid signature.

The surface string can vary without changing the logical content in any of several ways, including the following.

- Character encoding

  The character set in an XML document is defined as ISO/IEC 10646 in the XML 1.0 Recommendation. The Recommendation allows considerable freedom in terms of character encoding. Thus the same document can be represented in different ways depending on the character encoding used, for example, ISO 8859-1, UTF-16, UTF-8, ASCII, or Shift-JIS.

- Handling of whitespaces

  The number of whitespaces between attributes is insignificant in XML. XML processors are not required to preserve the number of spaces. Thus

  ```
  <order id="C763" date="1998-11-17">
  ```

  and

  ```
  <order id="C763"    date="1998-11-17">
  ```

  are treated as exactly the same. Also, #x0D and #x0A and #x0D-#x0A are converted into a single newline character (#x0A).

- Default values of attributes

  Attributes declared as fixed may be optionally present. For example, if the DTD declares the `status` attribute of the `order` element as

  ```
  <!ATTLIST order status CDATA #FIXED "closed">
  ```

  then `<order status="closed"/>` and `<order/>` are equivalent. Different XML processors might generate different surface strings. The same applies to attributes with default values.

- Empty elements

  An empty element may be expressed by using either an empty tag or a pair of start and end tags, for example, `<book/>` or `<book></book>`.

- Order of attributes

  The order of attributes is insignificant. For example, the following are the same:

  ```
  <order id="C763" date="1998-11-17">
  ```

  and

  ```
  <order date="1998-11-17" id="C763">
  ```

Suppose you compose a purchase order XML document and digitally sign it based on the surface string. Your purchase order received by your retailer will most likely be forwarded further to other parties, such as the manufacturer, the bank, and the distributor, all of whom might have different implementations of XML processor. Your signature is supposed to be verified by them. To preserve the validity of your signature, the retailer would have to keep the original surface string. Of course, XML was not designed for this. We discuss a solution to the dilemma next.

7.6.2 DOMHash: Hash Value Based on DOM Structure

One solution to the surface string deviation is to *canonicalize* an XML document to be signed. That is, we define a canonical form that guarantees that two XML representations are logically equal if and only if their canonical forms are identical. However, instead of our defining a hash value on the surface string, we propose a hash value based on the *DOM structure*. Using the DOM structure is more desirable than using the surface string for several reasons.

- The DOM API requires that all of the string data of `DOMString` type be encoded in UTF-16. Thus there is no deviation of character encoding.

- Nonessential whitespaces are not represented in a DOM tree.

- Fixed attributes are always present regardless of whether they appear in the surface string.

- With the standard DOM API, the method of calculating a hash value can be precisely defined.

DOMHash is our definition of the method of calculating the hash value of a DOM node. A hash value is attached on every DOM node. Two DOM nodes that share the same hash value can be considered to represent the exact same subtree, while different values indicate that at least some part of these two subtrees differ. This is shown in Figure 7.7.

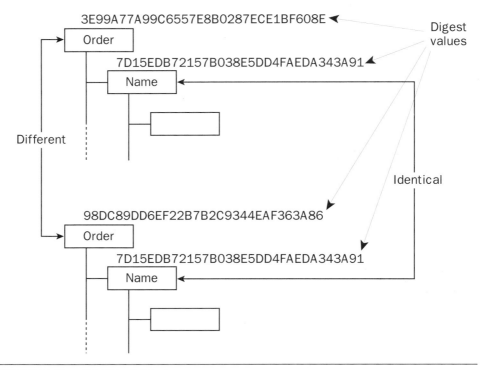

FIGURE 7.7 How DOMHash Works

In the figure, the name elements in the two DOM trees have the same hash value, 7D15EDB72157B038E5DD4FAEDA343A91, so we can be confident that the subtrees headed by these name elements are exactly the same, without our further checking the subelements of the trees. On the other hand, the order elements have different hash values, meaning that there are some differences within these trees (although not in the name elements).

The precise definition (specification) of DOMHash is given in Appendix F. XML for Java provides a DOMHash implementation, class TXNode, of org.w3.do.Node, whose getDigest() method returns the MD5 digest value of a DOM node, in accordance with the specification.

Example of a Digital Signature Based on DOMHash

As an example of using a digital signature based on DOMHash, we show a pair of simple programs for signing (Sign.java) and verification (Verify.java). We use the JDK's built-in cryptography package, Java Cryptography Architecture, for the cryptographic operations.

Signing and Verifying an XML Document

Suppose company A wants to purchase a PC from a mail order company, company B. The order document would look as follows.

```
<?xml version="1.0"?>
<root>
    <order>
        <item id="C763" date="1998-11-17">6883-JF3</item>
        <quantity>3</quantity>
        <name>company A</name>
    </order>
</root>
```

Before sending this order to a mail order company, we want to digitally sign it with our private key so that the company can be sure of the authenticity of the order. This is depicted in Figure 7.8.

Although it is possible to sign the entire document and send the signature separately, company A chooses to sign the `order` element using DOMHash and to include the signature within the document, as shown next.

```
<?xml version="1.0"?>
<root>
    <order>
        <item id="C763" date="1998-11-17">6883-JF3</item>
        <quantity>3</quantity>
        <name>Hiroshi Maruyama</name>
    </order>
```

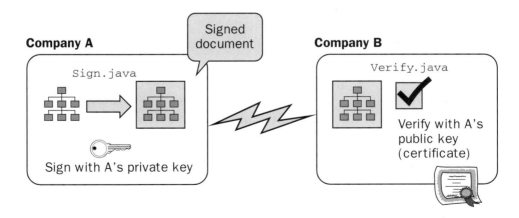

FIGURE 7.8 Signing and verifying using a digital signature

```
<signature>MC0CFQCTj78llAMpmM1qOk5swiFhODwV0gIUaPBclmQqKN/ZAZ2WjDX7Vv
BMG20=
    </signature>
</root>
```

Note that the `signature` element cannot be included in the `order` element. Doing that would change its digest value and thus invalidate the signature.

> **NOTE:** The simplified signature format used in this sample *must not* be used in production systems because attacks such as denial and forgery are possible against this simplified format. At the least, you need to include unambiguous algorithm identifiers (both for the digest algorithm and the signature algorithm) within the signed scope. The IETF and the W3C are working on defining digital signature for XML documents.

Java Cryptography Architecture

For the cryptographic operations in our example, we use **Java Cryptography Architecture** (JCA). JCA is designed to provide a single API for a number of different cryptographic algorithms and implementations (called *providers*). The U.S. Government prohibits the exportation of strong encryption technologies outside of the United States and Canada because it considers such technology to be strategic military technology. Thus people outside of those countries cannot obtain those providers that have strong encryption capability. However, in our example we use the JDK 1.1 default cryptography provider named SUN, which uses the DSA (Digital Signature Algorithm) as its digital signature algorithm. DSA is free and used only for signatures and so is not subject to export restrictions.

`Sign.java`

The `Sign.java` program is responsible for digitally signing an XML document. Before running the `Sign.java` program, however, we need to prepare a *key pair* for signing. JDK 1.1 has a utility called `javakey` for the basic key management functions. The following two commands create, respectively, a trusted identity named "company A" and generate a 1,024-bit DSA key pair for company A.

```
R:\samples\chap7>javakey -cs company-A true
R:\samples\chap7>javakey -gk company-A DSA 1024 c:\pubkey c:\privatekey
```

The identity and the key pair are stored in JDK's default key store. The generated public key and private key are also stored in the specified files for the purpose of exchanging keys. You can check the contents of the key store by using the following command.

```
R:\samples\chap7>javakey -1
Scope: sun.security.IdentityDatabase, source file: C:/WINDOWS\
   identitydb.obj

[Signer] company-A [identitydb.obj] [trusted]
```

Now we have a key pair for signing. The following command signs the XML document `order.xml` and writes the signed document to `c:\signedOrder.xml`.

```
R:\samples\chap7>java Sign Company-A order.xml c:\signedOrder.xml
```

Listing 7.4 shows the source code of `Sign.java`. The method `main()` reads an XML file and parses it and then calls the method `signIt()`. The next steps follow.

1. `signIt()` calculates the digest value using the `getDigest()` method of XML for Java.

2. Then a signing environment is set up. This step includes

    a. extracting the signer's private key from a key store and

    b. obtaining a `Signature` object that supports the specified algorithm from the installed providers (in this case, from the default provider).

3. The `sign()` method signs the digest value using the private key.

4. The resulting signature is Base64-encoded and inserted as a new child element of the root node.

Listing 7.4 `Sign.java`: Digitally signs an XML document

```
/**
 * Sign.java
 */
import com.ibm.xml.parser.*;
import java.io.*;
import org.w3c.dom.*;

import java.security.*;
import java.io.*;
import sun.security.*;
import java.util.*;
```

```
public class Sign {

    public static void main(String[] argv) {
        if (argv.length != 2) {
            System.err.println("Usage: java Sign signerId infile");
            System.exit(1);
        }
        try {
            FileInputStream is = new FileInputStream(argv[1]);
            Parser parser = new Parser(argv[1]);
            TXDocument doc = parser.readStream(is);
            if (parser.getNumberOfErrors() > 0) {
                System.exit(1);
            }

            signIt(doc, argv[0]);

            doc.print(new PrintWriter(System.out));
        } catch (Exception e) {
            e.printStackTrace();
        }
    }

    static void signIt(Document doc, String id) {
        try {
            // 1. Gets the first element under the root as the signing
            //    scope,
            // and obtains its digest value.
            Node root = doc.getDocumentElement();
            Node resource = root.getFirstChild();
            while (resource.getNodeType() != Node.ELEMENT_NODE) {
                resource = resource.getNextSibling();
            }
            byte digest[] = ((TXElement)resource).getDigest();

            // 2. Sets up the signing environment.
            IdentityScope is = sun.security.provider.IdentityDatabase.
              getSystemScope();
            Signer signer =  (Signer)is.getIdentity(id);
            if (signer==null) {
                System.err.println("Can't find the signer "+id);
                System.exit(-1);
            }
            Signature sig = Signature.getInstance("SHA/DSA");
```

```
        // 3. Signs it.
        sig.initSign(signer.getPrivateKey());
        sig.update(digest);
        String encodedSignatureString = (new sun.misc.
        BASE64Encoder()).encodeBuffer(sig.sign());

        // 4. Creates a new "signature" element, and appends it to
        //    the root.
        Element sigElement = new TXElement("signature");
        sigElement.appendChild(doc.createTextNode
        (encodedSignatureString));
        root.appendChild(sigElement);

    } catch (Exception e) {
        e.printStackTrace();
    }
  }
}
```

Verify.java

For signature verification, we need a trusted public key of the signer. This is usually obtained via a certificate signed by a trusted CA, but here, for simplicity, we use the public key generated in the previous subsection. We send our public key to the mail order company, B, for it to load into its own key store using the `javakey` utility.

The verification program, `Verify.java`, mirrors the structure of the signing program, `Sign.java`. First, it parses the input and then extracts the signature scope, followed by the signature element. Next, the verification environment is set up. Finally, the `verify()` method verifies whether the signature was in fact created by the given identity, returning `true` if it was.

Listing 7.5 shows the complete listing of `Verify.java`.

Listing 7.5 `Verify.java`: verifies the signature of an XML document.

```
/**
 * Verify.java
 */
import com.ibm.xml.parser.*;
import org.w3c.dom.*;
import java.io.*;
import java.security.*;
```

```java
public class Verify {

    /**
     * Parse a document and verify it.
     */
    public static void main(String[] argv) {
        if (argv.length != 2) {
            System.err.println("Usage: java Verify signerId infile ");
            System.exit(1);
        }
        try {
            FileInputStream is = new FileInputStream(argv[1]);
            Parser parser = new Parser(argv[1]);
            TXDocument doc = parser.readStream(is);
            if (parser.getNumberOfErrors() > 0) {
                System.exit(1);
            }

            verifyIt(doc,argv[0]);
        } catch (Exception e) {
            e.printStackTrace();
        }
    }

    /**
     * Verify a signed document.
     */
    public static void verifyIt(Document doc, String id) {
        try {
            // 1. Gets the first element under the root as the signed
            //    resource,
            //    and obtains its digest value.
            Node root = doc.getDocumentElement();
            Node resource = root.getFirstChild();
            while (resource.getNodeType() != Node.ELEMENT_NODE) {
                resource = resource.getNextSibling();
            }
            byte digest[] = ((TXElement)resource).getDigest();

            // 2. Finds the "signature" element, and decodes its
            //    value.
            while (resource.getNodeType() != Node.ELEMENT_NODE
                    || !resource.getNodeName().equals("signature")) {
                resource = resource.getNextSibling();
            }
```

```
            String signatureString = ((Text)resource.getFirstChild()).
            getNodeValue();
            sun.misc.BASE64Decoder dec = new sun.misc.BASE64Decoder();
            byte[] signature = dec.decodeBuffer(signatureString);

            // 3. Sets up the verification environment.
            Signature sig = Signature.getInstance("SHA/DSA");
            IdentityScope is = sun.security.provider.IdentityDatabase.
            getSystemScope();
            Signer signer = (Signer)is.getIdentity(id);
            if (signer==null) {
                System.err.println("Can't find the signer "+id);
                System.exit(-1);
            }

            // 4. Verifies the signature.
            sig.initVerify(signer.getPublicKey());
            sig.update(digest);
            if (sig.verify(signature)) {
                System.out.println("Signature verified.");
            } else {
                System.out.println("Signature did not verify.");
            }
        } catch (Exception e) {
            e.printStackTrace();
        }
    }
}
```

This program is run by entering the following command, where
`c:\signedOrder.xml` is the file containing the signed document.

```
R:\samples\chap7>java Verify company=A c:\signedOrder.xml
Signature verified.
```

Next, we modify the content of `c:\signedOrder.xml` and try to verify it. If we
change any essential part (such as the quantity from 3 to 4), the signature will
no longer verify. Nonessential changes, however, such as adding a space character between two attributes, does not affect the verifiability. Note that in XML,
whitespaces between elements are essential, so changing indentation will
invalidate the signature in this example.

Other Applications of DOMHash

In addition to serving as a basis for digital signatures, DOMHash has another important application: the synchronization of two DOM structures. Suppose that a server program generates a DOM structure that is to be rendered by clients. If the server makes frequent small changes on a large DOM tree, only the modified parts should be sent over to the client. A client can initiate a request by sending the root hash value of the structure in the cache memory. If that value matches the root hash value of the current server structure, nothing needs to be sent. Otherwise, the server compares the client hash value with the older versions in the server's cache. If it finds one that matches the client's version, then it locates differences with the current version by recursively comparing the hash values of each node. In this way, the client can receive only an updated portion of a large structure rather than the whole thing. A similar idea of minimizing the network communication for data replication was proposed in *The HTTP Distribution and Replication Protocol*.

7.7 Summary

In this chapter, we discussed the use of XML and HTTP as messaging mechanisms. The largest concern when using the Internet for B2B communication is security. We showed that by using SSL, you can achieve end-to-end security of communication. By using digital signatures, you also can provide nonrepudiatability of messages. Since the surface XML string might fluctuate depending on a number of factors, we proposed to use a hash value based on the underlying DOM structure.

CHAPTER 8

Developing Applications Using JavaBeans

8.1 Introduction

For more than a decade, there have always been fewer skilled software developers than needed. Programmers have gotten used to a large backlog of software to be developed. It is natural, then, that one of the most important themes in software engineering has been, and will be, *software reuse*, that is, reusing existing software as much as possible to build new applications.

In fact, virtually every newly developed application today reuses software to some degree. The reused software might be a small subroutine in a programmer's personal library or as big as a whole enterprise application. For example, XML-based messaging, discussed in Chapter 7, is a way of reusing already deployed applications as components of a new application.

In this chapter, we discuss *JavaBeans,* Java's software component architecture. We discuss how XML for Java can be componentized as JavaBeans and how visual builders are utilized for rapid application development.

After introducing the basics of JavaBeans, we consider how to provide the functionality of XML for Java as JavaBeans. Using the componentized XML for Java, we build a Travel Planning application that creates an itinerary by communicating with multiple other applications.

We use VisualAge for Java in our examples in this chapter. VisualAge for Java 2.0 Entry Version, which is limited to dealing with a maximum of 500 classes (enough for our sample programs!) is included on the CD-ROM so that you can try the examples with it.

8.2 Reusing Software

Before talking about JavaBeans, we first review the history of software reuse. One of the earliest instances of software reuse was the *subroutine*. Instead of the same task, for example sorting, being repeatedly coded, its initial code is abstracted as a subroutine that can be called from many different parts of a single program. Algorithms implemented as subroutines, too, are useful when shared across programs. It is easy to copy the source code, but compiling the same code again and again is expensive. Thus followed the idea of *linking*, which enables the reuse of compiled subroutines. For bookkeeping purposes, a set of interrelated subroutines are gathered into a *library*. Subroutine libraries are still the most widely used form of software reuse. Today, many software vendors provide subroutine libraries for various common tasks such as numerical analysis, computer graphics, and statistical analysis. A programmer looks for appropriate subroutines needed for an application from the documentation, learns about their API, and studies the header files. The programmer then writes the code, compiles it, and links it with the library.

The idea of *object-oriented programming*, which originated from Smalltalk-80, quickly gained popularity in the 1990s after C++, an object-oriented extension of C, was introduced. In this type of programming, an object encapsulates the implementation details by clearly separating its *interface* from its *implementation*. Programmers now need to know only the interface. Furthermore, a class can be reused by *inheriting* most of its features while modifying others by *overloading* them. Inheritance has proved to be particularly useful for building GUIs. A set of reusable object-oriented classes is called a *class library*.

Both subroutine libraries and class libraries are for experienced programmers. You need to read the documentation, understand the interface, code against it, and compile the code with the libraries. It is possible to create a tool that helps you to combine these parts, but it is very unlikely that your tool can also work with other vendors' subroutines and classes.

8.3 Software Components and JavaBeans

The term **software component** refers to a reusable piece of software that can be manipulated and combined with other components using a *builder tool*. Well-known successful software component systems include Borland's Delphi (based on the Pascal language) and Microsoft's COM (Component Object Model, whose components are called by the names of OLE controls, ActiveX controls, and so on). In Java, the standard component model is the JavaBean. Because the interactions between components, as well as interactions between components and the builder tool, are standardized, any component supplied by one vendor can work with other components by another vendor and within any builder.

When it comes to component software, there are two types of developers:

- Component suppliers, a relatively small group of skilled Java programmers (usually software vendors) who provide the reusable components

- Application developers, the much larger group of programmers who use those components to build end-user applications

It is for the application developer that component software is intended, since it is assumed that although they might need to write a few lines of code, they generally do not need an extensive knowledge about an underlying programming language such as Java. Software components are intended to minimize the burden on this group of developers.

Figure 8.1 shows a screen shot of using VisualAge for Java, one of the most popular JavaBeans builders. In this figure, a telephone book application is being built by using the Swing package. As you can see, the components are visually composed. Their look and feel are exactly what you get when you run the program because these components are actually running in the builder. In the figure, the features of the bean labeled "Open . . ." are shown in the pop-up property sheet window. You can inspect and modify these properties (such as background color and text font) without consulting the manual or the header files. You also can program dynamic behaviors (for example, if a button is pressed, the background color of another bean changes).

When a software component is running in a builder, it must reply to inquiries from the builder about the component itself, such as the name and type of

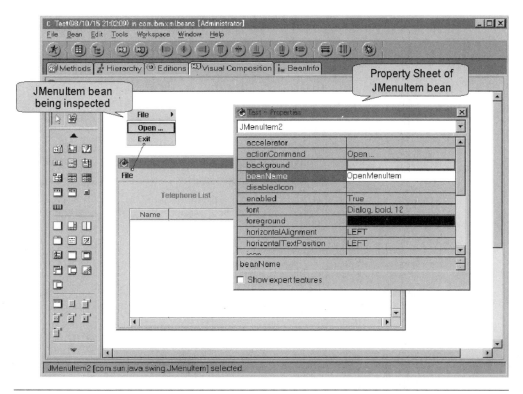

FIGURE 8.1 Sample of typical JavaBean builder usage (VisualAge for Java)

properties and the name and signature of methods. In JavaBeans, these kinds of information of class `Foo` are implemented in the class `FooBeanInfo`. (If the `BeanInfo` file is not present, the builder uses *reflection* to obtain the minimum information about the interface of the bean.) Because the `BeanInfo` file is not called (and thus not loaded) at runtime, it does not introduce additional runtime overhead.

A bean has three types of features that are published to other beans:

- Property

  A **property** is an instance variable that is published through a pair of accessing methods. For example, a property named `bar` will be accessed by the two methods `getBar()` and `putBar()`. A property can be declared *bound*, meaning it fires a `PropertyChange` event if its value is changed.

- Method

    This is the same as a public method.

- Event

    An **event** is a mechanism to notify other "listener" beans when something happens in a "source" bean. This is the standard way to pass around the control using a visual builder such as VisualAge for Java.

The detailed information (name, type, signature, and so on) about these features is recognized by the builder either through the `BeanInfo` class or through introspection, so you can browse, set values, and connect these features visually by using mouse clicks. Some builders such as VisualAge for Java even allow you to make property-to-property, event-to-method, and event-to-property connections by drawing lines between the beans. Thus most of the programming can be done without writing Java code.

People tend to think that software components are a technology for building GUIs. It is true that GUI components such as windows, menus, buttons, and so on are very useful in building a GUI quickly. However, nonvisual components that do not have visual graphics are as useful as visual ones. When you are composing an application with nonvisual components using a visual builder, the position of each component is insignificant. Only property sheets and connections between beans are meaningful visually. In the next section, we componentize XML for Java as invisible JavaBeans.

8.4 Componentizing XML for Java as JavaBeans

XML for Java is functionally very rich. Understanding all of it by reading the API document is not easy. What properties and options are available to control the behavior of the parser and the generator? How are the input and output data structures passed around? With the beans version of XML for Java, application developers can check the features with the help of the builder, inspect and set the property values via the property sheets, and connect events and methods.

As an XML processor, XML for Java has two major functions: parsing and generation. It is possible to define a single bean that can perform both functions with a *boolean* flag indicating which function to perform. However, this likely is not a good idea. This is because the resulting bean would have many more features than would two separate beans, and that would obscure the purpose of the bean. So we decided to create two beans, one for parsing and one for generation.

Another consideration is how to propagate an event and data. Suppose a parser finishes parsing and wants to pass the DOM tree to the next bean, such as a generator. There needs to be a mechanism to notify the generator that the DOM tree is ready, along with a way to pass the data (the DOM tree). JavaBeans provides a powerful event model to do this. We define a new event class called XMLEvent to contain a reference to a DOM tree during event propagation (Figure 8.2). The parser generates an XMLEvent and propagates the event to the generator. The generator receives the XMLEvent object and extracts the DOM tree contained in it. This is depicted in Figure 8.2.

To create a new event, you

- define an event class,
- define a listener interface, and
- for each event source, implement addXMLListener() and removeXMLListener() methods.

In case of VisualAge for Java, most of these steps are automatically taken care of by the builder. Using this event interface, we will create the following two beans:

- "XMLParser" bean
- "XMLGenerator" bean

Both of them are considered as wrappers of XML for Java. They will provide appropriate properties, methods, and events. They are all invisible beans. Next, we will describe these beans in turn.

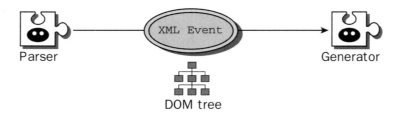

FIGURE 8.2 XMLEvent conveys the event and DOM tree

8.4.1 `XMLParser` **Bean**

The `XMLParser` bean is a wrapper of the parsing function of XML for Java. It does parsing when its only method `parse()` is called. Table 8.1 shows the features of this bean.

Note that these features can be created through the builder, as shown in Figure 8.3.

Although the properties and the event can be added with mouse clicks by using VisualAge for Java, the `parse()` method needs to call XML for Java to implement its functionality, so this part needs to be coded manually by the component supplier. Listing 8.1 shows the implementation of this method. Note that the parse result is set to the `document` property of `XMLEvent`. Then `fireHandleXMLEvent()` delivers the event to all of the listeners.

Listing 8.1 Method `parse()` in the `XMLParser` bean:

```
/**
 * Perform the parse method.
 */
public void parse() {
    // Perform the parse method.
    try {
        if (getInputStream()==null)
```

TABLE 8.1 Features of `XMLParser` Bean

FEATURE TYPE	FEATURE NAME	DATA TYPE	DESCRIPTION
Property	fileName	java.lang.String	A property to hold the input file-name. When `parse()` is called, the parser reads input from this file.
Property	inputStream	java.io.InputStream	A property to hold the input stream. If this property is non-null, the input comes from here instead of a file. This is an alternative way of specifying the input to this parser.
Event	handleXMLEvent (XMLEvent)	NA	An event generated when parsing is finished. The resulting DOM tree is set in the `XMLEvent`.
Method	parse()	NA	A method that starts parsing.

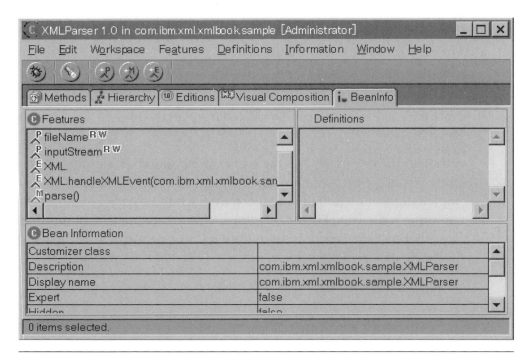

FIGURE 8.3 XMLParser bean in VisualAge for Java

```
        setInputStream(new java.io.FileInputStream(getFileName()));
    com.ibm.xml.parser.Parser parser = new com.ibm.xml.parser.
      Parser(getFileName());
    parser.setExpandEntityReferences(getExpandEntityReferences());
    org.w3c.dom.Document doc = parser.readStream(getInputStream());
    System.out.println("Parse finished");
    getInputStream().close();
    XMLEvent evt = new XMLEvent(this);
    evt.setDocument(doc);
    fireHandleXMLEvent(evt);
  } catch (java.io.IOException ioe) {
      ioe.printStackTrace();
  }
  return;
}
```

8.4.2 XMLGenerator **Bean**

XMLGenerator is a wrapper bean of the generation function of XML for Java.
This bean has three properties and two methods, as shown in Table 8.2.

TABLE 8.2 Features of the `XMLGenerator` Bean

FEATURE TYPE	FEATURE NAME	DATA TYPE	DESCRIPTION
Property	`fileName`	`java.lang.String`	A property to specify the output filename.
Property	`outputStream`	`java.io.OutputStream`	A property that if not null, redirects the output to this stream instead of a file. This is an alternative way of specifying the output of this generator.
Property	`encoding`	`java.lang.String`	A property to specify the character encoding of the output.
Method	`generate` `(XMLEvent)`	NA	A method to start generation from the `Document` pointed to by the `document` property of the `XMLEvent` parameter.
Method	`generate` `(Document)`	NA	A method to start generation from the `Document` parameter. This is an alternative way to start generation.

The property `encoding` is specified by a string such as "ISO-8859-1," not "USEnglish." The description string is defined in the `BeanInfo` class so that the builder can guide the application developer to decide what value is expected for this property. Figure 8.4 shows the property sheet of the `XMLGenerator` bean with the property encoding highlighted. Notice the short description at the bottom of the window explaining the expected value. Concise and self-descriptive strings are key to truly reusable components.

The method `generate()` calls XML for Java and is coded as in Listing 8.2.

Listing 8.2 Method `generate()` in the `XMLGenerator` bean:

```
/**
 * Perform the generate method.
 * @param doc org.w3c.dom.Document
 */
public void generate(org.w3c.dom.Document doc) {
    // Perform the generate method.
    if (doc == null)
        return;
    PrintWriter pw;
```

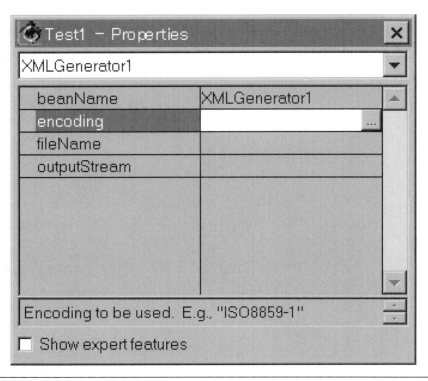

FIGURE 8.4 Property box of the XMLGenerator bean in VisualAge for Java

```
try {
    if (getOutputStream() != null) {
      pw = new PrintWriter(getOutputStream());
    } else
      if (getFileName() != null) {
        pw = new PrintWriter(new FileOutputStream(getFileName()));
      } else {
        pw = new PrintWriter(System.out);
      }
    if (getEncoding() != null && !getEncoding().equals("")) {
      ((TXDocument)doc).setEncoding(getEncoding());
      if (getHtmlGeneration()) {
        Writer writer = new OutputStreamWriter(System.
          out,getEncoding());
        Visitor visitor = new HTMLPrintVisitor(writer);
        new NonRecursivePreorderTreeTraversal(visitor).
          traverse(doc);
      } else {
```

```
            ((TXDocument)doc).printWithFormat(pw, getEncoding());
        }
    } else {
        if (getHtmlGeneration()) {
            Writer writer = new OutputStreamWriter(System.out);
            Visitor visitor = new HTMLPrintVisitor(writer);
            new NonRecursivePreorderTreeTraversal(visitor).
                traverse(doc);
        } else {
            ((TXDocument)doc).printWithFormat(pw);
        }
    }
} catch (Exception ioe) {
    ioe.printStackTrace();
}
return;
}
```

Now that we have both the parser and generator as JavaBeans, we can build a simple application.

8.4.3 `SimpleParseAndGenerate` with Beans

Although the `XMLParser` and `XMLGenerator` beans are invisible, it still makes a lot of sense to use the visual builder to build an application. As the simplest example, we develop an equivalent of `SimpleParseAndPrint` (Listing 2.2) from Chapter 2. This application reads an XML document from a file, parses it to a DOM tree, and regenerates an XML document from the DOM tree with formatting. It uses one `XMLParser` bean and one `XMLGenerator` bean, as shown in Figure 8.5.[1]

`XMLParser1` and `XMLGenerator1` are bean names. Bean names can be assigned arbitrarily. In this case, the names are automatically generated by the builder. The event propagation between the beans is shown by the line. Double-clicking the line shows the details of the connection, as shown in Figure 8.6. This connection propagates a `handleXMLEvent()` generated in the parser to the `generate(XMLEvent)` method of the generator. Note that the "Pass event data" check box is on, meaning that this event connection should carry the event object as the argument.

---

[1]Here, the word "bean" refers to an *instance* of JavaBean *class*. This is confusing but the word is used for both meanings.

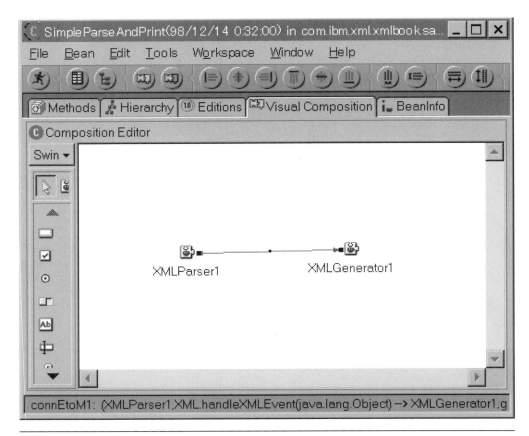

FIGURE 8.5 `SimpleParseAndPrint`: the beans version

How does VisualAge for Java convert the event-to-method connection into Java code? This implementation is rather complex. The container class `SimpleParseAndPrint.java` implements the `XMLListener` interface so that it can become an event listener for `XML` events. This interface requires the `handleXMLEvent()` method, which is implemented in the class `SimpleParseAndPrint.java`, as follows.

```
public void handleXMLEvent(XMLEvent evt) {
    if ((evt.getSource() == getXMLParser1()) ) {
        getXMLGenerator1().generate(evt);
    }
}
```

The event source, `XMLParser1` in this case, must have a set of methods that allow the adding and removing of `XMLListener` objects. These are automatically generated by VisualAge for Java when an event feature for a class is created.

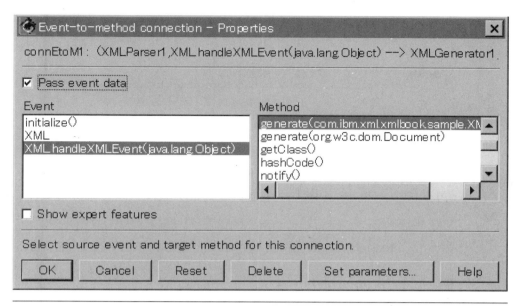

FIGURE 8.6 Event-to-method connection between `XMLParser1` and `XMLGenerator1`

When parsing is finished and a DOM tree is created, an `XMLEvent` is generated and propagated to all listeners. VisualAge for Java also creates the code for this. Note that even component suppliers do not need to know all of these details, as they are hidden beneath the simple and powerful event propagation model of JavaBeans.

The `SimpleParseAndGenerate` application is almost done because the core logic of parse and generate is now in place. Next, we write a simple main program to initiate the parsing. Listing 8.3 shows the method `main()` in `SimpleParseAndGenerate`. Since the skeleton of the method is also generated by the builder, we need only to fill in the middle three lines (lines [5] through [7] in Listing 8.3), which set the filenames to `XMLParser1` and `XMLGenerator1`, and then call `parse()`. Of course, it is also possible to use GUI components to supply these filenames, in which case there would be no need to write a single line of code.

Listing 8.3 Method `main()` in `SimpleParseAndGenerate`: initiates parsing

```
      public static void main(String[] args) {
         try {
            SimpleParseAndPrint aSimpleParseAndPrint;
            aSimpleParseAndPrint = new SimpleParseAndPrint();
[5]         aSimpleParseAndPrint.getXMLParser1().setFileName(args[0]);
```

```
            aSimpleParseAndPrint.getXMLGenerator1().setFileName(args[1]);
[7]         aSimpleParseAndPrint.getXMLParser1().parse();

    } catch (Throwable exception) {
       System.err.println("Exception occurred in main() of
       java.lang.Object");
       exception.printStackTrace(System.out);
    }
}
```

The complete generated code is in the chap8 directory on the CD-ROM. Thus you can execute the code by typing the following at the command prompt.

```
R:\samples\chap8>java SimpleParseAndGenerate test.xml test.out
```

Advanced readers might find it interesting to look at the generated Java source code, located in xmlsamplebeans.jar on the CD-ROM. See the readme.html file for instructions on how to run the program.

8.4.4 Using the LMX Bean

To do more useful tasks, you can make the LMX processor a bean. This bean differs from the previous XMLGenerator bean: It needs two input documents—the conversion rule and the document to be converted. We design so that both of these documents come in as XMLEvents. The features of this bean are given in Table 8.3.

As in the cases of XMLParser and XMLGenerator, we will create a wrapper bean of LMX, called XMLConverter, whose features are shown in Table 8.3.

TABLE 8.3 Features of the XMLConverter Bean

FEATURE TYPE	FEATURE NAME	DATA TYPE	DESCRIPTION
Method	convert (XMLEvent)	NA	A method that starts the conversion of the document held by the XMLEvent.
Method	setRule (XMLEvent)	NA	A method that sets the document held by the XMLEvent as the conversion rule.
Property	reverse	boolean	A property that when set to true applies the rule in the reverse direction.
Event	handleXMLEvent (XMLEvent)	NA	An event generated when parsing is finished. The resulting DOM tree is set in the XMLEvent.

But before doing so, we extended the functionality of LMX described in Chapter 4 in the several ways including the following:

- Variables can have names, such as `$address;`, instead of being limited to numbers (as in `$1;`).

- It runs with any DOM implementation (It is independent from XML for Java).

- It is now in the `com.ibm.xml.lmx` package.

The revised LMX code is on the CD-ROM under the directory `\lmx\src\com\ibm\xml\lmx`. The wrapper bean, `XMLConverter.java`, is included in a jar file named `xmlsamplebeans.jar` in the `chap8` directory.

A typical use of the `XMLConverter` bean is shown in Figure 8.7. This is again a command line processor, which does a conversion. This time, however, the input filename and the output filename are given as the property values at building time, rather than as command line arguments at runtime. As can be

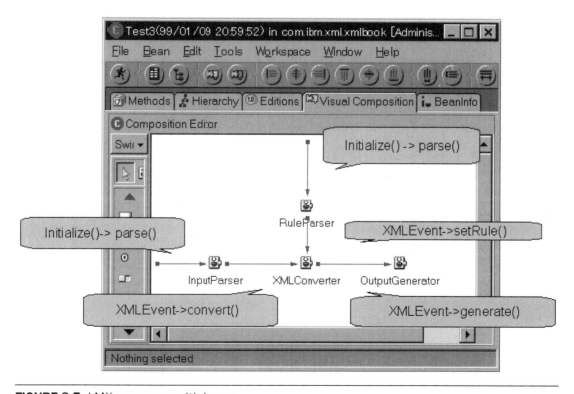

FIGURE 8.7 LMX processor with beans

seen in the figure, the `RuleParser` bean supplies the conversion rule, the `InputParser` bean supplies the input document, and the conversion result is propagated to the `OutputGenerator` bean as an `XMLEvent`.

Let us take a closer look at the event propagation in this application. The event connections are represented as arrows, to each of which we attach a balloon description. Following is the order of the events' firing.

1. `LMXProcessor.initialize() -> RuleParser.parse()`

   The `initialize()` event is fired when the container object, `LMXProcessor`, is instantiated. Since the `main()` method creates an instance of this object, this is the origin of the event propagation. Here, this event triggers `RuleParser` to parse an XML rule file and fires an `XMLEvent` when finished.

2. `RuleParser.handleXMLEvent -> XMLConverter.setRule()`

   `XMLEvent` propagates to `XMLConverter`, whose `Ruleset()` method is called. The `XMLConverter` analyzes the DOM tree held by the `XMLEvent` and prepares for conversion.

3. `LMXProcessor.initialize() -> InputParser.parse()`

   Next, the `parse()` method of `InputParser` is called. This method parses the input XML file and fires another `XMLEvent`.

4. `InputParser.handleXMLEvent -> XMLConverter.convert()`

   The `XMLEvent` triggers the `convert()` method of the `XMLConverter`. This method starts the conversion using the rule set by the `setRule()` method.

5. `XMLConverter.convert() -> OutputGenerator.generate()`

   After the conversion is completed, the resulting DOM tree is passed in a generated `XMLEvent` to `OutputGenerator`. The generated XML is stored in the file specified in the `fileName` property.

This example illustrates the use of visual, event-driven programming with JavaBeans. Not a single line of code is written to develop this application. All of the source code is included on the CD-ROM so that you can examine how it works with the low-level details. In the next section, we develop a more involved Web application.

8.5 Travel Planning Application

As the last and largest sample Web application, we develop a web automation application, shown in Figure 8.8, that accesses multiple Web sites using XML. Suppose that you are planning a trip and there are three Web sites that you want to access:

- An airline's site

- A hotel's site

- An intranet employee database site

Although you can access these sites one by one and plan your itinerary manually, our application will automatically pull information from the sites and create an itinerary for you.

We assume that these Web sites are already XML-enabled, meaning that they can reply in XML to an HTTP request, as follows.

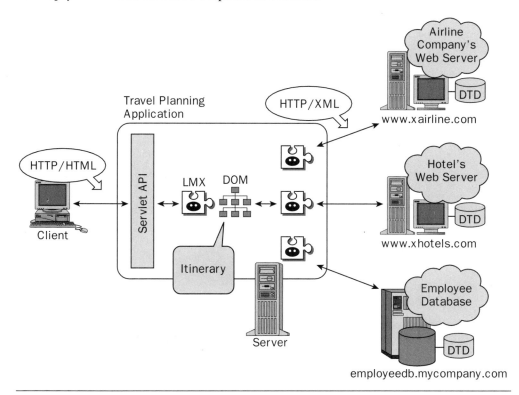

FIGURE 8.8 System structure of the Travel Planning application

1. The airline's flight schedule Web site

   Given dates, an origin airport, and a destination airport, this Web site returns available flights as an XML document.

   ```xml
   <?xml version="1.0" encoding="ISO-8859-1"?>
       <flights>
           <flight>
               <departure_time>0710</departure_time>
               <arrival_time>0840</arrival_time>
               <flight_number>ANA 244</flight_number>
               <class>
                   <super_seat>yes</super_seat>
                   <economy_seat>yes</economy_seat>
               </class>
           </flight>
       </flights>
   ```

2. Hotel's Web site

   This Web site returns the available hotel rooms in the specified city on the specified dates. The result again is in XML.

   ```xml
   <?xml version="1.0" encoding="ISO-8859-1"?>
       <accommodation>
           <hotel>
               <name>Graden Hotel Narita</name>
               <type>s</type>
               <charge>9900</charge>
               <station>Shuttle bus service from Keisei Narita
                 station</station>
               <information>
                   <tel>03-5123-4567</tel>
                   <fax>03-5123-4568</fax>
                   <URL>http://hotel.aska.or.jp/yoyaku/HOTEL/399/399.
                     html</URL>
               </information>
           </hotel>
       </accommodation>
   ```

3. Employee database site

   This intranet application returns an employee's information in an XML form.

   ```xml
   <?xml version="1.0" encoding="ISO-8859-1"?>
       <database>
           <name>Kazuyo Yagishita</name>
   ```

```
<number>123456</number>
<department>
    <dept_name>Network Applications</dept_name>
    <dept_code>A0000</dept_code>
</department>
<number>
    <extension>XXXX</extension>
    <external>0462-73-XXXX</external>
</number>
<mail_address>
    <e_mail>abc@jp.ibm.com</e_mail>
    <internal_mail>LAB-S00</internal_mail>
</mail_address>
<position>Researcher</position>
</database>
```

Since all of the information is available in the XML/DOM form, it should be relatively easy to build an itinerary document, which is also a DOM tree, by combining these parts. The itinerary DOM is converted into either HTML or other forms depending on the type of the client.

As shown in Figure 8.8, this is a Web application (that is, a servlet) that runs on a Web server. At the same time, it also is a client of the three existing Web applications. We will build this servlet named `TravelServlet` using visual composition.

In addition to the three beans we developed in the previous section, we need the following two new beans in our Travel Planning application.

- `XMLServer`. This bean accesses a Web server using HTTP, receives an XML document as the result, and returns the parsed DOM tree.

- `DOMExpander`. Given a "skeleton" document with slots and a set of "parts" documents, this bean fills in the slots with the parts and returns the expanded tree as a separate copy.

Using these components, we build our `TravelServlet` visually, as shown in Figure 8.9.

When this servlet is initialized, the following event propagation takes place.

1. The `skeletonFileName` property of `TravelServlet` is set to the `fileName` property of `SkeletonParser`.

2. The `xmlRuleFileName` property of `TravelServlet` is set to the `fileName` property of `RuleParser`.

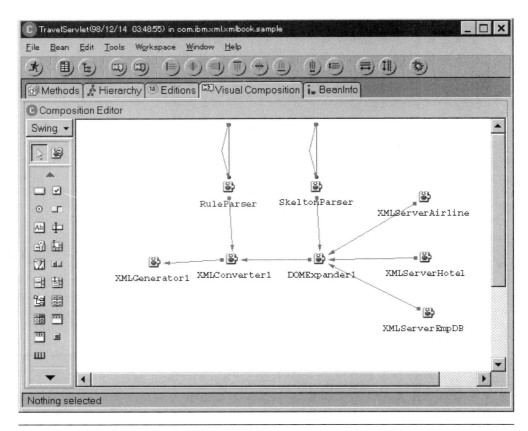

FIGURE 8.9 Visual composition of `TravelServlet`

3. The `parse()` method of `skeletonParser` is called, and the result is propagated to `DOMExpander`.

4. The `parse()` method of `ruleParser` is called, and the result is propagated to `XMLConverter1`.

Now the servlet is ready to process POST requests. For each POST request, the following event propagation occurs.

1. When an HTTP POST request is received by the servlet, `doPOST()` is executed. This first sets `HTTPOutputStream` to the `outputStream` property of `XMLGenerator1` and then calls the three `XMLServer` beans in turn.

2. Each `XMLServer` bean establishes an HTTP connection to the specified server, retrieves the XML document, parses it, and generates an `XMLEvent` to send it to `DOMExpander`.

3. When `DOMExpander` receives enough inputs (in this case, three), it makes a copy of the skeleton by replacing the slots with the values set in step 2. Once the result is created, another `XMLEvent` is sent to `XMLConverter1`.

4. `XMLConverter1` converts the received DOM to an HTML document by using the specified rule.

5. `XMLGenerator1` generates the HTML that goes into the output stream that was set in step 1.

We skip the details of these event connections because of space limitations. However, it is important to notice that these connections can be made by mouse clicks using builders such as VisualAge for Java. Next, we look at the implementations of the two new beans.

8.5.1 `XMLServer` Bean Implementation

The bean `XMLServer` encapsulates accesses to a Web site. The site's URL is given in the property `URL`. When the bean's `doIt()` method is called and parsing is finished, a `DOMEvent` is generated. The features of this bean are given in Table 8.4. Two methods, `clearParameters()` and `addParameters()`, are used to set the parameters attached to the HTTP request. The property `method` is used to specify the HTTP method.

TABLE 8.4 Features of the `XMLServer` Bean

FEATURE TYPE	FEATURE NAME	DATA TYPE	DESCRIPTION
Property	`URL`	`String`	The URL of the XML document to be fetched.
Method	`clearParameters()`		The method that clears the parameters to be sent along with the URL.
Method	`addParmeters` `(Name, Value)`	`String,` `String`	The method that adds a `name=value` parameter.
Property	`method`	`String`	The HTTP method, either `POST` or `GET`, used to connect to the server.
Event	`handleXMLEvent` `(XMLEvent)`	NA	An event generated when parsing is finished. The resulting DOM tree is set in the `XMLEvent`.
Method	`doIt()`	NA	The method that fetches the page and parses it.

The implementation of doIt() is shown in Listing 8.4. Here, only the POST method is shown. Implementing the GET method should be easy.

Listing 8.4 doIt(): Accesses the HTTP/XML server

```
/**
 * Perform the doIt method.
 * 1. Connects to the URL, and sends the parameters.
 * 2. Parses the result.
 * 3. Generates an XMLEvent.
 */
public void doIt() {
    try {
        java.net.URL url = new java.net.URL(getURL());
        java.net.URLConnection uc = url.openConnection();
        uc.setDoInput(true);
        if (getMethod().equals("GET")) {
                            // Handles the GET method (not supported).
        } else if (getMethod().equals("POST")) {
                            // Handles the POST method.
            uc.setDoOutput(true);
            java.io.PrintWriter pw = new java.io.PrintWriter(uc.
            getOutputStream());
            pw.println(getParameters());
            pw.close();
        }

                        // Invokes the XML Parser.
        java.io.InputStream is = uc.getInputStream();
        com.ibm.xml.parser.Parser parser = new com.ibm.xml.parser.
          Parser(getURL());
        org.w3c.dom.Document doc = parser.readStream(is);

                        // Generates an XMLEvent.
        XMLEvent evt = new XMLEvent(this);
        evt.setDocument(doc);
        fireHandleXMLEvent(evt);
        is.close();
    } catch (java.lang.Exception e) {
        e.printStackTrace();
    }
    return;
}
```

8.5.2 `DOMExpander` **Bean Implementation**

The `DOMExpander` bean is for replacing slots in a skeleton. A skeleton is an XML file with slots that have the following XLink-like syntax:

```
<embed href="urn:javabean:airline#child(3)"/>
```

The URN is interpreted as referring to a DOM tree by a name. The right-hand side of the hash sign is an XPointer that points to the element that is to be inserted as a replacement of this `embed` element. This example refers to the third child element of the root of the DOM tree named `airline`. The following code shows the skeleton that we use in our Travel Planning servlet. It has three slots (shown in bold type), corresponding respectively to the employee intranet database, the airline's Web site, and the hotel's Web site.

```
<?xml version="1.0" encoding="ISO-8859-1"?>
<!DOCTYPE schedule SYSTEM "schedule.dtd">
<schedule>
    <employee>
        <embed href="urn:javabean:employee#child(1)"/>
    </employee>

    <date>
        <departure_day>
            <year>1998</year>
            <month>9</month>
            <day>16</day>
        </departure_day>
        <return_day>
            <year>1998</year>
            <month>9</month>
            <day>18</day>
        </return_day>
    </date>

    <airport>
        <departure_airport>Fukuoka</departure_airport>
        <arrival_airport>Tokyo (Haneda)</arrival_airport>
    </airport>

    <flight>
        <embed href="urn:javabean:airline#child(1)"/>
    </flight>

    <accommodation>
        <embed href="urn:javabean:hotelWebSite#child(1)"/>
```

```
        </accommodation>
      </schedule>
```

The features of DOMExpander are listed in Table 8.5. The slot values are set by the addEntry() method. We keep these values in a hash table named valueTable.

The property numberOfEntry specifies how many values must be set with addEntry() before the expansion is carried out. Once the specified number of input values are set, the expand() method, described next, is called to create a new DOM tree. Then an XMLEvent is triggered.

The implementation of the method expand() in Listing 8.5 uses the com.ibm.xml.xpointer package to parse and deference XPointers.

Listing 8.5 Method expand(): Dereferences the XPointer in the skeleton

```
/**
 * Expand "urn:javabeans" links with the values set by addEntry().
 */
public void expand() {
    try {
        // 1. Creates a copy of the skeleton
        // (casting to TXDocument is necessary for cloning the whole
        //  document).
        Document result = (Document)((TXDocument)getSkeleton()).clone();
        Document root = null;
```

TABLE 8.5 Features of the DOMExpander Bean

FEATURE TYPE	FEATURE NAME	DATA TYPE	DESCRIPTION
Property	numberOfEntry	int	The number of entries to be filled in before doing expansion.
Property	skeleton	Document	The skeleton document.
Method	setSkeleton(evt)	XMLEvent	An alternative method to set the skeleton document.
Method	addEntry(evt,name)	XMLEvent, String	A method specifying a value with its name.
Method	addEntry(doc,name)	Document, String	An alternative method to specify a value with its name.
Method	clearEntry()	NA	A method that clears all of the values.
Event	handleXMLEvent(evt)	XMLEvent	An event generated when expansion is finished. The resulting DOM tree is set in the XMLEvent.

```
        Element source = null;
        Element parent = null;
        String domName = null;
        String pointer = null;

        // 2. Collects all of the "embed" elements.
        NodeList nodeList = result.getElementsByTagName("embed");

        // 3. Replace the "embed" elements with the values in the
        //    hashtable.
        for (int i = 0; i < nodeList.getLength(); i++) {
            Element elt = (Element) nodeList.item(i);
            String urn = elt.getAttribute("href");
            if (urn.startsWith("urn:javabean:")) {
                int fromIndex = "urn:javabean:".length();
                int index = urn.indexOf('#', fromIndex);
                domName = urn.substring(fromIndex, index);
                pointer = urn.substring(index + 1);
            } else
                return;
            root = (Document)valueTable.get(domName);
            if (root == null) {
                System.err.println("DOMExpander: "+domName+" not
                  found.");
            }

            // Dereferences the XPointer.
            XPointerParser xpp = new XPointerParser();
            source = (Element)xpp.parse(pointer).point(root).item(0).
              node;

            // Replaces the node.
            parent = (Element) elt.getParentNode();
            parent.insertBefore(source, elt);
            parent.removeChild(elt);
        }

        // 4. Generates an XMLEvent.
        XMLEvent evt = new XMLEvent(this);
        evt.setDocument(result);
        fireHandleXMLEvent(evt);
    } catch (Exception e) {
        e.printStackTrace();
    }
}
```

8.5.3 `TravelServlet`

The result of `DOMExpander` is a logical structure of the created itinerary, from which an XML document is created so that the client can feed the XML file to its own application. If the client has a browser only, we generate an HTML document instead that shows the contents of the itinerary nicely. As always, we use the LMX processor for converting XML to HTML. The LMX rules are shown next.

```xml
<?xml version="1.0" encoding="ISO-8859-1"?>
<lmx:rules>

    <!- ******************************************* ->
    <lmx:pattern>
        <lmx:lhs>
            <schedule>$1;</schedule>
        </lmx:lhs>

        <lmx:rhs>
            <HTML>
            <HEAD> <TITLE>Itinerary</TITLE> </HEAD>
            <BODY>
                <CENTER>
                    <H1><font color="Gray">ITINERARY</font></H1>
                </CENTER>
            $1;
            </BODY>
        </HTML>
        </lmx:rhs>
    </lmx:pattern>

    <!- ******************************************* ->
    <lmx:pattern>
        <lmx:lhs>
            <employee>
                <name>$name;</name>
            </employee>
        </lmx:lhs>
        <lmx:rhs>
            <div>
                <h2>Name</h2>
                <p>$name;</p>
            </div>
        </lmx:rhs>
    </lmx:pattern>
```

```
<!-- ******************************************** -->

<lmx:pattern>
    <lmx:lhs>
        <date>
            <departure_day>
            <year>$dyear;</year>
            <month>$dmonth;</month>
            <day>$dday;</day>
        </departure_day>
        <return_day>
            <year>$ryear;</year>
            <month>$rmonth;</month>
            <day>$rday;</day>
        </return_day>
    </date>
    </lmx:lhs>
    <lmx:rhs>
        <div>
            <h2>Date</h2>
            <table border="1">

<tr><td>Departure</td><td><b>$dmonth;</b>/<b>$dday;
  </b>/<b>$dyear;</b></td></tr>
<tr><td>Return</td><td><b>$rmonth;</b>/<b>$rday;
  </b>/<b>$ryear;</b></td></tr>
            </table>
        </div>
    </lmx:rhs>
</lmx:pattern>

<!-- ******************************************** -->

<lmx:pattern>
    <lmx:lhs>
        <airport>
            <departure_airport>$from;</departure_airport>
             <arrival_airport>$to;</arrival_airport>
        </airport>
    </lmx:lhs>
    <lmx:rhs>
        <div>
            <h2>Airports</h2>
            <table border="1">
            <tr><td>From:</td><td>$from;</td></tr>
```

```
                <tr><td>To:</td><td>$to;</td></tr>
                </table>
            </div>
        </lmx:rhs>
</lmx:pattern>


<!- ******************************************** ->


<lmx:pattern>
    <lmx:lhs>
        <flight>
            <flight>
                <departure_time>$deptime;</departure_time>
                <arrival_time>$arrtime;</arrival_time>
                <flight_number>$flno;</flight_number>
                <class>
                        <super_seat>$1;</super_seat>
                        <economy_seat>$2;</economy_seat>
                </class>
            </flight>
        </flight>
    </lmx:lhs>
    <lmx:rhs>
        <div>
            <h2>Flight</h2>
            <table border="1">
            <tr><td>Flight No:</td><td>$flno;</td></tr>
            <tr><td>Departure:</td><td>$deptime;</td></tr>
            <tr><td>Arrival:</td><td>$arrtime;</td></tr>
            </table>
        </div>
    </lmx:rhs>
</lmx:pattern>


<!- ******************************************** ->


<lmx:pattern>
    <lmx:lhs>
        <accommodation>
            <hotel>
                <name>$name;</name>
                <type>$1;</type>
                <charge>$price;</charge>
                <station>$2;</station>
                <information>
```

```
                                <tel>$3;</tel>
                                <fax>$4;</fax>
                                <URL>$5;</URL>
                        </information>
                    </hotel>
                </accommodation>
            </lmx:lhs>
            <lmx:rhs>
                <div>
                    <h2>Hotel</h2>
                    <table border="1">
                    <tr><td>Hotel Name:</td><td>$name;</td></tr>
                    <tr><td>Price:</td><td>$price;</td></tr>
                    <tr><td>Phone no:</td><td>$3;</td></tr>
                    <tr><td>Fax no:</td><td>$4;</td></tr>
                    </table>
                </div>
            </lmx:rhs>
        </lmx:pattern>

    </lmx:rules>
```

Now we complete `TravelServlet`. Most of the application programming has already been done by visually composing the beans and preparing the skeleton and LMX files. The only programming remaining is the implementation of the servlet's `doPost()` method, as shown in Listing 8.6. As you can see, very little has to be done by the application developer.

Listing 8.6 Method `doPOST()`: Main entry point of the servlet

```
public void doPost(HttpServletRequest request, HttpServletResponse
response)
    throws IOException, MalformedURLException {

    // 1. Sets the outputStream of the generator bean.
    getXMLGenerator1().setOutputStream(response.getOutputStream());

    // 2. Clears the parameters of the XMLServer beans.
    XMLServer airline = getXMLServerAirline();
    XMLServer hotel = getXMLServerHotel();
    XMLServer employee = getXMLServerEmpDB();
    airline.clearParameters();
    hotel.clearParameters();
    employee.clearParameters();
```

```
    // 3. Copies the POST parameters to the XMLServer beans.
    for (Enumeration e = request.getParameterNames(); e.
      hasMoreElements();) {
        String name = (String) e.nextElement();
        String value = request.getParameterValues(name)[0];
        airline.addParameter(name, value);
        hotel.addParameter(name, value);
        employee.addParameter(name, value);
    }

    // 4. Triggers all of the XMLServer beans.
    airline.doIt();
    hotel.doIt();
    employee.doIt();
}
```

Because of space limitations, we used a lot of restrictive assumptions in developing our sample Web automation application. In a real situation, however, you might need to do many things, including converting the tag names and the structure of returned flight information. Inserting an LMX bean between XMLServer and DOMExpander will do this for you. This can be done entirely visually without getting into the Java code. This flexibility is the real power of using software components. We believe that more and more software components to deal with XML documents and XML messages will soon be available to all developers.

8.6 Evolution of Web Applications

The potential of XML-enabled Web applications can be illustrated by the very simple Travel Planning application that we developed in this chapter. Airline and hotel companies have invested a lot to make their existing backend systems (typically based on Lotus Notes, SAP, and so on) accessible from Web browsers. This has been a tremendous success, now exerting greater reach to end users all over the world. However, that reach is limited to browsers (and thus to human users) because HTML is good only for displaying on the screen. For example, a travel agent who wants to put the flight information in a spreadsheet to combine it with other information for a customer must manually cut and paste individual pieces of information between the Web browser and the spreadsheet application.

8.6.1 Browser Clients

Figure 8.10 depicts a possible scenario of the evolution of a Web site powered by XML. Existing Web applications are typically designed to generate HTML pages directly from a database. The first step to establish an XML-enabled Web site is to generate a logical and presentation-neutral representation in XML/DOM, which is to be converted into HTML, as shown in case (1) in Figure 8.10. This covers all of the browser-based clients.

8.6.2 Office Clients

The second step is to convert the presentation-neutral representation into a format that is supported by office products. For example, if the travel agent receives the flight information in XML that is compatible with office products, that information can be fed into a spreadsheet, thereby eliminating tedious cut-and-paste operations. This is shown in case (2) in Figure 8.10. Microsoft and Lotus are quickly moving toward supporting XML in their office products. For example, Lotus e-Suite is already XML-enabled, so you can create an XML document that is directly loadable to an e-Suite spreadsheet.

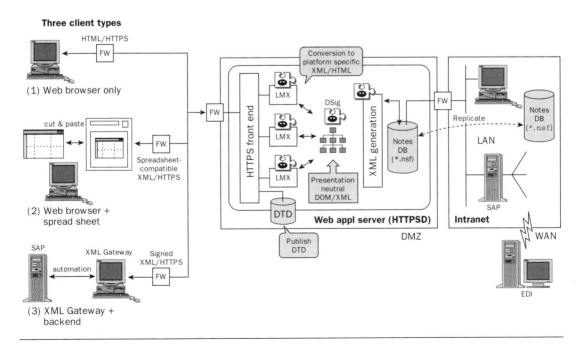

FIGURE 8.10 XML-powered Web site

8.6.3 Integrated B2B Applications

As the third step, the travel agency can connect the XML-enabled airline Web site to its backend system (such as SAP), thereby allowing agents to automatically check the flight availability and to issue orders. This is shown in case (3) in Figure 8.10. In this way, the XML-enabled Web site can be integrated into the agency's enterprise system as one of its components.

All of these transactions are made on the Internet using SSL, so maximum security is maintained, with no need for an expensive leased line (VAN). In addition, digital signatures build trust among business partners.

We believe many Web sites will be increasingly used as components of a more-or-less similar architecture in the near future. The technologies described in this book—XML, Java, XML processors, LMX processor, servlets, SQLX, SSL, digital signatures, and JavaBeans—are essential for realizing the coming world of Web applications.

8.7 Summary

In this chapter, we discussed the use of JavaBeans in the rapid development of Web applications. With well-designed components, application development can be done with very little code writing and manual consulting, thus significantly reducing development costs.

About the CD-ROM

The CD-ROM included with this book contains all of the source codes and resource files, as well as some useful XML tools. It also has the trial versions of three IBM products used in this book:

- IBM WebSphere, which provides a servlet environment in which to run the sample programs in Chapter 5

- IBM DB2 Universal Database, which can be used as the backend database of the sample programs described in Chapter 6

- IBM VisualAge for Java as a JavaBean building tool described in Chapter 8.

See the `index.html` and README files in the corresponding directories for detailed installation instructions. The directory structure of the CD-ROM is as follows

```
</>                    : root directory
  + index.html         : Top page of this CD-ROM that contains links to
                         other resources
  + links.html         : Useful links (Appendix C)
  + <samples>          : Source codes, XML documents, and other files used
                         in each chapter

    + <chap2>
    + <chap3>
    + <chap4>
    + <chap5>
    + <chap6>
    + <chap7>
    + <chap8>
  + <alphaworks>       : XML tools from IBM's alphaWorks
                         (http://www.alphaworks.ibm.com)
  + <udb>              : IBM DB2 Universal Database (trial version)
```

```
+ <vajava>         : IBM VisualAge for Java (trial version)
+ <websphere>      : IBM WebSphere (trial version)
+ <xml4j>          : XML for Java
   + <APIDOC>      : API of XML for Java (JavaDoc format)
+ <lmx>            : Language for Mapping XML (LMX): enhanced version
```

Using Other XML Processors

Downloadable XML Processors

Although the sample programs in this book were written with XML for Java, it is possible to use other XML processors in many cases. This appendix gives other available Java implementations of XML processors and tips on using them.

Note that the descriptions here are as of October, 1998. Many vendors are aggressive in refreshing their implementations. It is the reader's responsibility to check the latest release.

Note that some of the software packages do not allow commercial use without explicit licensing. You must carefully read the license agreement included in the downloaded package. Of the XML processors listed, Lark, AElfred, XP, and XML for Java grant royalty-free commercial uses.

Other software packages of interest are shown in Table B2.

TABLE B1 XML Processors in Java

PROCESSOR	LATEST VERSION	VALIDATING PROCESSOR	SAX	W3C DOM	COMMERCIAL USE WITHOUT FEE?	URL	Notes
Lark	1.0 beta (Jan. 5, 1998)	Yes	Requires a SAX driver	Requires Docuverse	Yes	http://www.textuality.com/Lark/	
AElfred	1.2a (May 2, 1998)	No	Yes	Requires Docuverse	Yes	http://www.microstar.com/XML/index.html	High-speed, compact
XP	0.5 (January 1999)	No	Yes	Requires Docuverse	Yes	http://www.jclark.com/xml/xp/index.html	
XML for Java (XML4J)	1.1.14 (January 1999) 2.0.0 (February 1999)	Yes	Yes	Yes	Yes	http://www.alphaworks.ibm.com/formula/xml	Rich functions, XPointer support
DataChannel—Microsoft XML Java Parser (dcxml)	Beta1 (August 1998)	Yes	No	No	No	http://www.datachannel.com/xml_resources/xml_form.html	
SXP	0.83 (January 1999)	Yes	Yes	Yes	No	http://www.loria.fr/projets/XSilfide/EN/sxp/	Rich functions, XPointer/ XLL support
Java Project X	ea2 (Nov. 25, 1998)	Yes	Yes	Yes	No	http://developer.javasoft.com/developer/earlyAccess/xml/index.html	High-speed

TABLE B2 Other Software/APIs

	LATEST VERSION	URL
Simple API for XML (SAX)	1.0	`http://www.megginson.com/SAX/`
Docuverse DOM SDK	1.0PR3B (12 Oct. 1998)	`http://www.docuverse.com/domsdk/ index.html`

Using the XML Processor with the SAX API

All of the XML processors listed in this appendix, except for dcxml, support SAX. With Lark, you need the sample SAX driver for Lark, which is available at the SAX home page. For the others, the SAX 1.0 package is included in the distribution, so no additional download for SAX support is necessary.

Following is a partial list of the criteria to consider when selecting an XML processor for SAX-based applications:

- Parse speed

- Error checking

  (some processors skip error checking to obtain a higher parsing speed)

- Support for attribute types

  If your application needs to know the type of a given attribute, you need a validating processor for which the `AttributeList#getType()` method returns the proper value.

Using the XML Processor with the DOM API

Even though some of the XML processors do not support DOM natively, you can use the Docuverse DOM SDK, which creates DOM trees from the SAX API calls.

XML for Java, SXP, and Sun Java Project X have their own DOM implementations. On the other hand, dcxml generates its own proprietary tree structures, which have an API similar to those of the package `org.w3c.dom`. XML for Java and SXP provide several useful methods in addition to the Level 1 DOM API.

The Parsing API

The W3C DOM Level 1 Recommendation does not specify the programming interface to start parsing and receiving a DOM tree. Following is a comparison of XML for Java and Docuverse DOM SDK.

XML for Java

```
String documenturi = ...
Parser parser = new Parser(documenturi);
Document doc = parser.readStream(parser.getInputStream(documenturi,
null, documenturi));
```

Docuverse DOM SDK

```
String documenturi = ...
DOM dom = new DOM();
dom.setProperty("sax.driver", "com.microstar.xml.SAXDriver"); //
AElfred
Document doc = dom.openDocument(documenturi);
```

The Generation API

Docuverse DOM SDK 1.0PR3B does not have an API for XML generation. You need to write a generation code for yourself that traverses the DOM tree. As described in Chapter 3, XML for Java provides simple generation as well as validating generation.

Useful Links and Books

This appendix is a compilation of links and books on the subjects mentioned in the book.

Standards

Standards bodies and pertinent documents mentioned in this book are listed in Table C.1. The status of these documents are as of February, 1999, and may have been changed after that. Please check the standards body's home pages for the latest information.

- World Wide Web Consortium (W3C): `http://www.w3.org`

  - `http://www.w3.org/`

    W3C Homepage

  - `http://www.w3.org/TR/`

    Lists all documents published by the W3C.

  - `http://www.w3.org/Submission/`

    Lists all documents submitted to the W3C.

- Internet Engineering Task Force (IETF): `http://www.ietf.org`

- International Organization for Standardization (ISO):
  `http://www.iso.ch/`

TABLE C.1 Alphabetical List of Links to Standard Documents

NAME	URL	STATUS	BODY
ASC X12	http://polaris.disa.org/		
CDF	http://www.w3.org/TR/NOTE-CDFsubmit.html	W3C Note	W3C
CORBA 2.2	http://www.omg.org/library/c2indx.html		OMG
DCD	http://www.w3.org/TR/NOTE-dcd	W3C Note	W3C
DOM Level 1	http://www.w3.org/TR/REC-DOM-Level-1	Recommendation (Oct. 1, 1998)	W3C
DOMHash	http://www.ietf.org/internet-drafts/ draft-hiroshi-dom-hash-01.txt	Internet Draft	IETF
DRP	http://www.w3.org/TR/NOTE-drp.html	W3C Note	W3C
EDIFACT	http://www.unece.org/trade/untdid/		
HTML 4.0	http://www.w3.org/TR/html140	Recommendation	W3C
HTTP 1.1 (RFC-2068)	http://www.ietf.org/rfc/rfc2068.txt	IETF RFC	IETF
IPSec	http://www.ietf.org/html.charters/ ipsec-charter.html		IETF
JavaBeans	http://java.sun.com/beans/index.html		Sun Micro Systems
MathML 1.0	http://www.w3.org/TR/REC-MathML/	Recommendation	W3C
Namespace	http://www.w3.org/TR/REC-xml-names/	Recommendation	W3C
P3P	http://www.w3.org/TR/WD-P3P10-syntax	Working Draft	W3C
PKCS Series	http://www.rsa.com/rsalabs/pubs/PKCS/		RSA Data Security
RDF Model and Syntax	http://www.w3.org/TR/PR-rdf-syntax	Proposed Recommendation	W3C
RDF Schema	http://www.w3.org/TR/WD-rdf-schema	Working Draft	W3C
SAX 1.0	http://www.megginson.com/SAX/		
Servlet 2.1	http://java.sun.com/products/servlet/ 2.1/index.html		Sun Micro Systems
SMIL 1.0	http://www.w3.org/TR/REC-smil/	Recommendation	W3C
SMTP, RFC822	http://www.ietf.org/rfc/rfc0822.txt	IETF RFC	IETF
SSL 3.0	http://home.netscape.com/eng/ssl3/ draft302.txt		Netscape
Unicode (ISO10464)	http://www.unicode.org/		
WebDAV	http://www.ietf.org/rfc/rfc2518.txt	IETF RFC	IETF
WML	http://www.wapforum.org/docs/technical/ wml-30-apr-98.pdf	1.0	WAP Forum
XLink	http://www.w3.org/TR/WD-xlink	Working Draft	W3C
XML 1.0	http://www.w3.org/TR/REC-xml	Recommendation (Feb. 10, 1998)	W3C
XPointer	http://www.w3.org/TR/WD-xptr	Working Draft	W3C
XSL	http://www.w3.org/TR/WD-xsl	Working Draft	W3C

Links of General XML Interests

- The SGML/XML Web page by Robin Cover:
  `http://www.oasis-open.org/cover/xml.html`

  Comprehensive links to XML and SGML, including articles, books, XML data, and tools.

- Annotated XML Specification by Tim Bray:
  `http://www.xml.com/axml/axml.html`

- `http://www.xml.com/`

  A rich mix of information for developers and beginners alike.

- `http://www.xmlu.com/`

  News and information on upcoming events.

- xml-dev mailing list:
  `http://www.lists.ic.ac.uk/hypermail/xml-dev/index.html`

  Very active mailing list for the discussion of XML specifications. Participants include people in W3C Working Groups and tool developers.

- IBM XML Web page: `http://www.ibm.com/xml/`

  White papers, links to IBM's downloadable technologies, and tutorials.

- Microsoft XML Web page: `http://www.microsoft.com/xml/`

  Good tutorials and demos.

- James Clark's Web page: `http://www.jclark.com/`

  The page of James Clark, author of XP, a highly conforming XML parser in Java. Page contains a set of XML test cases for testing the conformance of XML parsers.

- Graphic Communications Association (GCA): `http://www.gca.org/`

  A professional organization that organizes many conferences and seminars on XML.

- The Organization for the Advancement of Structured Information Standards (OASIS): `http://www.oasis-open.org/`

  A nonprofit, international consortium for discussing HTML/XML/SGML.

- XMLDevelopers.com: `http://www.xmldevelopers.com/`

  A site specialized for providing information to XML and Java developers. It has a comprehensible, program-development tutorial using XML for Java.

- XMLSoftware.com: `http://www.xmlsoftware.com/`

  A rich set of links to available XML tools.

Links to Product Home Pages

- Lotus eSuite: `http://www.lotus.com/home.nsf/tabs/esuite1/`
- Java Web Server: `http://jeeves.javasoft.com/products/java-server/index.html`
- JDBC drivers: `http://java.sun.com/products/jdbc/jdbc.drivers.html`
- DB2: `http://www.software.ibm.com/data/`
- MQSeries: `http://www.software.ibm.com/ts/mqseries/`
- Verisign: `http://www.verisign.com/`
- VisualAge for Java: `http://www.software.ibm.com/ad/vajava/`
- PGP: `http://www.pgp.com/`
- S/MIME: `http://www.rsa.com/rsa/S-MIME/`

Books

There are many books that cover Java or XML. Following is a partial list.

Java

1. The Java Series, Addison-Wesley: Reading, Mass. In particular, these:

   Arnold, Ken and James Gosling, *The Java Programming Language, Second Edition*, 1997. ISBN: 0-201-31006-6

   Campione, Mary and Kathy Walrath, *The Java Tutorial Second Edition*, 1998. ISBN: 0-201-31007-4

Chan, Patrick and Rosanna Lee, *The Java Class Libraries Second Edition, Volume 1*, 1998. ISBN: 0-201-31002-3

Chan, Patrick, Rosanna Lee, and Doug Kramer, *The Java Class Libraries Second Edition, Volume 2*, 1998. ISBN: 0-201-31003-1

Hamilton, Graham, Rick Cattell, and Maydene Fisher, *JDBC Database Access With Java: A Tutorial and Annotated Reference*, 1997. ISBN: 0-201-30995-5

2. Englander, Robert, *Developing Java Beans*, O'Reilly: Sebastopol, CA, 1997. ISBN:1-56592-289-1

3. Flanagan, David, *Java in a Nutshell, 2nd Edition*, O'Reilly: , 1997. ISBN 1-56592-262-X

4. Horstmann, Cay and Gray Cornel, *Core Java 1.1 Volume I—Fundamentals*, Prentice Hall: Upper Saddle River, NJ, 1997. ISBN: 0-13-766957-7

5. Horstmann, Cay and Gray Cornel, *Core Java 1.1 Volume II—Advanced Features*, Prentice Hall:, 1998. ISBN: 0-13-766965-8

6. Hunter, Jason and William Crawford, *Java Servlet Programming*, O'Reilly: Sebastopol, CA, 1997. ISBN:1-56592-391-X

7. Patel, Pratik, and Karl Moss, *Java Database Programming With JDBC*, The Coriolis Group: Scottsdale, AZ, 1997. ISBN: 1-57610-159-2

8. Reese, George E., and George H. Reese, *Database Programming With Jdbc and Java*, O'Reilly: Sebastopol, CA, 1997. ISBN: 1565922700

XML/SGML

1. Alschuler, Liora, *ABCD . . . SGML: A User's Guide to Structured Information*, International Computer Press: London/Boston, 1995. ISBN: 1-850-32197-3

2. Boumphrey, Frank, Olivia di Renzo, Jon Duckett, Joe Graf, Paul Houle, Trevor Jenkins, Peter Jones, Adrian Kingsley-Hughes, Kathie Kingsley-Hughes, Craig McQueen, Stephen Mohr, and Tad Murphy, *Professional XML Applications*, Wrox Press, Inc.: Chicago, 1998. ISBN: 1-861-00152-5

3. Bradley, Neil, *The XML Companion*, Prentice Hall Computer Books: Upper Saddle River, NJ, 1998. ISBN: 0-13-081152-1

4. Bradley, Neil, *The Concise SGML Companion* Addison-Wesley: Harlow, Essex, 1997. ISBN: 0-201-41999-8

5. DeRose, Steven J., *The SGML FAQ Book: Understanding the Foundation of HTML and XML*, Kluwer Academic Publishers: Dordrecht/Boston/London, 1997. ISBN: 0-7923-9943-9

6. Goldfarb, Charles F. and Yuri Rubinsky, *The SGML Handbook*, Clarendon Press: Oxford, 1991. ISBN: 0-19-853737-9

7. Goldfarb, Charles F., Steve Pepper, and Chet Ensign, *SGML Buyer's Guide: A Unique Guide to Determining Your Requirements and Choosing the Right SGML and XML Products and Services*, Prentice Hall: Upper Saddle River, NJ, 1998. ISBN: 0-13-681511-1

8. Harold, Elliotte Rusty, *XML: Extensible Markup Language*, IDG Books Worldwide: Foster City/Chicago/New York, 1998. ISBN: 0-764-53199-9

9. Jelliffe, Rick, *The XML and SGML Cookbook: Recipes for Structured Information*, Prentice Hall: Upper Saddle River, NJ, 1998. ISBN: 0-136-14223-0

10. Light, Richard and Tim Bray, *Presenting XML*, Sams: Indianapolis, IN, 1998. ISBN: 1-575-21334-6

11. Mayer, Eve and Jeanne Andaloussi, *Developing SGML DTDs: From Text to Model to Markup*, Prentice Hall: Upper Saddle River, NJ, 1996. ISBN: 0-13-309881-8

12. Megginson, David, *Structuring XML Documents*, Prentice Hall: Upper Saddle River, NJ, 1998. ISBN: 0-13-642299-3

13. Simpson, John E., *Just XML*, Prentice Hall Computer Books: Upper Saddle River, NJ, 1998. ISBN: 0-13-943417-8

14. Smith, Norman E., *Practical Guide to SGML/XML Filters*, Wordware Publishing: Plano, TX, 1998. ISBN: 1-556-22587-3

Other Topics

1. Gamma, Erich, Richard Helm, Ralph Johnson, and John Vlissides, *Design Patterns*, Addison-Wesley: Reading, Mass, 1995. ISBN: 0-201-63361-2

2. Garfinkel, Simson, and Gene Spafford, *Web Security & Commerce*, O'Reilly: 1997. ISBN: 1-565-92269-7

XML for Java API Reference

This appendix lists the public classes and methods of XML for Java. For further details, consult the APIDOC on the CD-ROM.

Package `com.ibm.xml.domutil`

Utility class for W3C DOM

Package `com.ibm.xml.parser`

XML4J core classes

Package `com.ibm.xml.parser.util`

XML4J utility classes

Package `org.w3c.dom`

W3C DOM interfaces

Package `org.xml.sax`

Package `org.xml.sax.helpers`

Simple API for XML (SAX) classes

Package `com.ibm.xml.domutil`

Class `DOMDuplicator`

```
public class DOMDuplicator {
    // Constructors
    public DOMDuplicator();
```

```
    // Methods
    public static org.w3c.dom.Node cloneNode(org.w3c.dom.Document
factory, org.w3c.dom.Node node);
}
```

Package com.ibm.xml.parser

Class AttDef

```
public class AttDef extends Child {
    // Fields
    public static final int CDATA;
    public static final int ID;
    public static final int IDREF;
    public static final int IDREFS;
    public static final int ENTITY;
    public static final int ENTITIES;
    public static final int NMTOKEN;
    public static final int NMTOKENS;
    public static final int NOTATION;
    public static final int NAME_TOKEN_GROUP;
    public static final String[] S_TYPESTR;
    public static final int FIXED;
    public static final int REQUIRED;
    public static final int IMPLIED;
    public static final int NOFIXED;
    public static final int UNKNOWN;
    // Constructors
    public AttDef(String name);
    // Methods
    public void acceptPost(Visitor visitor) throws Exception;
    public void acceptPre(Visitor visitor) throws Exception;
    public boolean addElement(String token);
    public synchronized Object clone();
    public boolean contains(String token);
    public String elementAt(int index);
    public java.util.Enumeration elements();
    public synchronized boolean equals(org.w3c.dom.Node arg, boolean
        deep);
    public int getDeclaredType();
    public String getDefaultStringValue();
    public int getDefaultType();
    public String getName();
```

```
        public String getNodeName();
        public short getNodeType();
        public void setDeclaredType(int declaredValueType);
        public void setDefaultStringValue(String value);
        public void setDefaultType(int defaultValueType);
        public void setName(String name);
        public int size();
    }
```

Class Attlist

```
    public class Attlist extends Child {
        // Constructors
        public Attlist(String name);
        // Methods
        public void acceptPost(Visitor visitor) throws Exception;
        public void acceptPre(Visitor visitor) throws Exception;
        public boolean addElement(AttDef attDef);
        public synchronized Object clone();
        public boolean contains(String attDefName);
        public AttDef elementAt(int index);
        public java.util.Enumeration elements();
        public synchronized boolean equals(org.w3c.dom.Node arg, boolean
          deep);
        public AttDef getAttDef(String attDefName);
        public String getName();
        public String getNodeName();
        public short getNodeType();
        public int size();
    }
```

Class CM1op

```
    public class CM1op extends CMNode {
        // Constructors
        public CM1op(int type, CMNode node);
        // Methods
        public boolean equals(Object obj);
        public CMNode getNode();
        public int getType();
        public int hashCode();
        public void setNode(CMNode node);
        public String toString();
    }
```

Class CM2op

```
public class CM2op extends CMNode {
    // Constructors
    public CM2op(int type, CMNode leftNode, CMNode rightNode);
    // Methods
    public boolean equals(Object obj);
    public CMNode getLeft();
    public CMNode getRight();
    public int getType();
    public int hashCode();
    public void setLeft(CMNode leftNode);
    public void setRight(CMNode rightNode);
    public String toString();
}
```

Class CMLeaf

```
public class CMLeaf extends CMNode {
    // Constructors
    public CMLeaf(String name);
    // Methods
    public boolean equals(Object obj);
    public String getName();
    public int hashCode();
    public String toString();
}
```

Class CMNode

```
public abstract class CMNode implements java.io.Serializable {
    // Constructors
    public CMNode();
}
```

Class Child

```
public abstract class Child implements org.w3c.dom.Node, Cloneable,
java.io.Serializable, Visitee {
    // Fields
    public static final int ELEMENT_DECL;
    public static final int ATTLIST;
    public static final int ATTDEF;
    public static final int PSEUDONODE;
    public static final String NAME_DOCUMENT;
    public static final String NAME_COMMENT;
```

```
public static final String NAME_TEXT;
public static final String NAME_CDATA;
public static final String NAME_DOCFRAGMENT;
public static final String NAME_ATTDEF;
public static final String NAME_ATTLIST;
public static final String NAME_ELEMENT_DECL;
public static final String NAME_PSEUDONODE;
// Constructors
public Child();
// Methods
public org.w3c.dom.Node appendChild(org.w3c.dom.Node newChild)
  throws org.w3c.dom.DOMException;
public void clearDigest();
public abstract Object clone();
public org.w3c.dom.Node cloneNode(boolean deep);
public abstract boolean equals(org.w3c.dom.Node node, boolean deep);
public org.w3c.dom.NamedNodeMap getAttributes();
public org.w3c.dom.NodeList getChildNodes();
public byte[] getDigest() throws LibraryException;
public TXDocument getFactory();
public org.w3c.dom.Node getFirstChild();
public org.w3c.dom.Node getFirstWithoutReference();
public org.w3c.dom.Node getLastChild();
public org.w3c.dom.Node getLastWithoutReference();
public org.w3c.dom.Node getNextSibling();
public org.w3c.dom.Node getNextWithoutReference();
public String getNodeValue();
public org.w3c.dom.Document getOwnerDocument();
public org.w3c.dom.Node getParentNode();
public org.w3c.dom.Node getParentWithoutReference();
public org.w3c.dom.Node getPreviousSibling();
public org.w3c.dom.Node getPreviousWithoutReference();
public String getText();
public boolean hasChildNodes();
public org.w3c.dom.Node insertBefore(org.w3c.dom.Node newChild,
  org.w3c.dom.Node refChild) throws org.w3c.dom.DOMException;
public com.ibm.xml.xpointer.XPointer makeXPointer();
public void print(java.io.Writer writer, String encoding) throws
  java.io.IOException, LibraryException;
public void print(java.io.Writer writer) throws java.io.IOException,
  LibraryException;
public org.w3c.dom.Node removeChild(org.w3c.dom.Node oldChild)
  throws org.w3c.dom.DOMException;
public org.w3c.dom.Node replaceChild(org.w3c.dom.Node oldChild,
  org.w3c.dom.Node newChild) throws org.w3c.dom.DOMException;
```

```
            public TXElement searchAncestors(String qName);
            public TXElement searchAncestors(int matchType, String uri, String
              qNameOrLocalName);
            public void setFactory(TXDocument factory);
            public void setNodeValue(String arg);
            public void toXMLString(java.io.Writer writer, String encoding)
              throws java.io.IOException, LibraryException;
            public void toXMLString(java.io.Writer writer) throws
              java.io.IOException, LibraryException;
      }
```

Class ContentModel

```
      public class ContentModel implements Cloneable, java.io.Serializable {
            // Constructors
            public ContentModel(int type);
            public ContentModel(CMNode modelGroupNode);
            // Methods
            public synchronized Object clone();
            public synchronized boolean equals(Object obj);
            public CMNode getContentModelNode();
            public TXDocument getFactory();
            public String getPseudoContentModel();
            public int hashCode();
            public void setContentModelNode(CMNode modelGroupNode);
            public void setFactory(TXDocument factory);
            public void setPseudoContentModel(String literal);
            public String toString();
      }
```

Class DTD

```
      public class DTD extends Parent implements org.w3c.dom.DocumentType {
            // Fields
            public static final String CM_EOC;
            public static final String CM_ERROR;
            public static final String CM_PCDATA;
            // Constructors
            public DTD();
            public DTD(String name, ExternalID externalID);
            // Methods
            public java.util.Enumeration IDs();
            public void acceptPost(Visitor visitor) throws Exception;
            public void acceptPre(Visitor visitor) throws Exception;
            protected void checkChildType(org.w3c.dom.Node child) throws
              org.w3c.dom.DOMException;
```

```
public boolean checkContent(TXElement element);
public org.w3c.dom.Element checkID(String id);
public Object clone();
public synchronized org.w3c.dom.Node cloneNode(boolean deep);
public synchronized boolean equals(org.w3c.dom.Node arg, boolean
  deep);
public java.util.Enumeration externalElements();
public java.util.Hashtable getAppendableElements(org.w3c.dom.Element
  element, java.util.Hashtable hashtable);
public AttDef getAttributeDeclaration(String elementName, String
  attributeName);
public java.util.Enumeration getAttributeDeclarations(String
  elementName);
public ContentModel getContentModel(String elementName);
public int getContentType(String elementName);
public ElementDecl getElementDeclaration(String elementName);
public java.util.Enumeration getElementDeclarations();
public org.w3c.dom.NamedNodeMap getEntities();
public EntityDecl getEntityDecl(String name, boolean isParameter);
public java.util.Enumeration getEntityEnumeration();
public ExternalID getExternalID();
public int getExternalSize();
public java.util.Hashtable getInsertableElements(org.w3c.dom.Element
  element, int index, java.util.Hashtable hashtable);
public java.util.Hashtable getInsertableElementsForValidContent(org.
  w3c.dom.Element element, int index, java.util.Hashtable hashtable);
public int getInternalSize();
public String getName();
public String getNodeName();
public short getNodeType();
public org.w3c.dom.Notation getNotation(String notationName);
public java.util.Enumeration getNotationEnumeration();
public org.w3c.dom.NamedNodeMap getNotations();
public java.util.Enumeration internalElements();
public boolean isAttributeDeclared(String elementName, String
  attributeName);
public boolean isElementDeclared(String elementName);
public boolean isParsingExternal();
public boolean isPrintInternalDTD();
public java.util.Vector makeContentElementList(String
  elementDeclName);
public java.util.Hashtable prepareTable(String elementName);
public void printExternal(java.io.Writer pw, String encoding) throws
  java.io.IOException;
```

```
        protected void realInsert(org.w3c.dom.Node newChild, int index)
           throws org.w3c.dom.DOMException;
        public boolean registID(org.w3c.dom.Element element, String id);
        public void setEncoding(String xmlEncoding);
        public void setExternalID(ExternalID externalID);
        public void setParsingExternal(boolean flag);
        public void setPrintInternalDTD(boolean flag);
    }
```

Class ElementDecl

```
    public class ElementDecl extends Child {
        // Fields
        public static final int EMPTY;
        public static final int ANY;
        public static final int MODEL_GROUP;
        // Constructors
        public ElementDecl(String name, ContentModel contentModel);
        // Methods
        public void acceptPost(Visitor visitor) throws Exception;
        public void acceptPre(Visitor visitor) throws Exception;
        public synchronized Object clone();
        public synchronized boolean equals(org.w3c.dom.Node arg, boolean
           deep);
        public int getContentType();
        public String getName();
        public String getNodeName();
        public short getNodeType();
        public void setContentType(int contentType);
        public void setName(String name);
    }
```

Interface ElementHandler

```
    public abstract interface ElementHandler {
        // Methods
        public TXElement handleElement(TXElement element);
    }
```

Class EndTraversalException

```
    public class EndTraversalException extends TreeTraversalException {
        // Constructors
        public EndTraversalException();
        public EndTraversalException(String msg);
    }
```

Class EntityDecl

```
public class EntityDecl extends Parent {
    // Constructors
    public EntityDecl(String name, String value, boolean isParameter);
    public EntityDecl(String name, ExternalID externalID, boolean
        isParameter, String ndata);
    // Methods
    public void acceptPost(Visitor visitor) throws Exception;
    public void acceptPre(Visitor visitor) throws Exception;
    protected void checkChildType(org.w3c.dom.Node child) throws org.
        w3c.dom.DOMException;
    public synchronized Object clone();
    public synchronized org.w3c.dom.Node cloneNode(boolean deep);
    public boolean equals(org.w3c.dom.Node arg, boolean deep);
        protected org.w3c.dom.Entity getEntityImpl();
    public ExternalID getExternalID();
    public String getNodeName();
    public short getNodeType();
    public String getNotationName();
    public String getPublicId();
    public String getSystemId();
    public String getValue();
    public boolean isExternal();
    public boolean isParameter();
}
```

Interface ErrorListener

```
public abstract interface ErrorListener {
    // Methods
    public int error(String fileName, int lineNo, int charOffset, Object
        key, String msg);
}
```

Class ExternalID

```
public class ExternalID implements java.io.Serializable {
    // Constructors
    public ExternalID(String systemID);
    public ExternalID(String publicID, String systemID);
    // Methods
    public boolean equals(Object obj);
    public String getPubidLiteral();
    public String getSystemLiteral();
    public int hashCode();
    public boolean isPublic();
```

```
        public boolean isSystem();
        public String toString();
    }
```

Class FormatPrintVisitor

```
    public class FormatPrintVisitor extends ToXMLStringVisitor implements
    Visitor {
        // Fields
        protected int currentIndent;
        protected int indent;
        protected boolean ispreserve;
        protected java.util.Stack preserves;
        protected boolean isprevtext;
        // Constructors
        public FormatPrintVisitor(java.io.Writer writer, String encoding,
          int indent);
        public FormatPrintVisitor(java.io.Writer writer, String
          encoding);
        public FormatPrintVisitor(java.io.Writer writer);
        // Methods
        public void visitAttlistPre(Attlist attlist) throws Exception;
        public void visitCommentPre(TXComment comment) throws Exception;
        public void visitDTDPost(DTD dtd) throws Exception;
        public void visitDTDPre(DTD dtd) throws Exception;
        public void visitDocumentPost(TXDocument document) throws
          Exception;
        public void visitElementDeclPre(ElementDecl elementDecl) throws
          Exception;
        public void visitElementPost(TXElement element) throws Exception;
        public void visitElementPre(TXElement element) throws Exception;
        public void visitEntityDeclPre(EntityDecl entityDecl) throws
          Exception;
        public void visitNotationPre(TXNotation notation) throws
          Exception;
        public void visitPIPre(TXPI pi) throws Exception;
        public void visitTextPre(TXText text) throws Exception;
    }
```

Class GeneralReference

```
    public class GeneralReference extends Parent implements
    org.w3c.dom.EntityReference {
        // Constructors
        public GeneralReference(String name);
        // Methods
```

```
    public void acceptPost(Visitor visitor) throws Exception;
    public void acceptPre(Visitor visitor) throws Exception;
    protected void checkChildType(org.w3c.dom.Node child) throws
        org.w3c.dom.DOMException;
    public Object clone();
    public synchronized org.w3c.dom.Node cloneNode(boolean deep);
    public void collectNamespaceAttributes();
    public void collectNamespaceAttributes(org.w3c.dom.Node parent);
    public synchronized boolean equals(org.w3c.dom.Node arg, boolean
        deep);
    public String getLanguage();
    public String getName();
    public String getNodeName();
    public short getNodeType();
    public void removeOverlappedNamespaceAttributes();
}
```

Class InsertableElement

```
    public class InsertableElement {
        // Fields
        public String name;
        public boolean status;
        public int index;
        // Constructors
        public InsertableElement(String name);
        public InsertableElement(String name, boolean status);
        public InsertableElement(int index);
        // Methods
        public String toString();
    }
```

Class InvalidEncodingException

```
    public class InvalidEncodingException extends java.io.IOException {
        // Constructors
        public InvalidEncodingException();
        public InvalidEncodingException(String msg);
    }
```

Class LibraryException

```
    public class LibraryException extends RuntimeException {
        // Constructors
        public LibraryException();
        public LibraryException(String msg);
    }
```

Class MIME2Java

```
public class MIME2Java {
    // Methods
    public static String convert(String mimeCharsetName);
    public static String reverse(String encoding);
}
```

Class MakeDigestVisitor

```
public class MakeDigestVisitor extends NOOPVisitor implements Visitor
{
    // Fields
    protected java.security.MessageDigest messageDigest;
    // Constructors
    public MakeDigestVisitor(java.security.MessageDigest
      messageDigest);
    // Methods
    public void visitAttributePre(TXAttribute attribute) throws
      Exception;
    public void visitCommentPre(TXComment comment) throws Exception;
    public void visitElementPost(TXElement element) throws Exception;
    public void visitElementPre(TXElement element) throws Exception;
    public void visitGeneralReferencePre(GeneralReference
      generalReference) throws Exception;
    public void visitPIPre(TXPI pi) throws Exception;
    public void visitTextPre(TXText text) throws Exception;
}
```

Class Match

```
public class Match {
    // Fields
    public static final int QNAME;
    public static final int NSLOCAL;
    public static final int NS;
    // Constructors
    public Match();
    // Methods
    public static boolean matchName(Namespace target, int matchType,
    String uri, String qNameOrLocalName);
}
```

Interface Namespace

```
public abstract interface Namespace {
    // Methods
    public String createExpandedName();
```

```
        public String getNSLocalName();
        public String getNSName();
        public String getName();
    }
```

Interface NoRequiredAttributeHandler

```
    public abstract interface NoRequiredAttributeHandler {
        // Methods
        public TXElement handleNoRequiredAttribute(TXElement element,
          String attributeName);
    }
```

Class NonRecursivePreorderTreeTraversal

```
    public class NonRecursivePreorderTreeTraversal extends TreeTraversal
    {
        // Constructors
        public NonRecursivePreorderTreeTraversal(Visitor visitor);
        // Methods
        public void traverse(org.w3c.dom.Node startNode) throws
          Exception;
    }
```

Interface PIHandler

```
    public abstract interface PIHandler {
        // Methods
        public void handlePI(String name, String data);
    }
```

Class Parent

```
    public abstract class Parent extends Child {
        // Constructors
        public Parent();
        // Methods
        public synchronized org.w3c.dom.Node appendChild(org.w3c.dom.Node
          newChild);
        protected abstract void checkChildType(org.w3c.dom.Node child)
          throws org.w3c.dom.DOMException;
        public java.util.Enumeration elements();
        public void expandEntityReferences();
        public org.w3c.dom.NodeList getChildNodes();
        public Child[] getChildrenArray();
```

```
         public org.w3c.dom.Node getFirstChild();
         public org.w3c.dom.Node getFirstWithoutReference();
         public org.w3c.dom.Node getLastChild();
         public org.w3c.dom.Node getLastWithoutReference();
         public String getText();
         public boolean hasChildNodes();
         public synchronized void insert(org.w3c.dom.Node child, int index)
           throws org.w3c.dom.DOMException;
         public synchronized org.w3c.dom.Node insertAfter(org.w3c.dom.Node
           newChild, org.w3c.dom.Node refChild) throws org.w3c.dom.
           DOMException;
         public synchronized org.w3c.dom.Node insertBefore(org.w3c.dom.Node
           newChild, org.w3c.dom.Node refChild) throws org.w3c.dom.
           DOMException;
         public synchronized org.w3c.dom.Node insertFirst(org.w3c.dom.Node
           newChild);
         public synchronized org.w3c.dom.Node insertLast(org.w3c.dom.Node
           newChild);
         protected void processAfterRemove(org.w3c.dom.Node oldChild);
         protected void realInsert(org.w3c.dom.Node child, int index) throws
           org.w3c.dom.DOMException;
         public synchronized org.w3c.dom.Node removeChild(org.w3c.dom.Node
           oldChild) throws org.w3c.dom.DOMException;
         public synchronized org.w3c.dom.Node replaceChild(org.w3c.dom.Node
           newChild, org.w3c.dom.Node oldChild) throws org.w3c.dom.
           DOMException;
       }
```

Class Parser

```
     public class Parser {
       // Constructors
       public Parser(String name);
       public Parser(String name, ErrorListener errorListener,
         StreamProducer streamProducer);
       // Methods
       public void addElementHandler(ElementHandler elementHandler);
       public void addElementHandler(ElementHandler elementHandler, String
         elementTagName);
       public void addNoRequiredAttributeHandler(NoRequiredAttributeHandler
         noRequiredAttributeHandler);
       public void addPIHandler(PIHandler piHandler);
       public void addPreRootHandler(PreRootHandler preRootHandler);
       public void closeInputStream(Source source);
       public Source getInputStream(String name, String publicID, String
         systemID) throws java.io.IOException;
```

```
         public int getNumberOfErrors();
         public int getNumberOfWarnings();
         public int getReaderBufferSize();
         public void loadCatalog(java.io.Reader reader) throws java.io.
            IOException;
         public DTD readDTDStream(java.io.InputStream inputStream) throws
            java.io.IOException;
         public DTD readDTDStream(java.io.Reader reader) throws java.io.
            IOException;
         public DTD readDTDStream(Source source) throws java.io.
            IOException;
         public TXDocument readStream(java.io.InputStream inputStream);
         public TXDocument readStream(java.io.Reader reader);
         public TXDocument readStream(Source source);
         public void setAllowJavaEncodingName(boolean
            isAllowJavaEncodingName);
         public void setElementFactory(TXDocument elementFactory);
         public void setEndBy1stError(boolean isEndBy1stError);
         public void setErrorNoByteMark(boolean isErrorNoByteMark);
         public void setExpandEntityReferences(boolean
            isExpandEntityReferences);
         public void setKeepComment(boolean isKeepComment);
         public void setLocale(java.util.Locale locale);
         public void setPreserveSpace(boolean isPreserveSpace);
         public void setProcessExternalDTD(boolean isProcessExternalDTD);
         public void setProcessNamespace(boolean isProcessNamespace);
         public void setReaderBufferSize(int readerBufferSize);
         public void setReferenceHandler(ReferenceHandler
            referenceHandler);
         public void setTagHandler(TagHandler tagHandler);
         public void setWarningNoDoctypeDecl(boolean
            isWarningNoDoctypeDecl);
         public void setWarningNoXMLDecl(boolean isWarningNoXMLDecl);
         public void setWarningRedefinedEntity(boolean
            isWarningRedefinedEntity);
         public void stop();
    }
```

Interface PreRootHandler

```
    public abstract interface PreRootHandler {
        // Methods
        public void handlePreRoot(TXDocument document, String rootName);
    }
```

Class PseudoNode

```
public class PseudoNode extends TXCharacterData {
    // Constructors
    public PseudoNode(String data);
    // Methods
    public void acceptPost(Visitor visitor) throws Exception;
    public void acceptPre(Visitor visitor) throws Exception;
    public synchronized Object clone();
    public boolean equals(org.w3c.dom.Node arg, boolean deep);
    public String getNodeName();
    public short getNodeType();
    public String getText();
}
```

Interface ReferenceHandler

```
public abstract interface ReferenceHandler {
    // Methods
    public void endReference(String entityName);
    public void startReference(String entityName);
}
```

Class SAXDriver

```
public class SAXDriver implements org.xml.sax.Parser, org.xml.sax.
AttributeList, ErrorListener, TagHandler, StreamProducer {
    // Constructors
    public SAXDriver();
    // Methods
    public void closeInputStream(Source source);
    public int error(String fileName, int lineNo, int charOffset,
        Object key, String msg) throws RuntimeException;
    public Source getInputStream(String name, String publicID, String
        systemID) throws java.io.IOException, RuntimeException;
    public int getLength();
    public String getName(int i);
    public String getType(int i);
    public String getType(String name);
    public String getValue(int i);
    public String getValue(String name);
    public void handleEndTag(TXElement el, boolean empty) throws
        RuntimeException;
    public void handleStartTag(TXElement element, boolean empty)
        throws RuntimeException;
    public void loadCatalog(java.io.Reader reader) throws
        java.io.IOException;
```

```
    public void parse(org.xml.sax.InputSource isrc) throws
      org.xml.sax.SAXException;
    public void parse(String systemId) throws org.xml.sax.
      SAXException;
    public void setDTDHandler(org.xml.sax.DTDHandler handler);
    public void setDocumentHandler(org.xml.sax.DocumentHandler
      handler);
    public void setEntityResolver(org.xml.sax.EntityResolver
      handler);
    public void setErrorHandler(org.xml.sax.ErrorHandler handler);
    public void setLocale(java.util.Locale locale) throws org.xml.
      sax.SAXException;
}
```

Class Source

```
public class Source {
    // Constructors
    public Source(java.io.InputStream inputStream);
    public Source(java.io.InputStream inputStream, String encoding);
    public Source(java.io.Reader reader);
    // Methods
    public String getEncoding();
    public java.io.InputStream getInputStream();
    public java.io.Reader getReader();
}
```

Class Stderr

```
public class Stderr implements ErrorListener, StreamProducer {
    // Fields
    public static java.io.PrintWriter printer;
    protected String name;
    protected java.net.URL url;
    protected java.util.Stack stack;
    protected java.util.Hashtable catalog;
    protected boolean isPrintWarning;
    // Constructors
    public Stderr(String name);
    // Methods
    public void closeInputStream(Source source);
    public int error(String file, int lineNo, int charOffset, Object
      key, String msg);
    public static java.net.URL file2URL(String file) throws java.net.
      MalformedURLException;
```

```
    public Source getInputStream(String name, String publicID, String
      systemID) throws java.io.IOException;
    public void loadCatalog(java.io.Reader reader) throws java.io.
      IOException;
    public void setPrintWarning(boolean isPrintWarning);
}
```

Interface StreamProducer

```
public abstract interface StreamProducer {
    // Methods
    public void closeInputStream(Source source);
    public Source getInputStream(String name, String publicID, String
      systemID) throws java.io.IOException;
    public void loadCatalog(java.io.Reader reader) throws java.io.
      IOException;
}
```

Class StylesheetPI

```
public class StylesheetPI extends TXPI {
    // Fields
    public static final String S_XMLSTYLESHEET;
    public static final String S_XMLALTSTYLESHEET;
    public static final String S_STYLESHEET;
    public static final String S_ALTSTYLESHEET;
    public static final String S_TEXTCSS;
    // Constructors
    public StylesheetPI(String hrefURI);
    public StylesheetPI(String type, String hrefURI, String title);
    public StylesheetPI(String name, String type, String hrefURI,
      String title);
    public StylesheetPI(String name, String data, String type, String
      hrefURI, String title) throws LibraryException;
    // Methods
    public synchronized Object clone();
    public String getHref();
    public String getTitle();
    public String getType();
}
```

Class TXAttribute

```
public class TXAttribute extends Parent implements org.w3c.dom.Attr,
Namespace {
    // Constructors
    public TXAttribute(String name, String value);
    // Methods
    public void acceptPost(Visitor visitor) throws Exception;
    public void acceptPre(Visitor visitor) throws Exception;
    protected void checkChildType(org.w3c.dom.Node child) throws org.
      w3c.dom.DOMException;
    public Object clone();
    public synchronized org.w3c.dom.Node cloneNode(boolean deep);
    public String createExpandedName();
    public synchronized boolean equals(org.w3c.dom.Node arg, boolean
      deep);
    public boolean equals(Object object);
    public String getNSLocalName();
    public String getNSName();
    public String getName();
    public org.w3c.dom.Node getNextSibling();
    public String getNodeName();
    public short getNodeType();
    public String getNodeValue();
    public org.w3c.dom.Node getParentNode();
    public org.w3c.dom.Node getPreviousSibling();
    public boolean getSpecified();
    public int getType();
    public String[] getTypedValue();
    public String getValue();
    public int hashCode();
    protected void realInsert(org.w3c.dom.Node child, int index)
      throws LibraryException;
    public org.w3c.dom.Node removeChild(org.w3c.dom.Node oldChild)
      throws org.w3c.dom.DOMException;
    public org.w3c.dom.Node replaceChild(org.w3c.dom.Node newChild,
      org.w3c.dom.Node oldChild) throws org.w3c.dom.DOMException;
    public void setNodeValue(String value);
    public void setSpecified(boolean specified);
    public void setType(int type, String[] typedValue);
    public void setValue(String value);
    public String toString();
    public String toXMLString(String encoding);
    public String toXMLString();
}
```

Class TXCDATASection

```
public class TXCDATASection extends TXText implements
org.w3c.dom.CDATASection {
    // Constructors
    public TXCDATASection(String data);
    // Methods
    public synchronized Object clone();
    public synchronized boolean equals(org.w3c.dom.Node arg, boolean
      deep);
    public String getNodeName();
    public short getNodeType();
}
```

Class TXCharacterData

```
public abstract class TXCharacterData extends Child implements
org.w3c.dom.CharacterData {
    // Constructors
    public TXCharacterData();
    // Methods
    public synchronized void appendData(String data) throws org.w3c.
      dom.DOMException;
    public synchronized void deleteData(int offset, int count) throws
      org.w3c.dom.DOMException;
    public String getData();
    public int getLength();
    public String getNodeValue();
    public synchronized void insertData(int offset, String data)
      throws org.w3c.dom.DOMException;
    public synchronized void replaceData(int offset, int count,
      String data) throws org.w3c.dom.DOMException;
    public void setData(String data);
    public void setNodeValue(String data);
    public synchronized String substringData(int start, int count)
      throws org.w3c.dom.DOMException;
}
```

Class TXComment

```
public class TXComment extends TXCharacterData implements
org.w3c.dom.Comment {
    // Constructors
    public TXComment(String data);
    // Methods
    public void acceptPost(Visitor visitor) throws Exception;
```

```
    public void acceptPre(Visitor visitor) throws Exception;
    public synchronized Object clone();
    public synchronized boolean equals(org.w3c.dom.Node arg, boolean
      deep);
    public String getNodeName();
    public short getNodeType();
    public String getText();
}
```

Class TXDocument

```
public class TXDocument extends Parent implements
org.w3c.dom.Document {
    // Fields
    public String expandedNameSeparator;
    // Constructors
    public TXDocument();
    // Methods
    public void acceptPost(Visitor visitor) throws Exception;
    public void acceptPre(Visitor visitor) throws Exception;
    protected void checkChildType(org.w3c.dom.Node child) throws org.
      w3c.dom.DOMException;
    public Object clone();
    public synchronized org.w3c.dom.Node cloneNode(boolean deep);
    public AttDef createAttDef(String name);
    public Attlist createAttlist(String name);
    public org.w3c.dom.Attr createAttribute(String name) throws org.
      w3c.dom.DOMException;
    public org.w3c.dom.CDATASection createCDATASection(String data)
      throws org.w3c.dom.DOMException;
    public org.w3c.dom.Comment createComment(String data);
    public ContentModel createContentModel(int type);
    public ContentModel createContentModel(CMNode modelGroupNode);
    public DTD createDTD();
    public DTD createDTD(String name, ExternalID externalID);
    public org.w3c.dom.DocumentFragment createDocumentFragment();
    public org.w3c.dom.Element createElement(String name) throws org.
      w3c.dom.DOMException;
    public ElementDecl createElementDecl(String name, ContentModel
      contentModel);
    public org.w3c.dom.Entity createEntity();
    public EntityDecl createEntityDecl(String name, String value,
      boolean isParameter);
    public EntityDecl createEntityDecl(String name, ExternalID
      externalID, boolean isParameter, String ndata);
```

```
public org.w3c.dom.EntityReference createEntityReference(String name)
  throws org.w3c.dom.DOMException;
public java.security.MessageDigest createMessageDigest() throws
  java.security.NoSuchAlgorithmException;
public TXNotation createNotation(String name, ExternalID externalID);
public org.w3c.dom.ProcessingInstruction createProcessingInstruction(
  String name, String data) throws org.w3c.dom.DOMException;
public StylesheetPI createStylesheetPI(String name, String data,
  String type, String hrefURI, String title);
public org.w3c.dom.Text createTextNode(String data);
public TXText createTextNode(String data, boolean
  isIgnorableWhitespace);
public TXText createTextNode(char[] charArray, int offset, int
  length, boolean isIgnorableWhitespace);
public synchronized boolean equals(org.w3c.dom.Node arg, boolean
  deep);
public DTD getDTD();
public org.w3c.dom.DocumentType getDoctype();
public org.w3c.dom.Element getDocumentElement();
public org.w3c.dom.NodeList getElementsByTagName(String qName);
public String getEncoding();
public TXDocument getFactory();
public org.w3c.dom.DOMImplementation getImplementation();
public static TXDocument getInstance();
public String getNodeName();
public short getNodeType();
public org.w3c.dom.Document getOwnerDocument();
public String getRootName();
public String getStandalone();
public String getText();
public String getVersion();
public boolean isAddFixedAttributes();
public boolean isCheckNodeLoop();
public boolean isCheckOwnerDocument();
public boolean isCheckValidity();
public boolean isProcessNamespace();
public boolean isStandalone();
public void printWithFormat(java.io.Writer pw) throws java.io.
  IOException, LibraryException;
public void printWithFormat(java.io.Writer pw, String encoding)
  throws java.io.IOException, LibraryException;
public void printWithFormat(java.io.Writer pw, String encoding, int
  indent) throws java.io.IOException, LibraryException;
protected void realInsert(org.w3c.dom.Node child, int index) throws
  LibraryException;
```

```
    public org.w3c.dom.Node removeChild(org.w3c.dom.Node oldChild)
        throws org.w3c.dom.DOMException;
    public org.w3c.dom.Node replaceChild(org.w3c.dom.Node newChild,
        org.w3c.dom.Node oldChild) throws org.w3c.dom.DOMException;
    protected void resetCheckValidity();
    public void setAddFixedAttributes(boolean addFixedAttributes);
    public void setCheckNodeLoop(boolean doCheck);
    public void setCheckOwnerDocument(boolean doCheck);
    public void setDigestAlgorithm(String defDigestAlgorithm);
    public void setEncoding(String xmlEncoding);
    public void setPrintInternalDTD(boolean printInternalDTD);
    public void setProcessNamespace(boolean isProcessNamespace);
    public void setStandalone(String standalone);
    public void setVersion(String xmlVersion);
}
```

Class TXDocumentFragment

```
public class TXDocumentFragment extends Parent implements
org.w3c.dom.DocumentFragment {
    // Constructors
    public TXDocumentFragment();
    // Methods
    public void acceptPost(Visitor visitor) throws Exception;
    public void acceptPre(Visitor visitor) throws Exception;
    protected void checkChildType(org.w3c.dom.Node child) throws org.
        w3c.dom.DOMException;
    public Object clone();
    public synchronized org.w3c.dom.Node cloneNode(boolean deep);
    public synchronized boolean equals(org.w3c.dom.Node arg, boolean
        deep);
    public String getNodeName();
    public short getNodeType();
}
```

Class TXElement

```
public class TXElement extends Parent implements org.w3c.dom.Element,
Namespace {
    // Fields
    public static final String S_XMLNS;
    public static final String S_XMLNAMESPACEURI;
    // Constructors
    public TXElement(String tagName);
    // Methods
```

```
public void acceptPost(Visitor visitor) throws Exception;
public void acceptPre(Visitor visitor) throws Exception;
public void addTextElement(TXText text);
public java.util.Enumeration attributeElements();
protected void checkChildType(org.w3c.dom.Node child) throws org.
   w3c.dom.DOMException;
public synchronized Object clone();
public org.w3c.dom.Node cloneNode(boolean deep);
public synchronized TXElement cloneWithoutChildren();
public void collectNamespaceAttributes();
public void collectNamespaceAttributes(org.w3c.dom.Node parent);
public String createExpandedName();
public boolean equals(org.w3c.dom.Node arg, boolean deep);
public String getAttribute(String name);
public TXAttribute[] getAttributeArray();
public org.w3c.dom.Attr getAttributeNode(String name);
public org.w3c.dom.NamedNodeMap getAttributes();
public TXElement getElementNamed(String qName);
public TXElement getElementNamed(String uri, String localName);
public TXElement getElementNamed(int matchType, String uri,
   String qNameOrLocalName);
public org.w3c.dom.NodeList getElementsByTagName(String qName);
public org.w3c.dom.NodeList getElementsNamed(String qName);
public org.w3c.dom.NodeList getElementsNamed(String uri, String
   localName);
public org.w3c.dom.NodeList getElementsNamed(int matchType,
   String uri, String qNameOrLocalName);
public String getLanguage();
public static String getLocalNameForQName(String qname);
public String getNSLocalName();
public String getNSName();
public String getNamespaceForPrefix(String prefix);
public String getNamespaceForQName(String qname);
public String getNodeName();
public short getNodeType();
public TXElement getNthElementNamed(int nth, String qName);
public TXElement getNthElementNamed(int nth, String uri, String
   localName);
public TXElement getNthElementNamed(int nth, int matchType,
   String uri, String qNameOrLocalName);
public String getTagName();
public boolean isPreserveSpace();
public void normalize();
public void removeAttribute(String name);
```

```
     public org.w3c.dom.Attr removeAttributeNode(org.w3c.dom.Attr
        attribute);
     public void removeOverlappedNamespaceAttributes();
     protected void resetDefaultAttribute(String name);
     public TXElement[] searchChildrenAll(String qName);
     public TXElement searchDescendants(String qName);
     public TXElement searchDescendants(int matchType, String uri,
        String qNameOrLocalName);
     public TXElement[] searchDescendantsAll(String qName);
     public TXElement[] searchDescendantsAll(int matchType, String uri,
        String qNameOrLocalName);
     public void setAttribute(String name, String value) throws
        org.w3c.dom.DOMException;
     public org.w3c.dom.Attr setAttributeNode(org.w3c.dom.Attr
        attribute);
     public void setPreserveSpace(boolean isPreserveSpace);
     public void setTagName(String tagName);
  }
```

Class TXNotation

```
  public class TXNotation extends Child {
     // Constructors
     public TXNotation(String name, ExternalID externalID);
     // Methods
     public void acceptPost(Visitor visitor) throws Exception;
     public void acceptPre(Visitor visitor) throws Exception;
     public synchronized Object clone();
     public synchronized boolean equals(org.w3c.dom.Node arg, boolean
        deep);
     public ExternalID getExternalID();
     public String getNodeName();
     public short getNodeType();
     protected org.w3c.dom.Notation getNotationImpl();
     public String getPublicId();
     public String getSystemId();
  }
```

Class TXPI

```
  public class TXPI extends Child implements
  org.w3c.dom.ProcessingInstruction {
     // Constructors
     public TXPI(String name, String data);
```

```
        // Methods
        public void acceptPost(Visitor visitor) throws Exception;
        public void acceptPre(Visitor visitor) throws Exception;
        public synchronized Object clone();
        public synchronized boolean equals(org.w3c.dom.Node arg, boolean
          deep);
        public String getData();
        public String getNodeName();
        public short getNodeType();
        public String getNodeValue();
        public String getTarget();
        public String getText();
        public void setData(String data);
        public void setNodeValue(String data);
        public void setTarget(String arg);
    }
```

Class TXText

```
    public class TXText extends TXCharacterData implements org.w3c.dom.
    Text {
        // Constructors
        public TXText(String data);
        // Methods
        public void acceptPost(Visitor visitor) throws Exception;
        public void acceptPre(Visitor visitor) throws Exception;
        public synchronized Object clone();
        public boolean equals(org.w3c.dom.Node arg, boolean deep);
        public boolean getIsIgnorableWhitespace();
        public String getLanguage();
        public String getNodeName();
        public short getNodeType();
        public String getText();
        public static String makePrintable(String string);
        public void setIsIgnorableWhitespace(boolean isIgnorableWhitespace);
        public org.w3c.dom.Text splitText(int offset) throws org.w3c.dom.
          DOMException;
        public static String trim(String string);
        public static String trim(String string, boolean trimHead, boolean
          trimTail);
    }
```

Interface TagHandler

```
    public abstract interface TagHandler {
        // Methods
```

```
    public void handleEndTag(TXElement element, boolean empty);
    public void handleStartTag(TXElement element, boolean empty);
}
```

Class ToNextSiblingTraversalException

```
public class ToNextSiblingTraversalException extends
TreeTraversalException {
    // Constructors
    public ToNextSiblingTraversalException();
    public ToNextSiblingTraversalException(String msg);
}
```

Class TreeTraversal

```
public abstract class TreeTraversal {
    // Constructors
    public TreeTraversal(Visitor visitor);
    // Methods
    public Visitor getVisitor();
    public abstract void traverse(org.w3c.dom.Node startNode) throws
        Exception;
}
```

Class TreeTraversalException

```
public class TreeTraversalException extends Exception {
    // Constructors
    public TreeTraversalException();
    public TreeTraversalException(String msg);
}
```

Class Util

```
public class Util {
    // Constructors
    public Util();
    // Methods
    public static String backReference(String string, String
        encoding);
    public static String backReference(String string, String
        specials, String encoding);
    public static String backReferenceForEntity(String string, String
        encoding);
    public static boolean checkAllSpace(String string);
```

```
        public static boolean checkEncoding(String xmlEncoding);
        public static boolean checkLanguageID(String languageID);
        public static boolean checkNCName(String name);
        public static boolean checkName(String name);
        public static boolean checkNmtoken(String nmtoken);
        public static boolean checkVersionNum(String versionNum);
        public static int getInvalidURIChar(String uri);
        public static void indent(java.io.Writer pw, int n) throws java.
          io.IOException;
        public static boolean isURN(String uri);
        public static String normalizeURN(String urn);
        public static void printSpace(java.io.Writer pw, int n) throws
          java.io.IOException;
        public static java.util.Vector sortStringVector(java.util.Vector
          vector);
    }
```

Class Version

```
    public class Version {
        // Fields
        public static final String S_VERSION;
        public static final int MAJOR;
        public static final int MINOR;
        public static final int SUBMINOR;
        // Constructors
        public Version();
    }
```

Interface Visitee

```
    public abstract interface Visitee {
        // Methods
        public void acceptPost(Visitor visitor) throws Exception;
        public void acceptPre(Visitor visitor) throws Exception;
    }
```

Interface Visitor

```
    public abstract interface Visitor {
        // Methods
        public void visitAttDefPost(AttDef attDef) throws Exception;
        public void visitAttDefPre(AttDef attDef) throws Exception;
        public void visitAttlistPost(Attlist attlist) throws Exception;
```

```
public void visitAttlistPre(Attlist attlist) throws Exception;
public void visitAttributePost(TXAttribute attribute) throws
    Exception;
public void visitAttributePre(TXAttribute attribute) throws
    Exception;
public void visitCommentPost(TXComment comment) throws Exception;
public void visitCommentPre(TXComment comment) throws Exception;
public void visitDTDPost(DTD dtd) throws Exception;
public void visitDTDPre(DTD dtd) throws Exception;
public void visitDocumentFragmentPost(TXDocumentFragment
    documentFrag) throws Exception;
public void visitDocumentFragmentPre(TXDocumentFragment
    documentFrag) throws Exception;
public void visitDocumentPost(TXDocument document) throws
    Exception;
public void visitDocumentPre(TXDocument document) throws
    Exception;
public void visitElementDeclPost(ElementDecl elementDecl) throws
    Exception;
public void visitElementDeclPre(ElementDecl elementDecl) throws
    Exception;
public void visitElementPost(TXElement element) throws Exception;
public void visitElementPre(TXElement element) throws Exception;
public void visitEntityDeclPost(EntityDecl entityDecl) throws
    Exception;
public void visitEntityDeclPre(EntityDecl entityDecl) throws
    Exception;
public void visitGeneralReferencePost(GeneralReference
    generalReference) throws Exception;
public void visitGeneralReferencePre(GeneralReference
    generalReference) throws Exception;
public void visitNotationPost(TXNotation notation) throws
    Exception;
public void visitNotationPre(TXNotation notation) throws
    Exception;
public void visitPIPost(TXPI pi) throws Exception;
public void visitPIPre(TXPI pi) throws Exception;
public void visitPseudoNodePost(PseudoNode pseudoNode) throws
    Exception;
public void visitPseudoNodePre(PseudoNode pseudoNode) throws
    Exception;
public void visitTextPost(TXText text) throws Exception;
public void visitTextPre(TXText text) throws Exception;
}
```

Class XMLChar

```
public final class XMLChar {
    // Fields
    public static final String S_SPACES;
    // Methods
    public static boolean isChar(int ch);
    public static boolean isLetter(int ch);
    public static boolean isNameChar(int ch);
    public static boolean isSpace(int ch);
}
```

Class XMLCharGen

```
public class XMLCharGen {
    // Constructors
    public XMLCharGen();
    // Methods
    public static boolean isChar(int ch);
    public static boolean isCombiningChar(int ch);
    public static boolean isDigit(int ch);
    public static boolean isExtender(int ch);
    public static boolean isIgnorable(int ch);
    public static boolean isLetter(int ch);
    public static boolean isNameChar(int ch);
    public static boolean isSpace(int ch);
    public static void main(String[] argv);
}
```

Package com.ibm.xml.parser.util

Class HTMLPrintVisitor

```
public class HTMLPrintVisitor extends
com.ibm.xml.parser.ToXMLStringVisitor {
    // Fields
    protected int level;
    protected String doctype;
    // Constructors
    public HTMLPrintVisitor(java.io.Writer writer, String encoding,
        String doctype);
    public HTMLPrintVisitor(java.io.Writer writer, String encoding);
    public HTMLPrintVisitor(java.io.Writer writer);
    // Methods
```

```
        public void visitAttDefPre(com.ibm.xml.parser.AttDef attDef)
          throws Exception;
        public void visitAttlistPre(com.ibm.xml.parser.Attlist attlist)
          throws Exception;
        public void visitAttributePre(com.ibm.xml.parser.TXAttribute
          attribute) throws Exception;
        public void visitDTDPost(com.ibm.xml.parser.DTD dtd) throws
          Exception;
        public void visitDTDPre(com.ibm.xml.parser.DTD dtd) throws
          Exception;
        public void visitDocumentPost(com.ibm.xml.parser.TXDocument
          document) throws Exception;
        public void visitDocumentPre(com.ibm.xml.parser.TXDocument
          document) throws Exception;
        public void visitElementDeclPre(com.ibm.xml.parser.ElementDecl
          elementDecl) throws Exception;
        public void visitElementPost(com.ibm.xml.parser.TXElement
          element) throws Exception;
        public void visitElementPre(com.ibm.xml.parser.TXElement element)
          throws Exception;
        public void visitEntityDeclPre(com.ibm.xml.parser.EntityDecl
          entity) throws Exception;
        public void visitGeneralReferencePre(com.ibm.xml.parser.
          GeneralReference generalReference) throws Exception;
        public void visitNotationPre(com.ibm.xml.parser.TXNotation
          notation) throws Exception;
        public void visitPIPre(com.ibm.xml.parser.TXPI pi) throws
          Exception;
        public void visitTextPre(com.ibm.xml.parser.TXText text) throws
          Exception;
    }
```

Package org.w3c.dom

Interface Attr

```
    public abstract interface Attr extends Node {
        // Methods
        public String getName();
        public boolean getSpecified();
        public String getValue();
        public void setValue(String value);
    }
```

Interface Attribute

```
public abstract interface Attribute extends Node {
    // Methods
    public String getName();
    public boolean getSpecified();
    public String getValue();
    public void setValue(String arg);
}
```

Interface CDATASection

```
public abstract interface CDATASection extends Text {
}
```

Interface CharacterData

```
public abstract interface CharacterData extends Node {
    // Methods
    public void appendData(String arg) throws DOMException;
    public void deleteData(int offset, int count) throws
      DOMException;
    public String getData() throws DOMException;
    public int getLength();
    public void insertData(int offset, String arg) throws
      DOMException;
    public void replaceData(int offset, int count, String arg) throws
      DOMException;
    public void setData(String data) throws DOMException;
    public String substringData(int offset, int count) throws
      DOMException;
}
```

Interface Comment

```
public abstract interface Comment extends CharacterData {
}
```

Class DOMException

```
public abstract class DOMException extends RuntimeException {
    // Fields
    public short code;
    public static final short INDEX_SIZE_ERR;
    public static final short DOMSTRING_SIZE_ERR;
```

```
        public static final short HIERARCHY_REQUEST_ERR;
        public static final short WRONG_DOCUMENT_ERR;
        public static final short INVALID_CHARACTER_ERR;
        public static final short NO_DATA_ALLOWED_ERR;
        public static final short NO_MODIFICATION_ALLOWED_ERR;
        public static final short NOT_FOUND_ERR;
        public static final short NOT_SUPPORTED_ERR;
        public static final short INUSE_ATTRIBUTE_ERR;
        // Constructors
        public DOMException(short code, String message);
    }
```

Interface DOMImplementation

```
    public abstract interface DOMImplementation {
        // Methods
        public boolean hasFeature(String feature, String version);
    }
```

Interface Document

```
    public abstract interface Document extends Node {
        // Methods
        public Attr createAttribute(String name) throws DOMException;
        public CDATASection createCDATASection(String data) throws
          DOMException;
        public Comment createComment(String data);
        public DocumentFragment createDocumentFragment();
        public Element createElement(String tagName) throws DOMException;
        public EntityReference createEntityReference(String name) throws
          DOMException;
        public ProcessingInstruction createProcessingInstruction(String
          target, String data) throws DOMException;
        public Text createTextNode(String data);
        public DocumentType getDoctype();
        public Element getDocumentElement();
        public NodeList getElementsByTagName(String tagname);
        public DOMImplementation getImplementation();
    }
```

Interface DocumentFragment

```
    public abstract interface DocumentFragment extends Node {
    }
```

Interface DocumentType

```
public abstract interface DocumentType extends Node {
    // Methods
    public NamedNodeMap getEntities();
    public String getName();
    public NamedNodeMap getNotations();
}
```

Interface Element

```
public abstract interface Element extends Node {
    // Methods
    public String getAttribute(String name);
    public Attr getAttributeNode(String name);
    public NodeList getElementsByTagName(String name);
    public String getTagName();
    public void normalize();
    public void removeAttribute(String name) throws DOMException;
    public Attr removeAttributeNode(Attr oldAttr) throws
      DOMException;
    public void setAttribute(String name, String value) throws
      DOMException;
    public Attr setAttributeNode(Attr newAttr) throws DOMException;
}
```

Interface Entity

```
public abstract interface Entity extends Node {
    // Methods
    public String getNotationName();
    public String getPublicId();
    public String getSystemId();
}
```

Interface EntityReference

```
public abstract interface EntityReference extends Node {
}
```

Interface NamedNodeMap

```
public abstract interface NamedNodeMap {
    // Methods
    public int getLength();
```

```
    public Node getNamedItem(String name);
    public Node item(int index);
    public Node removeNamedItem(String name) throws DOMException;
    public Node setNamedItem(Node arg) throws DOMException;
}
```

Interface Node

```
public abstract interface Node {
    // Fields
    public static final short ELEMENT_NODE;
    public static final short ATTRIBUTE_NODE;
    public static final short TEXT_NODE;
    public static final short CDATA_SECTION_NODE;
    public static final short ENTITY_REFERENCE_NODE;
    public static final short ENTITY_NODE;
    public static final short PROCESSING_INSTRUCTION_NODE;
    public static final short COMMENT_NODE;
    public static final short DOCUMENT_NODE;
    public static final short DOCUMENT_TYPE_NODE;
    public static final short DOCUMENT_FRAGMENT_NODE;
    public static final short NOTATION_NODE;
    // Methods
    public Node appendChild(Node newChild) throws DOMException;
    public Node cloneNode(boolean deep);
    public NamedNodeMap getAttributes();
    public NodeList getChildNodes();
    public Node getFirstChild();
    public Node getLastChild();
    public Node getNextSibling();
    public String getNodeName();
    public short getNodeType();
    public String getNodeValue() throws DOMException;
    public Document getOwnerDocument();
    public Node getParentNode();
    public Node getPreviousSibling();
    public boolean hasChildNodes();
    public Node insertBefore(Node newChild, Node refChild) throws
       DOMException;
    public Node removeChild(Node oldChild) throws DOMException;
    public Node replaceChild(Node newChild, Node oldChild) throws
       DOMException;
    public void setNodeValue(String nodeValue) throws DOMException;
}
```

Interface NodeList

```
public abstract interface NodeList {
    // Methods
    public int getLength();
    public Node item(int index);
}
```

Interface Notation

```
public abstract interface Notation extends Node {
    // Methods
    public String getPublicId();
    public String getSystemId();
}
```

Interface ProcessingInstruction

```
public abstract interface ProcessingInstruction extends Node {
    // Methods
    public String getData();
    public String getTarget();
    public void setData(String data) throws DOMException;
}
```

Interface Text

```
public abstract interface Text extends CharacterData {
    // Methods
    public Text splitText(int offset) throws DOMException;
}
```

Package org.xml.sax

Interface AttributeList

```
public abstract interface AttributeList {
    // Methods
    public int getLength();
    public String getName(int i);
    public String getType(int i);
    public String getType(String name);
    public String getValue(int i);
    public String getValue(String name);
}
```

Interface `DTDHandler`

```
public abstract interface DTDHandler {
    // Methods
    public void notationDecl(String name, String publicId, String
        systemId) throws SAXException;
    public void unparsedEntityDecl(String name, String publicId, String
        systemId, String notationName) throws SAXException;
}
```

Interface `DocumentHandler`

```
public abstract interface DocumentHandler {
    // Methods
    public void characters(char[] ch, int start, int length) throws
        SAXException;
    public void endDocument() throws SAXException;
    public void endElement(String name) throws SAXException;
    public void ignorableWhitespace(char[] ch, int start, int length)
        throws SAXException;
    public void processingInstruction(String target, String data) throws
        SAXException;
    public void setDocumentLocator(Locator locator);
    public void startDocument() throws SAXException;
    public void startElement(String name, AttributeList atts) throws
        SAXException;
}
```

Interface `EntityResolver`

```
public abstract interface EntityResolver {
    // Methods
    public InputSource resolveEntity(String publicId, String systemId)
        throws SAXException, java.io.IOException;
}
```

Interface `ErrorHandler`

```
public abstract interface ErrorHandler {
    // Methods
    public void error(SAXParseException exception) throws SAXException;
    public void fatalError(SAXParseException exception) throws
        SAXException;
    public void warning(SAXParseException exception) throws
        SAXException;
}
```

Class HandlerBase

```
public class HandlerBase implements EntityResolver, DTDHandler,
DocumentHandler, ErrorHandler {
    // Constructors
    public HandlerBase();
    // Methods
    public void characters(char[] ch, int start, int length) throws
      SAXException;
    public void endDocument() throws SAXException;
    public void endElement(String name) throws SAXException;
    public void error(SAXParseException e) throws SAXException;
    public void fatalError(SAXParseException e) throws SAXException;
    public void ignorableWhitespace(char[] ch, int start, int length)
      throws SAXException;
    public void notationDecl(String name, String publicId, String
      systemId);
    public void processingInstruction(String target, String data)
      throws SAXException;
    public InputSource resolveEntity(String publicId, String
      systemId) throws SAXException;
    public void setDocumentLocator(Locator locator);
    public void startDocument() throws SAXException;
    public void startElement(String name, AttributeList attributes)
      throws SAXException;
    public void unparsedEntityDecl(String name, String publicId,
      String systemId, String notationName);
    public void warning(SAXParseException e) throws SAXException;
}
```

Class InputSource

```
public class InputSource {
    // Constructors
    public InputSource();
    public InputSource(String systemId);
    public InputSource(java.io.InputStream byteStream);
    public InputSource(java.io.Reader characterStream);
    // Methods
    public java.io.InputStream getByteStream();
    public java.io.Reader getCharacterStream();
    public String getEncoding();
    public String getPublicId();
    public String getSystemId();
    public void setByteStream(java.io.InputStream byteStream);
```

```
        public void setCharacterStream(java.io.Reader characterStream);
        public void setEncoding(String encoding);
        public void setPublicId(String publicId);
        public void setSystemId(String systemId);
    }
```

Interface Locator

```
    public abstract interface Locator {
        // Methods
        public int getColumnNumber();
        public int getLineNumber();
        public String getPublicId();
        public String getSystemId();
    }
```

Interface Parser

```
    public abstract interface Parser {
        // Methods
        public void parse(InputSource source) throws SAXException, java.
          io.IOException;
        public void parse(String systemId) throws SAXException, java.io.
          IOException;
        public void setDTDHandler(DTDHandler handler);
        public void setDocumentHandler(DocumentHandler handler);
        public void setEntityResolver(EntityResolver resolver);
        public void setErrorHandler(ErrorHandler handler);
        public void setLocale(java.util.Locale locale) throws
          SAXException;
    }
```

Class SAXException

```
    public class SAXException extends Exception {
        // Constructors
        public SAXException(String message);
        public SAXException(Exception e);
        public SAXException(String message, Exception e);
        // Methods
        public Exception getException();
        public String getMessage();
        public String toString();
    }
```

Class SAXParseException

```
public class SAXParseException extends SAXException {
    // Constructors
    public SAXParseException(String message, Locator locator);
    public SAXParseException(String message, Locator locator,
      Exception e);
    public SAXParseException(String message, String publicId, String
      systemId, int lineNumber, int columnNumber);
    public SAXParseException(String message, String publicId, String
      systemId, int lineNumber, int columnNumber, Exception e);
    // Methods
    public int getColumnNumber();
    public int getLineNumber();
    public String getPublicId();
    public String getSystemId();
}
```

Package org.xml.sax.helpers

Class AttributeListImpl

```
public class AttributeListImpl implements org.xml.sax.AttributeList {
    // Constructors
    public AttributeListImpl();
    public AttributeListImpl(org.xml.sax.AttributeList atts);
    // Methods
    public void addAttribute(String name, String type, String value);
    public void clear();
    public int getLength();
    public String getName(int i);
    public String getType(int i);
    public String getType(String name);
    public String getValue(int i);
    public String getValue(String name);
    public void removeAttribute(String name);
    public void setAttributeList(org.xml.sax.AttributeList atts);
}
```

Class LocatorImpl

```
public class LocatorImpl implements org.xml.sax.Locator {
    // Constructors
    public LocatorImpl();
    public LocatorImpl(org.xml.sax.Locator locator);
```

```
    // Methods
    public int getColumnNumber();
    public int getLineNumber();
    public String getPublicId();
    public String getSystemId();
    public void setColumnNumber(int columnNumber);
    public void setLineNumber(int lineNumber);
    public void setPublicId(String publicId);
    public void setSystemId(String systemId);
}
```

Class ParserFactory

```
public class ParserFactory {
    // Constructors
    public ParserFactory();
    // Methods
    public static org.xml.sax.Parser makeParser() throws
      ClassNotFoundException, IllegalAccessException,
      InstantiationException, NullPointerException,
      ClassCastException;
    public static org.xml.sax.Parser makeParser(String className)
      throws ClassNotFoundException, IllegalAccessException,
      InstantiationException, ClassCastException;
}
```

XML-Related Standardization Activities

The XML 1.0 Recommendation issued in February 1998 defines the basic building blocks, such as the syntax of XML documents and DTDs. Originally, XML was intended to be a family of specifications that cover the core syntax, linking, and stylesheets. These activities are still going on in the W3C. The XML "family" consisted of the following components:

- XML (Xtensible Markup Language), which specifies the base syntax of documents and DTDs

- XLL (Extensible Linking Language), which specifies links among documents

- XSL (Extensible Stylesheet Language), which specifies the appearance of a document

A result of continued efforts of the W3C, XLL since has been split into two parts, *XPointer* and *XLink*. At the time of this writing, only XML is a Recommendation; the others are still Working Drafts, but they are expected to be promoted to Proposed Recommendation and then Recommendation very soon.

XPointer

XPointer supports addressing into the internal structures of XML documents. Links in HTML documents are tagged with `<a href="http://...">`, where the value of the `href` attribute refers to the entire document. XPointer allows references to elements, character strings, and other parts of XML documents, whether or not they bear an explicit ID attribute (an attribute named id, such as id="section2"). The following example is a combination of a URL and an XPointer and refers to the seventh child of the third SECTION under the root element (example based on W3C XPointer Working Draft, March 3, 1998).

```
http://www.foo.com/bar.html#root().child(3,SECTION).child(7)
```

XLink

XLink specifies constructs that may be inserted into XML documents to describe links between objects. In HTML, a link is unidirectional from one resource to another and has no special meaning, except it brings up the referred document when clicked in a browser. With XLink, a document author can do the following, among others:

- Associate semantics to a link by giving a "role" to the link.

- Define a link that connects more than two resources.

- Define a bidirectional link.

In the following example, the link <commentary> connects three resources to the document containing this link with three different roles: "Essay," "Rebuttal," and "Comparison" (example based on W3C XLink Working Draft, March 3, 1998).

```
<commentary xml:link="extended" inline="false">
    <locator href="smith2.1" role="Essay"/>
    <locator href="jones1.4" role="Rebuttal"/>
    <locator href="robin3.2" role="Comparison"/>
</commentary>
```

Roles are particularly useful when searching. Suppose that you want to search a document foo.html to see whether it contains the word "Tokyo." If foo.html is an index page and the body of each chapter is in a separate file linked from foo.html, you want the search program to follow these links and locate the word. However, not all links in foo.html refer to its body. You do not want to follow links to referenced materials. By giving appropriate roles to each type of link, you can have the search program distinguish these. Note that in HTML, both <A HREF="...">tags and <IMG SRC="...">tags are links but with different roles.

Namespace

The purpose of Namespace is to allow multiple sets of tags to coexist in the same document. It is not easy to define a good DTD (or schema) that receives widespread support for a long period of time. Defining your DTD by reusing some of these good DTDs would enable it to receive more support than it would otherwise. In the following example, the `<price>` tag is borrowed from the schema defined in `http://ecommerce.org/edi` (example based on W3C Namespace Recommendation, January 14, 1999).

```
<?xml version="1.0"?>
    <order:x
        xmlns:order='http://ecommerce.org/order'
        xmlns:edi='http://ecommerce.org/edi'>
        <edi:price>14.95</edi:price>
    </order:x>
```

The namespace specification is extremely important because many other standards based in the XML syntax require a namespace in order for them to be properly defined.

XSL

Since XML defines only syntax, a program does not know how to format an XML document without having explicit instructions on styles. For example, what typeface and font size should be used for text in the `<CurrTemp>` tag? How can a program lay it out on the screen? XSL is a stylesheet language for formatting XML documents. An XSL stylesheet is composed of a set of rules. The following example rule matches all XML elements whose name is `para`, and translates them into flow objects (objects to be displayed) with the specified attributes. As you can see in this example, XSL itself is written in the XML syntax (example based on W3C XSL Working Draft, December 16, 1998).

```
<xsl:template match="para">
    <fo:block font-size="10pt" space-before="12pt">
        <xsl:apply-templates/>
    </fo:block>
</xsl:template>
```

In addition to rendering, XSL can also transform an XML document into another XML document. This general XML transformation capability could be particularly useful when dealing with documents that are logically similar but have slightly different DTDs.

The XPointer, XLink, and XSL specifications are not yet Recommendation as of this writing. Check the W3C site periodically to see how they evolve.

Document Object Model (DOM)

The DOM specifies an API to the object representation of XML documents. It is explained in detail in Chapters 2 and 4. As for programming language bindings, IDL (CORBA), Java, and ECMAScript (JavaScript) interfaces are defined. DOM Level 1 was issued as a W3C Recommendation October 1, 1998.

Simple API for XML (SAX)

SAX is another API for XML (explained in Chapter 2). Unlike the DOM and other specifications, it is not from W3C. Instead, David Megginson and the xml-dev mailing list collaboratively developed the SAX 1.0 Specification. It is a lightweight, event-driven API.

Other XML-Related Specifications

In addition to these core specifications, a number of related specifications and standards are being proposed and discussed. Some of the important ones are listed next.

- Resource Description Framework (RDF)

  RDF is a language for expressing metacontent in general. Unlike an XML document that is represented as a tree, an RDF document has a graph-based data structure.

- Document Content Description (DCD)

  Like the DTD, the DCD is a schema facility that defines the structure and content of XML documents. Unlike the DTD, the DCD is given in the XML syntax. The DCD was proposed by Microsoft and a few other companies. At the time of this writing, it is a note (NOTE-dcd-19980731).

- Platform for Privacy Preferences Project (P3P)

  The P3P enables the automatic interchange of personal information on HTTP. It proposes to use XML and the RDF for structured data exchange and privacy practice assertions.

- Web Distributed Authoring and Versioning (WebDAV)

  HTTP is good for distributing content to clients. For publishing to a Web server, on the other hand, more primitive protocols, such as FTP, are usually used. WebDAV, which is being defined by the IETF, tries to address this issue by extending the existing HTTP protocol. In particular, it will support locking and versioning for distributed authoring. XML is used as the data format for exchanging complex queries and responses on such properties as authors, versions, and locks. The following example shows a simple query in XML along with the extended HTTP header (example based on RFC 2518).

  ```
  PROPFIND /container/ HTTP/1.1
  Host: www.foo.bar
  Content-Length: xxxx
  Content-Type: text/xml

  <?xml version="1.0"?>
  <D:propfind xmlns:D="DAV:">
      <D:allprop/>
  </D:propfind>
  ```

- Wireless Markup Language (WML)

  WML is a markup language based on XML that is intended for specifying content and the user interface for narrowband devices, including cellular phones and pagers. It is being defined by the Wireless Application Protocol Forum (WAP Forum). A unit of delivery in WML is called a *deck*, which consists of multiple primitive pages called *cards*. Thus no communication is necessary as long as the user is navigating within a deck. The following simple example shows a deck comprised of two cards (example based on WML Version April 30, 1998).

  ```
  <WML>
      <CARD>
          <DO TYPE="ACCEPT">
              <GO URL="#card2"/>
          </DO>
  ```

```
        Hello world!    This is the first card...
    </CARD>
    <CARD NAME="card2">
        This is the second card.    Goodbye.
    </CARD>
</WML>
```

In addition to these specifications, many others are being proposed, including a Channel Definition Format (CDF) for representing channels of push publishing, an Open Software Description (OSD) for representing software distributions for installation over the Internet, a Synchronized Multimedia Integration Language (SMIL) for creating synchronized multimedia contents, and MathML for describing complex mathematical formulas. Moreover, industries such as banking and finance, manufacturing, distribution, and transportation are about to jump into defining industry-specific document and message formats based on XML.

F

DOMHASH Definition

Hash values in our proposal (see Chapter 7) are defined on the DOM type `Node`. We consider the following four node types that are used for representing a DOM document structure:

- Element (`Element`)
- Attribute (`Attr`)
- PI (`ProcessingInstruction`)
- Text (`Text`)

> **NOTE:** Comment nodes and Document Type Definitions (DTDs) do not participate in the digest value calculation. This is because DOM does not require a conformant processor to create data structures for these. DOMHash is designed so that it can be computed with any XML processor conformant to the DOM or SAX specification.

Here, we give the precise definitions of the digest for these types. We describe the format of the data to be supplied to a hash algorithm using a figure and a simple description, followed by a Java code fragment using the DOM API and the JDK 1.1 Platform Core API only. Therefore the semantics should be unambiguous.

As the rule of thumb, all strings are to be in UTF-16 in the network byte order (big-endian) with no byte order mark. If there is a sequence of text nodes without any element node in between, these text nodes are merged into one by concatenating them. A zero-length `Text` node is always ignored.

The code fragments in the following definitions assume that they are in implementation classes of `Node`. Therefore a method call without an explicit object reference is for the node itself. For example, `getData()` returns the text data of the current node if it is a `Text` node. The parameter `digestAlgorithm` is to be replaced by an identifier of the digest algorithm, such as MD5 (Message Digest 5) and SHA (Secure Hash Algorithm).

The computation should begin with a 4-byte integer that represents the type of the node, such as `Node.TEXT_NODE` or `Node.ELEMENT_NODE`.

To avoid the dependence on the namespace prefix, we use "expanded names" to do digest calculation. If an element name or an attribute name is qualified either by an explicit namespace prefix or by a default namespace, the name's LocalPart is prepended by the URI of the namespace (the *namespace name* as defined in the Namespace specification) and a colon before digest calculation. In the following example, the default qualified name "order" is expanded into "http://ecommerce.org/schema:order" while the explicit qualified name "book:title" is expanded into "urn:loc.gov:books:title" before digest calculation.

```
<?xml version="1.0"?>
<root xmlns='http://ecommerce.org/schema'
          xmlns:book='urn:loc.gov:books'>
    <order>
        <book:title> ... </book:title>
            :
    </order>
</root>
```

We define an *expanded name* (either for element or attribute) as follows:

If a name is not qualified, the expanded name is the name itself.

If a name is qualified with the prefix "xmlns", the expanded name is undefined.

If a name is qualified either by default or by an explicit namespace prefix, the expanded name is *URI bound to the namespace* + ":" + *LocalPart*

In the following definitions, we assume that the `getExpandedName()` method (which returns the expanded name as defined above) is defined in both `Element` and `Attr` interfaces of DOM.

Note that the digest values are not defined on namespace declarations. In other words, the digest value is not defined for an attribute when

- the attribute name is "xmlns", or

- the namespace prefix is "xmlns".

In the above example, the two attributes which are namespace declarations do not have digest values and therefore will not participate in the calculation of the digest value of the "root" element.

Text **Nodes**

The hash value of a `Text` node is computed on the 4-byte header followed by the UTF-16 encoded text string.

Format:

- `Node.TEXT_NODE` (3) in 32-bit network-byte-ordered integer

- Text data in UTF-16 stream (variable length)

Java Code:

```
public byte[] getDigest(String digestAlgorithm) {
    MessageDigest md = MessageDigest.getInstance(digestAlgorithm);
    md.update((byte)((Node.TEXT_NODE>>24) & 0xff));
    md.update((byte)((Node.TEXT_NODE>>16) & 0xff));
    md.update((byte)((Node.TEXT_NODE>>8) & 0xff));
    md.update((byte)(Node.TEXT_NODE & 0xff));
    md.update(getData().getBytes("UnicodeBigUnmarked"));
    return md.digest();
}
```

Here, `MessageDigest` is in the package `java.security.*`, one of the built-in packages of JDK 1.1.

PI (`ProcessingInstruction`) **Nodes**

A PI node has two components: the target and the data. The hash is computed on the concatenation of both. Note that the data contains the leading space character, so there is no ambiguity even if there is no separator between the target and the data.

Format:

- `Node.PROCESSING_INSTRUCTION_NODE` (7) in 32-bit network-byte-ordered integer

- PI target and data in UTF-16 stream (variable length)

Java Code:

```
public byte[] getDigest(String digestAlgorithm) {
    MessageDigest md = MessageDigest.getInstance(digestAlgorithm);
    md.update((byte)((Node.PROCESSING_INSTRUCTION_NODE>>24) & 0xff));
    md.update((byte)((Node.PROCESSING_INSTRUCTION_NODE>>16) &
      0xff));
    md.update((byte)((Node.PROCESSING_INSTRUCTION_NODE>>8) & 0xff));
    md.update((byte)(Node.PROCESSING_INSTRUCTION_NODE & 0xff));
    md.update(getName().getBytes("UnicodeBigUnmarked"));
    md.update(getData().getBytes("UnicodeBigUnmarked"));
    return md.digest();
}
```

Attribute (`Attr`) Nodes

Attribute nodes are similar to PI nodes, except that there must be a separator between the attribute name and the attribute value. Note that the 0x0000 value in UTF-16 is not allowed in an XML document, so it can serve as an unambiguous separator.

Format:

- `Node.ATTRIBUTE_NODE` (2) in 32-bit network-byte-ordered integer

- Attribute name in UTF-16 stream (variable length)

- 0x00 0x00

- Attribute value in UTF-16 stream (variable length)

Java Code:

```
public byte[] getDigest(String digestAlgorithm) {
    MessageDigest md = MessageDigest.getInstance(digestAlgorithm);
    md.update((byte)((Node.ATTRIBUTE_NODE>>24) & 0xff));
```

```
            md.update((byte)((Node.ATTRIBUTE_NODE>>16) & 0xff));
            md.update((byte)((Node.ATTRIBUTE_NODE>>8) & 0xff));
            md.update((byte)(Node.ATTRIBUTE_NODE & 0xff));
            md.update(getName().getBytes("UnicodeBigUnmarked"));
            md.update((byte)0);
            md.update((byte)0);
                // getValue() returns String instance in WD-DOM-19980416
            md.update(getValue().getBytes("UnicodeBigUnmarked"));
            return md.digest();
        }
```

Element **Nodes**

Element nodes are the most complex because they consist of other nodes recursively. Hash values of these component nodes are used to calculate the node's digest so that computation can be saved when the structure is partially changed.

First, all the attributes except for namespace declarations must be collected. This list is sorted by expanded attribute names. The sorting is done in ascending order in terms of the UTF-16 encoded expanded attribute names, using the string comparison operator defined as String.compareTo() in Java. The semantics of this sorting operation should be clear (no "ties" are possible because of the unique attribute name constraint).

- Node.ELEMENT_NODE (1) in 32-bit network-byte-ordered integer

- Element name in UTF-16 stream (variable length)

- 0x00 0x00

- A number of attributes in 32-bit network-byte-ordered unsigned integer

- Sequence of digest values of attribute, sorted by String#compareTo() for attribute names

- A number of child nodes in 32-bit network-byte-ordered unsigned integer

- Sequence of digest values of each child nodes (variable length)

(A sequence of child texts is merged into one text. A zero-length text is not counted as a child.)

Java Code:

```java
public byte[] getDigest(String digestAlgorithm) {
    MessageDigest md = MessageDigest.getInstance(digestAlgorithm);
    ByteArrayOutputStream baos = new ByteArrayOutputStream();
    DataOutputStream dos = new DataOutputStream(baos);
    dos.writeInt (Node.ELEMENT_NODE);  // This is stored in the
      network byte order.
    dos.write(getExpandedName() .getBytes ("UnicodeBigUnmarked"));
    dos.write((byte)0);
    dos.write((byte)0);
    // Collect all attributes except for namespace declarations
    NamedNodeMap nnm = this.getAttributes();
    int len = nnm.getLength()
          // Find "xmlns" or "xmlns:foo" in nnm and omit it.
    ...
    dos.writeInt(len);   // This is sorted in the network byte order
    // Sort attributes by String#compareTo() on expanded attribute
      names.
    ...
    // Assume that 'Attr[] aattr' has sorted Attribute instances.
    for (int i = 0; i < len; i ++)
       dos.write(aattr[i].getDigest(digestAlgorithm));
    Node n = this.getFirstChild();
    // Assume that adjoining Texts are merged and no 0-length Text
      and no Comment.
    len = this.getChildNodes() .getLength();
    dos.writeInt(len);    // This is stored in the network byte order
    while (n != null) {
       dos.write(n.getDigest(digestAlgorithm));
       n = n.getNextSibling();
    }
    dos.close();
    md.update(baos.toByteArray());
    return md.digest();
}
```

Thus a hash value of a DOM element can be strictly defined without the need to rely on generating a surface character string.

Index

Java™ Technology from Addison-Wesley

ISBN 0-201-37949-X

ISBN 0-201-37963-5

ISBN 0-201-60446-9

ISBN 0-201-43329-X

ISBN 0-201-48543-5

ISBN 0-201-61563-0

ISBN 0-201-30972-6

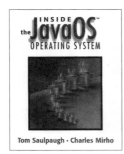

ISBN 0-201-18393-5

ISBN 0-201-32573-X

ISBN 0-201-32582-9

http://www.awl.com/cseng
✦ Addison-Wesley

Addison-Wesley Computer and Engineering Publishing Group

How to Register Your Book

Register this Book

Visit: **http://www.awl.com/cseng/register**

Enter this unique code: **csng-zcqk-bydb-wkow**

Then you will receive:

- Online updates about *XML and Java: Developing Web Applications*
- Exclusive offers on other Addison-Wesley books
- Access to our online book contest*

Visit our Web site

http://www.awl.com/cseng

When you think you've read enough, there's always more content for you at Addison-Wesley's web site. Our web site contains a directory of complete product information including:

- Chapters
- Exclusive author interviews
- Links to authors' pages
- Tables of contents
- Source code

You can also discover what tradeshows and conferences Addison-Wesley will be attending, read what others are saying about our titles, and find out where and when you can meet our authors and have them sign your book.

We encourage you to patronize the many fine retailers who stock Addison-Wesley titles. Visit our online directory to find stores near you or visit our online store: **http://store.awl.com/** or call **800-824-7799**.

Contact Us via Email

cepubprof@awl.com
Ask general questions about our books.
Sign up for our electronic mailing lists.
Submit corrections for our web site.

bexpress@awl.com
Request an Addison-Wesley catalog.
Get answers to questions regarding your order or our products.

innovations@awl.com
Request a current Innovations Newsletter.

webmaster@awl.com
Send comments about our web site.

mary.obrien@awl.com
Submit a book proposal.
Send errata for an Addison-Wesley book.

cepubpublicity@awl.com
Request a review copy for a member of the media interested in reviewing new Addison-Wesley titles.

Addison Wesley Longman
Computer and Engineering Publishing Group
One Jacob Way, Reading, Massachusetts 01867 USA
TEL 781-944-3700 • FAX 781-942-3076

*See web site for contest rules and duration

Warranty

Addison Wesley Longman warrants the enclosed disc to be free of defects in materials and faulty workmanship under normal use for a period of ninety days after purchase. If a defect is discovered in the disc during this warranty period, a replacement disc can be obtained at no charge by sending the defective disc, postage prepaid, with proof of purchase to:

Addison Wesley Longman, Inc.
Computer and Engineering Publishing Group
One Jacob Way
Reading, MA 01867

After the 90-day period, a replacement will be sent upon receipt of the defective disc and a check or money order for $10.00, payable to Addison Wesley Longman, Inc.

Addison Wesley Longman makes no warranty or representation, either express or implied, with respect to this software, its quality, performance, merchantability, or fitness for a particular purpose. In no event will Addison Wesley Longman, its distributors, or dealers be liable for direct, indirect, special, incidental, or consequential damages arising out of the use or inability to use the software. The exclusion of implied warranties is not permitted in some states. Therefore, the above exclusion may not apply to you. This warranty provides you with specific legal rights. There may be other rights that you may have that vary from state to state.

System Requirements

The CD-ROM included with this book is browsable on Windows 95, 98, NT, Macintosh, and UNIX platforms. Some of the software programs have individual requirements. Most of the Java technologies run on any platforms, provided that the appropriate Java environment is present.